D1715069

Advance praise for **Tune In to WOW Leadership**

"Today's most fertile landscape for creativity and nuance might just be American television, and Sheri Staak puts those imaginative visions to good use. Examples and counter-examples of effective leadership, steadfast integrity, and strength in the face of adversity abound on television, and Staak's clear, powerful connections are useful to anyone in a leadership position today. Accessible, intelligent, even fun, *Tune In to WOW Leadership* is not to be missed!"

—**Marshall Goldsmith,** Thinkers 50 Top Ten Global Business Thinker, top-ranked executive coach, and author of *New York Times* best-seller *What Got You Here Won't Get You There*

"Young professionals will find *Tune In to WOW Leadership* a primer in how to lead and manage not only others, but themselves."

—**Margaret H. Greenberg,** best-selling coauthor of *Profit from the Positive: Proven Leadership Strategies to Boost Productivity and Transform Your Business* and positive business columnist for *Live Happy Magazine*

"Those of you who are television enthusiasts will be enthralled by Sheri Staak's analysis of what it takes to have integrity as a leader. Staak profiles many stories of leadership—from Piper Chapman's indiscretions in *Orange Is the New Black* to Kevin Spacey's evil-doing Frank Underwood in the political drama *House of Cards*—to give the reader a WOW experience of what to do (and what not to do) in order to be a trustworthy leader. Enjoy this captivating read, full of valuable reminders on how to lead effectively."

—**Kathy Cramer, Ph.D.,** author of *Lead Positive: What Highly Effective Leaders See, Say, and Do*, founder and managing partner, The Cramer Institute

"*Tune In to WOW Leadership* is the 'TV guide' to visualizing leadership skills that will WOW!"

—**Sylvia McBrinn,** board director, former CEO and president, Axerion Therapeutics, Inc.

"Often the most memorable way to communicate ideas is through stories. Staak does this by linking her leadership concepts to TV characters we either love or hate. It's a fun way to highlight traits that are important for successful leaders."

—**Mike Kaufmann,** CEO, pharmaceutical segment, Cardinal Health

"Sheri Staak has created a fun, easy to grasp leadership book with *Tune In to WOW Leadership.* As a leader of a major lighting company for TV and feature films, I really connected with the way Sheri is able to share with us leadership skills through our favorite TV characters. I was totally impressed with this approach, not only because I come from TV and film, but also because anyone who is in a leadership role and who watches TV will relate to the concepts put before them. *Tune In to WOW Leadership* is a must read for anyone who has to display any leadership skills whether in the work place or out in the world."

—**Roy McDonald,** CEO, Briteshot

"*Tune In to WOW Leadership* is written in a relatable style and is great for current and future leaders as it is easy and fun to read. It is a good reminder of what it takes to be successful and respected! By sharing examples from popular TV shows, it really depicts the behavior needed to be a WOW leader."

—**Laurie Kahn,** president and founder, Media Staffing Network

"In her new book, *Tune In to WOW Leadership,* Sheri Staak gives us a 'Prime Time' read that reminds us of the qualities we admire in WOW leaders and of the leader we all set out to become."

—**Gregory Schofield,** CEO of Sales Performance Consulting and former executive VP sales for Novartis Pharmaceuticals

"As an entrepreneur and leader of a small business, I understand the value of leadership. Staak's book is a refreshing take on the tired topic of leadership. *Tune In to WOW Leadership* presents it in a way that is fun, engaging, and informative for all."

—**Mary White,** founder & CEO, BnBFinder.com

"*Tune In to WOW Leadership* is an adventure in leadership learning that is a must read for any leader, whether you are just beginning your leadership journey or you've been at it for a long time. You can open this book to any page and find a wealth of helpful guidance and food for thought. *Tune In to WOW Leadership* is chock full of practical, actionable advice that is sure to expand your capacity to lead in every area of your life. I highly recommend it to anyone who wants to take their leadership influence and impact to the next level."

—**David A. O'Brien,** president of WorkChoice Solutions and best-selling author of
The Navigator's Handbook: 101 Leadership Lessons for Work and Life

"Engaging, insightful, and inspiring. This book challenges leaders to rethink the effectiveness of their current methods and established organizational rules of engagement."

—**Ward Clapham,** author, *Lead Big: Discovering the
Upside of Unconventional Leadership*

"Using a refreshingly unconventional approach, Sheri Staak takes a look at what makes today's leadership qualities truly stand out. Pulling lessons from some of the most memorable TV episodes and characters, Staak shows us tangible ways to improve our communication skills, build trust with our colleagues, and earn the respect of others. Millenials and Baby Boomers alike will find ways to incorporate these learnings and truly 'WOW' as leaders. By utilizing the helpful 'WOW in Action' exercises, I'm already seeing a positive difference in the way I approach and solve issues with my team."

—**BJ Jones,** head of sales, AstraZeneca Diabetes

"You will never view television in quite the same way again after reading this special book. Staak pulls fascinating insights and life lessons from our favorite television shows and their well-known characters. *Tune In to WOW Leadership* is a unique and fun way to learn about how to become the 'WOW' leader of your own career and life."

—**Betsy Myers,** founding director of the Center for Women and Business,
author of *Take the Lead*, and senior adviser to two US presidents

Tune IN

to

WOW

LEADERSHIP

Tune IN

to

WOW

LEADERSHIP

10 LESSONS LEARNED FROM
AMERICA'S FAVORITE SHOWS

SHERI STAAK

with Kim LaPat

BOOK GROUP PRESS

Published by Greenleaf Book Group Press
Austin, Texas
www.greenleafbookgroup.com

Distributed by Greenleaf Book Group

For ordering information or special discounts for bulk purchases, please contact Greenleaf Book Group at PO Box 91869, Austin, TX 78709, 512.891.6100.

Design and composition by Greenleaf Book Group
Cover design by Greenleaf Book Group

Cover and interior images:
©shutterstock.com/J. Helgason
©shutterstock.com/Aleksandr Bryliaev

Publisher's Cataloging-In-Publication Data

Staak, Sheri.
    Tune in to WOW leadership : 10 lessons learned from America's favorite shows / Sheri Staak, with Kim LaPat.—First edition.

    pages ; cm

    Issued also as an ebook.

    1. Leadership. 2. Management. 3. Television programs—Social aspects—United States. 4. Characters and characteristics on television. 5. Success in business. I. LaPat, Kim. II. Title.

HD57.7 .S73 2014
658.4/092   2014939664

ISBN 13: 978-1-62634-099-2

Part of the Tree Neutral® program, which offsets the number of trees consumed in the production and printing of this book by taking proactive steps, such as planting trees in direct proportion to the number of trees used: www.treeneutral.com

Printed in the United States of America on acid-free paper   TreeNeutral

14 15 16 17 18 19   10 9 8 7 6 5 4 3 2 1

First Edition

I dedicate this book to my future WOW leaders, Emma and Spencer. Thank you for allowing me to teach you life skills and for giving me the greatest leadership title of my life—Mom!

A big thanks also goes out to my husband, Ed. Without your unrelenting daily encouragement, big ideas, and unwavering support, a leadership blog and book would never have come to fruition. You made it possible.

Contents

Acknowledgments

Through the journey of my life and career, I have never walked alone. Thankfully, for more than twenty years, I have had my husband by my side. He was the catalyst and the energy behind the creation of this book. Without his encouragement and total unwavering belief, I would have never created the leadership blog—*The Staak Report*—that led to the writing of this book. It was Ed's idea to use television shows and characters to punctuate the leadership qualities I wanted to focus on. Ed is a BIG thinker, and the bigger the idea, the more he likes it. When the world sends challenges my way, Ed manages to turn those challenges into a fun learning experience. For me, writing a book seemed impossible. I thank my husband for helping create a vision, continually encouraging me to create, and essentially allowing my vision of leadership to come to life in this book.

A special thank you to Kim LaPat, my editor and the person who helped me find my voice. Without Kim, this book would not have been brought to life. I want to especially thank Kim for her dedication, drive, continual input, and support through this entire process. She helped pull together the thoughts and ideas that I wanted to share. I had no idea of the amount of time, effort, work, and perspiration that goes into writing a book—I couldn't have done it without Kim.

I thank my dad for giving me the fundamentals, values, and drive to become a leader. He instilled in me the energy and perseverance needed to fight the fight and to never give up. Most of all, my father gave me the skills to bring people together and form them into a team. He taught me the power of giving and focusing on others besides myself.

Many authors have a life goal to write a book. I did not. Many authors write a book to support a consulting business. I did not. I wrote this book for emerging leaders who are hungry for insights into becoming a WOW leader. I wrote this book for leaders who may be stuck in a rut and in need of a positive boost. I wrote this book for the mature leader who wants to make sure she continues to grow her leadership skills and become a WOW leader. This acknowledgment goes out to all of you. You invested in this book because you want to be a WOW leader. I have complete confidence that you will be the best leader you can be—today and in the future. Go be a WOW leader!

Pitching the Concept—WOW Leadership

In today's business landscape, there are lots of good leaders, and even more bad ones. But where are all the WOW leaders? Leaders who inspire, motivate, and make a difference not just in their field, but in the lives of those they lead? Leaders who click, resonate, and relate to the real people? Where are the leaders who, instead of merely doling out orders, empower and encourage, eliciting creativity, strength, and excellence from their team?

If you've ever been an employee, you know what I mean. You've probably worked for (and with) a variety of leaders—some so horrible you would like to forget, and others so ordinary they were soon forgotten entirely. But have you ever had a great boss? Not decent, okay, fine, nice, or better-than-most, but really, truly outstanding? Odds are, you haven't. But why? Because the climb to the so-called top can be challenging, unpredictable, and downright exhausting. And while most leaders want to be WOWs, they often hit so many obstacles that they run out of steam before reaching the pinnacle of greatness. They plant their flag on the mountain of mediocrity, succumbing to the notion that good enough is good enough. Rather than excelling, they stagnate.

To really tap into your leadership potential, you've got to keep moving, growing, changing, and bettering yourself, regardless of your rank or title. Even when you've "arrived," you're still not there. Leadership, like life, is a journey, not a destination. Whether you're the newbie at the conference table, an experienced middle manager, or the veteran bigwig at the helm, you're all on the same leadership path; at least, you should be, if you want to WOW.

Real-world examples of exceptional leaders are few and far between, since so many would-be WOWs stop short of their full potential. But in the fictional world of television, where anything is possible, there are a plethora of examples from which to draw inspiration. Although I'm not a television junkie, I've learned quite a bit as a casual but regular viewer. I've found that while TV's primary function is entertainment, there's value and substance at its core. The story lines that are developed and the characters that are created often mirror and reflect humanity at its worst and its best. If we look beneath the surface of the drama, comedy, sentimentality, and occasional horror of what we see on TV, we find layers of truth. We can relate to it, understand it, and learn from it.

If you've never had a great boss, you're not alone. The majority of people tend to do little more than tolerate their bosses. But can you imagine working for someone as dependable, trustworthy, and humble as Leroy Jethro Gibbs, the *NCIS* top cop? How about *Star Trek*'s polyester prince, the decisive Captain James T. Kirk? Or *CSI*'s fair and team-focused Catherine Willows? In the TV realm, there are countless examples of characters with WOW leadership qualities. Think about the patient, integrity-solid Captain Frank Furillo of *Hill Street Blues*; New York's ideal (and therefore fictional) police commissioner Frank Reagan of *Blue Bloods*; approachable people-person and intuitive decision maker Commander Bill Adama, top-ranking officer on *Battlestar Galactica*; or Captain Claudette Wyms, the veteran police detective who serves as a moral guidepost on *The Shield*. The list goes on and on. How much better could we become under the wing of these fictional greats?

Leaders: WOWs and DUDs

TV leaders might not be the real deal, but many portray very real qualities, attributes, and ideals to which we might aspire. WOW leaders aren't perfect, but they're constantly striving to be better. They're not your ordinary, run-of-the-mill, cookie-cutter bosses who run the show with dreary, dispassionate authority. Instead, WOW leaders possess a certain something, an extra oomph that makes you stand up and take notice. There's an aura, a *je ne sais quoi*, about them that inspires their followers in a profound way.

WOW leaders embody the qualities they want to see in others; they lead by example, displaying an impressive work ethic and an attitude of confidence, fearlessness, and positivity. They have the ability to listen and to lead, and they have the fortitude to skillfully navigate a team, even around the bumps that inevitably turn up along every road to success.

WOW leaders are:

- Honest and trustworthy
- Humble and respectful
- Dedicated to self-improvement
- Authentic
- Goal-driven visionaries
- Effective communicators
- Invested in others
- Inspirational motivators
- Agents of change
- Bold decision makers and problem solvers

WOWs don't simply gain a following due to a promotion or by possessing the personality skills to persuade others into believing in their actions and choices. At their core, they're focused on doing right by being the right person and leading in the right way. When you tune in to WOW leadership, you're not only setting a vision and a goal for yourself, you're committed to the betterment of a business, a team, and the individuals you lead. WOW leaders aren't just good bosses, they're good people with a great purpose: not to elevate themselves above everyone around them, but rather to help those around them rise to their own potential.

On the other end of the leadership spectrum—nowhere near good, and far from WOW—are the DUD leaders. On TV, DUDs are those power-hungry, greedy, egotistical personalities who would rank among the worst bosses you'd ever meet. They may be persuasive and charismatic, but such charm often masks a self-serving, one-sided quest to attain power and personal success—even if it comes at the expense of the team. Think Monty Burns, the power plant overlord who serves as Homer's boss on *The Simpsons* or the negative, pugnacious Louie DePalma, the cage-dwelling boss/dispatcher on *Taxi*. How about the shrewd, morally challenged lawyer Patty Hewes from *Damages*?

Although everyone loves to hate the bad guy on TV, most of us would despise working for the likes of money-hungry Mr. Krabs (*SpongeBob SquarePants*), ego-inflated Michael Scott (*The Office*), or self-righteous and socially inept Dr. Gregory House (*House*). Nor would we want to be compared to any of these DUDs.

Unfortunately, however, real life is chock full of manipulative, ladder-climbing bosses who'll trample over anyone to get ahead. Their bottom-line goals of money, power, and prestige trump any positive leadership attributes. They don't care about what's right, only what's best for them. In any given industry or office around the country, I guarantee you'll find DUDs in positions of power.

As the anti-WOW, DUD leaders possess qualities that are completely contrary to their WOW counterparts. Where WOWs shine, DUDs cast negative shadows on those around them. Where WOWs lift and motivate, DUDs suppress and alienate. Like WOWs, DUDs may possess a certain presence that elevates them in the eyes of those they lead. But they use their charismatic ways to their own advantage, not for the betterment of the group, team, or company.

Remember J. R. Ewing, the villainous oil baron of mega prime-time soap opera *Dallas* (1978–1991)? Talk about egomaniacal. This cowboy-hat-wearing mogul was notoriously loved by audiences for his over-the-top schemes, tricks, and manipulations in the boardroom, bedroom, and beyond. Moral correctness was never a factor in any of his decisions. Financial gain and personal victory were always J. R.'s motives, even if it meant the destruction of his family or friends. While America tuned in week after week to revel in his jaw-dropping DUD antics, he wouldn't have been so adored as a real-life boss, relative, or acquaintance.

Like the J. R. Ewings of the world, DUDs can be fairly easy to identify. They aren't mediocre, underachieving leaders aiming to improve, nor are they potential WOWs trying to find themselves, or new leaders just starting out in a power position. In fact, in most cases, DUDs have been around for quite some time, firmly positioning themselves as untouchable, top-tier players. Sometimes the actions and attitudes of DUD leaders have been rewarded and reinforced by other DUD leaders—people who can identify with the same level of unimpressive leadership.

DUD leaders are:

- Narcissistic and egotistical
- Dishonest
- Manipulative
- Self-serving
- Closed-off; inaccessible
- Quick to pass blame
- Hostile fear-mongers
- Bullies
- Inconsistent
- Unable to connect with people
- Uninspired
- Negative and demeaning
- Quirky or odd

Dealing with a DUD leader can be tricky, if not dangerous to your career health. While many people have left jobs due to poor management or outright bad leadership, you may have no choice but to work with a boss who has sketchy morals, questionable strategies, and awkward or absent communication practices. Learning to maintain your own integrity and stay on the path to becoming a WOW is the challenge when you encounter a DUD, like trying to resist the powers of the devil himself. Don't sell out, though, because once you do, it's hard to salvage your soul. Never align with a DUD. In fact, if at all possible, run as fast as you can in the opposite direction and never look back!

WOW and DUD Shows

The qualities of a WOW leader are like the qualities of a much-loved TV show that moves you, stays with you, and stands the test of time. WOWs are like a classic TV series that has a certain X-factor or degree of originality that clicks with the audience, making it an instant hit and sustaining its popularity years later, even in syndication.

WOW TV shows don't go out of style. They are picked up as reruns, sold as DVD collections, and remembered for story lines and characters that resonate. Shows like *M*A*S*H*, *Friends*, *I Love Lucy*, *Seinfeld*, *The Sopranos*, *Cheers*, *Lost*, and so many others that are unique and cutting edge, that are successful not only in their day, but maintain staying power for years and even decades, are akin to WOW leaders who leave their mark within their industry or group.

However, no one remembers DUD TV shows. And for good reason: DUD television programs are often canceled early on because they don't have an audience. Perhaps these shows have awkward dialogue, unbelievable or uninteresting formats, or casting and acting that aren't up to par.

A standout among the DUDs was the 1990 British sitcom *Heil Honey, I'm Home!* This extremely short-lived series (if a single aired episode qualifies as a series) featured a fictional Adolf Hitler and Eva Braun as *Honeymooners*-esque suburbanites living next door to a Jewish couple. The nonhumorous antics in this unlikely scenario included Nazi salutes and offensive, cringe-worthy dialogue. How a DUD concept like this ever made it past the pitch room is beyond comprehension. But the same can be said for DUD leaders. It defies logic how ineffective, self-righteous leaders rise to power—but they do.

Unfortunately, while most DUD shows are quickly pulled from network lineups, DUD leaders are regularly retained in their positions, even when they should, in fact, be canceled! Due to politics, company ownership, tenure, or any number of other factors, DUD bosses routinely avoid the corporate axe. Similarly, although DUD TV shows are soon forgotten, DUD characters often thrive on WOW TV shows. In fact, many series are built around DUD individuals or use them as a tool to increase viewership. Why? Because people can relate to DUDs.

Everyone has dealt with negative, unlikable, and downright mean individuals at one time or another. On TV, evil and morally incomprehensible behavior can be quite entertaining. In real life, however, it's quite another story. People who find themselves influenced by DUD leaders in the workplace must be able to maneuver around the negativity and triumph in the end—which isn't always easy. A company and its workers, like a TV show and its cast, cannot simply be defined by the worst character. They must exist simultaneously, but also independently of their own flaws and weaknesses, to shine the spotlight on the positive and leave the negatives in the shadows.

The Leadership Journey: Working Your Way to WOW

In between the two extremes of WOW and DUD lies the vast majority of the leadership workforce currently in existence. Along the continuum are those poised to WOW and those on the brink of falling into DUD territory. There are fledgling leaders trying to gain their footing, more experienced leaders floundering with who they are or who they want to become, and a wide range of mediocre, lackluster wannabes. There are also exceptional leaders on the rise who haven't quite achieved WOW leader status but are good, well-respected leaders in their own right. For those near-WOWs, it's often only a matter of time before they absorb enough experience and open enough doors to bring them into the realm of WOW. Regardless of where you are on your leadership journey, you can begin working your way to WOW.

Let's take another look at the ten characteristics of WOW leaders:

- Honest and trustworthy
- Humble and respectful
- Dedicated to self-improvement
- Authentic
- Goal-driven visionaries
- Effective communicators
- Invested in others
- Inspirational motivators
- Agents of change
- Bold decision makers and problem solvers

Read from the top down, these ten traits first define a WOW leader's intrinsic qualities and then begin focusing on how those traits extend outward to positively impact those being led. Want to know why that's important? It's simple: WOW leadership starts on the inside, from the leader's heart, soul, and mind. Everything else builds from that. So, as long as you possess an innate moral soundness, you can become a WOW. By embracing the notion that leading is not merely a gift that is given, but a learned skill that can be strengthened and expanded, you can move from good to great.

However, if your goal is to acquire power, fame, fortune, and status above all else—things external to the heart, soul, and mind—you're heading into DUD territory. Sure, a WOW leader can have all the financial and professional rewards that the DUDs grasp for, but they're side effects of the WOW's primary focus: achieving success for the sake of accomplishment, self-improvement, and the collective good of a business or team.

While most of us want to make money—and there's no shame in admitting it would be nice to collect the big paychecks—a WOW leader isn't necessarily cashing in. You can be a WOW at the local McDonald's, managing the night shift; you can be a WOW volunteer who organizes and oversees philanthropic endeavors; or you can be a high-profile, multimillion-dollar WOW CEO. Your present circumstances aren't as critical as your attitude and inner motivation.

The fundamentals of being a WOW are the same regardless of

position or stature. If you're a WOW, you're achieving something great within your field of choice. You're making a difference. You're leading the way for those seeking direction now, as well as for those who come after you.

The title character of Bob Kane's TV series *Batman* (1966–68) is a WOW leader who cares nothing about acquiring fame or accolades for his superhero deeds. Already a millionaire, money was never Bruce Wayne's goal; serving the community by thwarting the nefarious criminals of Gotham City was always his motivation. Using a secret identity and working from his hidden Bat Cave, the hero never sought to receive awards, recognition, or pats on the back for ridding the city of crime. The intrinsic rewards were always enough for him.

While you may not have the tools on Batman's utility belt at your disposal, you can easily wear the suit of a WOW if you choose to. If you want be a WOW, you need to understand what it is, why it's important, and how to achieve it. You must be open to new perspectives and be willing to pursue new methodologies and leadership strategies. And you must be willing to make positive changes by tuning in to who you are as a leader. Like anything worth having, WOW leadership can be achieved with determination, drive, understanding, and of course, practice. With the right mix of confidence, humility, and willingness to learn and adapt along the way, you can begin to stand out as a leader worth following.

Thriving . . . or Just Surviving?

Throughout your career, there are bound to be ups and downs along the way. You may not always find yourself in the ideal position at a dream company, working with the perfect team. But that doesn't mean you can't always put your best foot—and your best attitude—forward. Regardless of your title or your position, or whether you are currently where you want to be career-wise, make sure you're thriving as a leader, and not just surviving.

If you're thriving, you're more likely to bring out the best in others, helping those you lead to thrive as well. However, if you're just drudging along, phoning in the leadership, you're doing little more than surviving—and I guarantee no one beneath you in the organization is inspired or thriving.

Are you a leader who's thriving? Check your answers to these questions:

- Do you wake up energized and eager to start the day?
- Are you excited about what new challenges you may face?
- Have you set up goals that you are actively working toward achieving?
- Is your office, cubicle, or desk space an organized, productive environment?
- Do you put in 100–110 percent effort on every task?
- Is your attitude positive and encouraging, not defeatist and negative?
- Do you try new approaches, make suggestions, and step up when needed?
- Are you focused on what you can give rather than on what you can get?

Or are you just surviving? Check your answers to these questions:

- Do you wake up unmotivated and dreading the day?
- Are you avoiding new challenges or wishing you could skip out on work?
- Is the only goal you've set at work focused on "getting out of here" or finding a new job?
- Do you find yourself "phoning it in" or putting forth minimal effort?
- Is your attitude negative, dismal, or indifferent?
- Do you pass off assignments to others or fail to contribute anything new?
- Are you more focused on your paycheck, the weekend, or lunchtime than on adding value to the company?

If you're merely surviving, you're not doing anyone any favors . . . including yourself. A WOW leader displays WOW qualities at every stage on the journey toward success. Even when conditions aren't optimal, the job isn't perfect, or the struggle seems impossibly difficult, a WOW will rise to the challenge and make the best of every situation. Today, tomorrow, and every day, harness your inner WOW and remind yourself to not just survive, but to thrive.

Ask yourself and answer honestly: What kind of leader are you now? What kind of leader do you want to become? Good enough—or extraordinary? The same-old cliché boss—or a respected role model worthy of being followed? What business needs today, now more than ever, are people with the passion, drive, and determination not just to lead, but to WOW.

How to Use This Book

All TV shows may not be created equal—think *The Blacklist* versus *The Bachelor*—but their journey to the screen follows a similar set of steps. First, a concept is conceived and pitched to network execs. After the green light is given, the behind-the-scenes building blocks of the program are constructed—actors are cast, scripts are written, sets are built, and the creative direction is determined. Next, a pilot show is produced, and if it hits the mark, it's picked up as a regular series. Once in production, those behind-the-scenes fundamentals come together to create the action and formulate each episode. Finally, the show goes on the air and begins its quest to entertain, captivate, and hold its audience.

Like the production journey of a great TV show, a WOW leader's journey begins with what's inside them (*behind the scenes*), expands to bring their skills into action (*in production*), and then sustains success by continuing to learn, grow, and evolve (*on the air*). In *Tune In to WOW Leadership*, I'll help you define and shape your own leadership experience using real-world insights fortified by fictional TV show character examples and comparisons.

Throughout this book are lists, exercises ("WOW in Action"), and bullet points that provide quick tips, useful techniques, and

WOW-building strategies. I've also included several sections called "Tune In" in which other areas of the TV universe demonstrate ways that WOW leadership can be successfully achieved and maintained.

The road to WOW leadership can be exciting, fulfilling, and full of surprises—but the path isn't the same for everyone. Your individualized experience depends on countless factors—varied obstacles, circumstances, and goals that are unique to your own life mission. But while no two journeys are identical, most people are headed in the same direction—upwards—toward their own paradigm of success. Making the commitment to improve your leadership skills using the tenets of this book will help you achieve your own brand of WOW.

Like watching the unfolding of a powerful TV drama, attaining WOW leadership can be a nail-biting, edge-of-your-seat adventure. It can challenge your thinking and push you to new levels of understanding. At other times, the quest can be more like a sitcom, enabling you to laugh at yourself and accept that even when you make mistakes, you can still make progress.

No matter what television genre you prefer, or what TV shows you're currently tuned in to, this book will help you view them in a whole new light. By examining some of the most popular television series and characters, both current and classic, you'll gain insight into WOW and DUD behaviors—which in turn will help you green-light your own leadership potential.

So, sit back, tune in, and set your internal DVR to WOW!

Part I

Behind the Scenes—
The WOW Within

Chapter 1

WOW Leaders Are Honest and Trustworthy

"If you don't have integrity, you have nothing. You can't buy it. You can have all the money in the world, but if you are not a moral and ethical person, you really have nothing."
—Henry Kravis

The WOW within each of us begins with a core set of fundamental, intrinsic qualities. Every WOW leader should—first, foremost, and always—be honest. A leader needs to be trusted, without question, in order to be followed. Without a steady moral compass and a strong ethical backbone, it's impossible to inspire, motivate, and encourage best practices in others.

Honesty takes courage, consistency, and confidence. Great leaders don't need to be perfect, but they need to possess a self-assuredness and fearlessness at all times that enable them to act truthfully, acknowledge their shortcomings, and admit their mistakes. Only then can they garner the respect of their team members and, by way of example, teach them to conduct themselves with the same level of integrity.

WOW leaders do what's right, not what they can get away with. They keep their integrity intact, maintaining a truthful, honest approach in all decisions and actions. WOW leaders don't make choices based solely on personal gain, and they don't cover up mistakes in an effort to improve their own image.

In Netflix's *Orange Is the New Black*, protagonist Piper Chapman's temporary lapse of integrity lands her in federal prison—derailing the life she'd created years after the fact. Had she maintained her moral ground ten years prior to her incarceration, she would not have agreed to be an occasional mule for her drug-smuggling, then-girlfriend Alex. And she wouldn't be sporting the orange jumpsuit now. While Piper inevitably did the right thing by refusing to partake in illegal activities and cutting ties with Alex, the damage was already done. Her bad decisions caught up with her—right when her life was back on track.

For leaders, there may come a time when bending the rules, cutting corners, or altering the truth seems like a tempting option. You may even be asked to lie or participate in illegal or immoral business practices by a higher-up. If your moral compass starts wavering in the wrong direction, get your bearings and head to the true north of what's right—every time. Only then will you keep your integrity and WOW foundation secure.

Having a solid base of morality is essential in a leadership position. As a rule, being the one in charge affords certain perks that can be hard to resist. But WOW leaders do not use their authority to line their wallets or improve their own standing at the expense of others. Leadership comes with responsibility that relies on trust by those who follow. Being honest and trustworthy is everything when it comes to leadership—you can't be a WOW without it.

There are many loyal, morally solid leaders portrayed on TV, characters who conduct themselves with integrity, grit, and determination, even in the most dire situations. Like many shows in the cop-drama genre, *Hawaii Five-0* and *NCIS* feature leaders who head up groups of investigators and detectives operating in powder-keg environments of conflict, frustration, and confusion (not unlike many real-life corporations or offices).

Steve McGarrett is the top cop of Hawaii Five-0, a fictional Hawaii State Police unit empowered by the governor to act on all seven islands in the chain. Special Agent Leroy Jethro Gibbs is the head of the *NCIS* Major Case Response Team, stationed at Washington Navy Yard in Washington, DC. Although their leadership styles differ, both are extremely loyal and supportive characters who operate with unwavering integrity and devotion to their teams. Both are WOW leaders in their own right.

Throughout his tenure, *NCIS*'s Gibbs has always stayed true to his team members, backing them up against attacks from both inside and outside the agency. He stands by his people regardless of perceived mistakes or potential fallout. With Gibbs, if one person on the team falls, they all tumble after like dominoes, including the leader; no one stands alone.

Similarly, McGarrett displays respect and loyalty to his team members, standing above them in terms of rank, but beside them when it comes to getting the job done. The *Hawaii Five-0* leader has put himself on the line in many instances, displaying not only his integrity, but also his trust in the people he leads.

In the fictional land of TV, as well as in the real world, it takes a WOW leader to be strong enough to operate successfully with that kind of vulnerability. Only exceptional leaders refrain from installing a protective shield around themselves so that all blame bounces off them and lands only on those around them. Hollywood's depiction of leadership characters who do the right thing at all costs is something to aspire to. While not all real-life endings wrap up as perfectly as those on many formulaic TV shows, the idea behind the stories is, fundamentally, on the right track: If you operate with integrity, honesty, and loyalty, you'll gain the respect and admiration of your team and will ultimately become more successful.

Alternatively, DUDs lack integrity and will sell their souls to get ahead. The methods by which their goals are achieved, whether honest or fair, is of low priority to them. DUDs lack accountability and are quick to blame others. They're perfectly willing to throw team members under the bus while they jump safely out of harm's way. They're also inconsistent with their standards and rules, often playing favorites to those who suck up. In short, DUD leaders can't be trusted.

The cult favorite *Arrested Development* expertly portrays a manipulative, morally corrupt DUD who goes to great lengths to keep up appearances and social status. Lucille Bluth, the family matriarch, cares about herself over everything and everyone else, including her own children. In season one's episode "My Mother, the Car," Lucille blames a car accident on her son, Michael, after she tries to run down a man who is riding a Segway and ultimately crashes. Later, at the doctor's office, with Michael suffering from short-term memory loss and lethargic from medication, Lucille repeatedly slaps him whenever he starts showing signs of remembrance. Nice mom.

No matter how intelligent or successful you are, if you're not trustworthy, you'll never gain the respect of those who follow you . . . and therefore, you'll never WOW. People follow those they like and trust. Leaders who have been consistent with their words and actions, showing that they care in both good and bad times, will earn the trust of the people they lead. When taking a leap of faith, as a company or as an individual, you have to believe in and trust that the outcome will be good, or you probably won't move forward. When people trust their leaders, they will move confidently in the right direction. But even the most astute visionary stumbles from time to time, and when that happens, a leader who is respected will still be trusted.

Gain and Sustain Trust

During campaign season, political hopefuls put on their best faces in an attempt to earn the public's votes. Somewhere along the line, the candidates inevitably assert that they can be trusted as a leader. Unfortunately, most of us have become too jaded to wholeheartedly trust any politician. We've been burned before, so we know the drill. But, still, we must cast a vote, so we go with the leader in whom we have the most faith—or the least mistrust. Just as it's important to trust those who run our government, it's also essential to have a trusting relationship with the leaders we report to on a daily basis. We need to trust our bosses—really, truly believe in them.

As a leader, you naturally want your team to have faith in you. But being trusted is more than a luxury; it's a necessity. When your team members don't believe in what you say or do, they won't fully commit to following you. In turn, success becomes nearly impossible. You must gain the respect and trust of your team members so they can confidently and securely follow your lead. By earning and maintaining that trust, you will ultimately elicit their best performance.

Among TV's most consistently trustworthy characters is Reverend Eric Camden from Aaron Spelling's hit show *7th Heaven*. The deeply faithful, honest, and well-intentioned father and minister guides his congregation and his family through the trials and tribulations of real-life issues. As a church and family leader, the reverend's psychology and theology backgrounds come in handy when helping others with their problems. But beyond any professional training or skills, it is his innate integrity, trustworthiness, and drive to always do the right thing that makes him a respected and impactful motivator, adviser, and role model.

There are several key ways that you, as a leader, can build trust with your team:

Be yourself 24/7. As we discuss in more detail in chapter 4, "WOW Leaders Are Authentic," presenting yourself in a clear, steady, and consistent manner is vital to building trust. Be yourself at all times and in all situations, and you will earn the respect of those you lead. Understand that part of being strong is allowing yourself a certain degree of vulnerability. Stay true to yourself and be honest with your team, even when you make mistakes.

Focus on strengths. Look for the positive values of everyone on your team. Sure, every person has weaknesses, but don't forget that he or she also has attributes of strength. Identify and embrace those qualities and learn to reinforce and build on them. Negativity can drive a team down very quickly, so be sure to praise and compliment successes before pointing out weaknesses or missteps. In that way, those you lead will learn to trust that you are out to help them, support them, and guide them rather than simply pouncing on their shortcomings. They will trust you as a competent leader.

Let them speak! Someone once said, "The king may be naked, but pity the poor person who tells the king the truth!" Don't become a pampered monarch who can only be curtsied to and never, ever challenged. Encourage free and open lines of communication. Let your team members speak freely about their ideas, opinions, and even their problems. Make sure they are comfortable and willing to discuss opposing ideas without fear of reprisals. If you let them speak, you earn their trust.

Macro-manage. Your team is not a pack of dogs that needs to be harnessed for the Iditarod. They are talented individuals who are better served when you refrain from micromanaging their every move. Engage your staff without focusing on the minutiae. To build trust, learn to macro-manage and give your team members the freedom they have earned. Allow them to manage the small stuff, showing them that you have faith in their abilities.

Encourage calculated risks. Don't discourage your team members from taking risks or pushing themselves to try new things. By encouraging calculated risk-taking, you demonstrate your belief in the team's decision-making skills.

Share the spotlight. Don't hog the limelight or steal your team's thunder! When possible, proudly announce team and individual achievements to the public or share those successes with colleagues and other staff. Praising your employees openly will help them trust in your character, integrity, and leadership ability.

Accept responsibility. If quotas or results fall short of expectations, take responsibility as the leader. Show your people that you understand when failures or setbacks occur. Leaders build trust quickly when they acknowledge their own accountability promptly and without exception.

Protect your people. The more you stand up for your staff, the more trust you build. People lose trust quickly when they sense their boss will hang them out to dry if disaster occurs. When outsiders try to undermine team members, leaders of merit defend and protect them.

Follow through. When you say that you're going to do something—do it! The same applies to what you say you won't do—don't! Establish a standard of sticking to your word. That's the only way you can be trusted as the boss.

Trust is built and absorbed over time, founded on actions and a proven record of cooperation and integrity. It can't be taught, directed, or dictated. The only way to earn trust is, in fact, to be trustworthy.

Broken Trust

Trust—or lack thereof—is a pivotal theme in the hit show *Homeland*, especially in terms of the relationship between Nicholas Brody and CIA agent Carrie Mathison. The series kicks off with the "hero's return" of Brody, who had previously been held for eight years as an al-Qaeda prisoner of war. As a U.S. Marine and family man, Brody is embraced by the public as a military hero who's endured the unthinkable and triumphantly survived. But the troubled soldier has, in fact, been turned by his captors, and his loyalty no longer lies with his own country. While the savvy CIA agent Mathison almost immediately suspects that Brody is embroiled in a terrorist plot, it takes a while for the rest of the agency to catch on.

Convinced of Brody's al-Qaeda ties, Carrie goes off the grid and begins unsanctioned surveillance on him. The spying brings her closer to the truth but also more connected to the brooding and handsome enigma. Meanwhile, Brody lies repeatedly to his wife, children, and friends, hiding his Muslim conversion and concealing his intention to commit treason against his country. While Brody himself at times seems torn and tortured by his own dishonesty, the lies continue to pile up, and only a last-minute call from home keeps him from activating a suicide vest at the White House.

With Brody clearly unraveling, and Carrie torn between her growing affection and her sustained suspicion of him, they become romantically involved by the close of the first season. However, just as Brody begins to trust her, one misstep reveals her spying ways, and he betrays her instantly by turning her in to the powers that be. By the second season, Carrie has been relieved of duty, but once the CIA is onto Brody, they want her back in the picture. To reestablish her connection with the would-be terrorist, she needs to repair the broken trust between them.

But in the world of *Homeland*, trust is a shaky proposition at best. The relationship is a series of lies, betrayals, and eventual disclosures from both sides. Neither one can truly trust the other, so the relationship is ultimately doomed.

In the world of business, national security might not be the underlying issue, but it is still a fact that when trust is broken it is exceedingly difficult to recover. Even if you're a trustworthy and honest WOW leader, you may not always be surrounded by other upstanding WOWs. You'll probably encounter a backstabbing DUD more than once throughout your career, so you'll need to be prepared to defend yourself and your honor.

Trust can be broken in any number of ways: a previously trusted coworker suddenly breaks a confidence; a new hire with an opposing set of values and philosophies upsets the balance of the team; a misguided, integrity-deficient colleague makes a false claim against you in an attempt to ruin your reputation; a power- and praise-hungry associate purposely takes all the credit for a team effort. In the working world, these scenarios are all too real. When a confidence is broken, you're naturally left wondering how and why it happened. You'll likely feel a number of conflicting emotions: anger, fear, hurt, disappointment, frustration, confusion. When someone crosses you for no apparent reason, it can be especially disheartening, even more than when the offense is committed to gain favor for a promotion or other accolades.

Think about the betrayal that sets the story for the espionage-thriller *Burn Notice*. CIA operative Michael Westen has been "burned" by an unknown betrayer and now finds himself blacklisted, disgraced, and left to wonder why he was set up in the first place. The show follows Westen as he searches for who did the "burning" and why that trust was broken.

Betrayals of trust can be minor, but they can also be catastrophic. When trust is broken between colleagues, it may be difficult to bring the relationship back to where it had been prior to the breach. But work is work, and you must move on. You have to make the attempt to salvage what you can and reestablish an amicable or, at the very least, tolerable rapport with those who've let you down.

Your reaction and approach to dealing with the betrayal and ultimately mending fences will vary depending on the severity of the situation. It's best to be as fair and transparent as possible, but each case is different, and when the offense is job-threatening, it will be extremely difficult to repair the relationship.

As a WOW leader, you need to be able to deal with personal trust issues. You must also have the skills required to step in when trusts are broken within your team. It's one thing not to trust in a nebulous, nameless someone or something that you have no personal relationship with; it's quite another to lose faith in someone you rely on, depend on, and interact with on a regular basis.

There are countless ways trust is broken in the workplace, but most fit into two categories: opportunistic betrayal and premeditated betrayal.

Opportunistic Betrayal

Opportunistic betrayal usually takes the form of a careless, cowardly, and sometimes knee-jerk action that, although not preplanned, happens when the opportunity for betrayal presents itself. This kind of affront often occurs casually, randomly, and without much thought as to the consequences or severity of what is being done. When the betrayal is opportunistic, your colleague acts thoughtlessly and demonstrates a weakness of character. Opportunistic betrayal includes:

- Gossiping or spreading rumors
- Backstabbing or breaking a confidence
- Taking credit for work that they did not do
- Blaming coworkers for their mistakes

On television, the situation-based lie is a common plot developer, especially in comedies. When generally well-liked characters fib, mislead someone, or misrepresent themselves, all sorts of humorous antics ensue. Think of all those times the platonic roommates on *Three's Company* had to lie to Mr. Roper to keep Jack Tripper on the lease. Likewise, lovable buffoon Doug Heffernan from the comedy *The King of Queens* often gets into trouble with his precocious wife, Carrie. In the 2001 episode "Inner Tube," Doug lies about having to work late so he can play football instead of attending a seminar with Carrie. Although the opportunistic lie wasn't meant to hurt or betray his wife, Doug later realizes it was a selfish, cowardly way out. His guilt eventually gets the best of him, as does a football-in-the-rain-induced fever, and he dreams about being in a series of classic TV shows with his father-in-law, Arthur. One of the most memorable sequences is when he dreams he's on *Wheel of Fortune* and the puzzle solution is "Doug Heffernan Is a Big Fat Liar." In the end, he admits his lie to Carrie in an attempt to set things right.

Opportunistic lies and betrayals can be humorous in the world of TV, but when jobs are on the line in the real world, it's not quite as funny. Lies hurt, no matter how innocuous they may at first seem. If you want to be a WOW leader, the truth, no matter how difficult, is always the best option.

Premeditated Betrayal

A premeditated betrayal is a carefully thought-out, preplanned scheme or act that not only violates the trust of a colleague but also intentionally hurts them. When one coworker deliberately betrays another, the motives are often driven by the possibility of career advancement, money, or other accolades. An individual who carries out a premeditated betrayal is often a DUD or one in the making, clearly exhibiting a lack of integrity.

Premeditated betrayal includes:

- Character assassination
- False claims about serious workplace violations
- Sabotage: setting someone up to fail or causing failure

Kevin Spacey's evil-doing Frank Underwood in the political drama *House of Cards* is prone to premeditated betrayal to further his own career. In an effort to secure a candidacy for vice president, he sets up an elaborate scheme to first lift up and then tear down Peter Russo, a young gubernatorial hopeful. The manipulative Underwood sets Russo up for failure, then seals his fate by first ensuring his public humiliation and then his death. Talk about extreme DUD behavior!

While real-world boardroom betrayals aren't generally as severe as outright homicide, a deliberate breach of trust of any kind can be hard to deal with, understand, or forgive. The less-offensive opportunistic betrayal can often be addressed and repaired, but rebounding from a premeditated backstabbing is an uphill battle that might be impossible to win. Even if the victim is willing to work on rebuilding trust, when a colleague stoops to that level of betrayal, he or she may not be open to or interested in forgiveness. If such a person is willing to damage your reputation and hang you out to dry in the first place, the individual probably won't want to shake hands and move on after the fact—at least, not willingly or easily.

In either case, once a trust is broken, how can it be repaired? Think of what it's like to lose a customer. Not only is the relationship severed, but often the customer begins spreading the word, negatively influencing other clients in the process. Once customers are lost, how do you get them back? It's hard. It takes persistence, determination, and a variety of creative approaches. And still it doesn't always work.

When it comes to repairing a broken trust, persistent, determined motivation is required. Trust within a team is so crucial to success that an attempt to repair relationships must be made. But everyone involved, including the WOW leader, needs to be on board and willing to tend to the wounds.

Dealing with Broken Team Trust

When trust issues arise between team members, WOW leaders need to be proactive in keeping the situation from escalating. They also need to be actively involved or ensure that HR is a part of the recovery and repair process between the parties.

Although many team situations are better served by a hands-off, on-the-sidelines approach from the boss, infighting and angst between colleagues is not one of those instances. A leader must deal with betrayal and trust issues, especially if those involved are stuck in a loop of hurtful behaviors.

If the issues are not dealt with, the whole team will suffer. When emotions fester beneath the surface or when they are outwardly displayed with anger or inappropriate, uncooperative behaviors, a number of negative consequences result, including:

- Decreased productivity
- Emotional exhaustion
- General distrust and cynicism, causing a snowball effect of paranoia and fear
- Lack of trust in leadership to manage a team
- Avoidance and lack of teamwork/collaboration
- Loss of top talent in the event that the "wronged" person leaves the organization
- Hostile, unproductive work environment

On the business-competition reality series *The Apprentice*, team dynamics often escalate into backstabbing, name-calling, and overall hostilities. Since the contestants are being judged in the boardroom after each team challenge and one or more are fired based on his or her performance, tensions tend to run high. While this TV-created situation is unique, the breakdown of trust happens just as often in real-world teams.

In the episode "Jingle All the Way Home" from the "Celebrity" edition of the series, two teams of three are tasked with writing a jingle for an ad campaign. Both teams have communication and respect problems right from the start, but team Forte (consisting of team manager Dayana Mendoza and teammates Clay Aiken and Lisa Lampanelli) experiences a total breakdown as accusations and curse words fly between colleagues. As things continue to escalate, Dayana calls Lisa "loud," and Lisa calls her team leader "passive aggressive," among other choice words. Lisa demands an apology from Dayana but then refuses to accept it when it's not heartfelt enough. Later, Lisa says if "someone lies about or misrepresents" her she considers them "a vicious animal and attacks." Needless to say, this team lost the challenge, and in the end, the team leader was fired and sent on her way.

Trust Strategies

A leader's role is vital to keep situations of broken trust from spiraling out of control. Here are some methods you can employ to ensure the best possible outcome:

Be fair. First and foremost, a leader must be seen as an impartial, fair, and trusted adviser who looks out for the best interests of all employees.

Be self-aware. Realize that your business objectives will never be met when there's a culture of conflict or lack of trust among your team members. Be aware of the kind of team you want to lead, and know that you must lead completely to keep the team productive and intact.

Keep in touch. When you stay in the loop, you can recognize and identify issues early on and recognize when conflicts are affecting performance. When more than one team member is telling you there's a problem, it's probably more than a minor personality conflict. Regardless, you'll want to assess the severity of the conflict.

Face the facts. Be honest with yourself when things aren't going well within the team. Be willing to deal with conflict management head-on by asking for help from your HR department or overseeing a conflict resolution intervention. If a problem hasn't resolved itself in a few weeks or months, it probably never will—without your guidance.

Communicate and investigate. Talk to those involved, as well as to team members around the situation. Get the story from multiple angles, as it's likely that other colleagues know the truth. Although those on the periphery of the problems may not want to get involved or take sides, you or HR will need to delicately extract information and gain their insights and observations to get to the heart of the matter.

Be the bridge. When a conflict resolution intervention is initiated, you or HR must serve as the bridge between the parties, helping them reach out and move little by little toward a middle ground of cooperation. You must remain impartial and focused on a solution rather than taking sides or making rash judgments. Listen and carefully steer the coworkers in the right direction.

Trust your instincts. When dealing with conflicts, it will often be a matter of he said/she said, with little proof as to who is telling the truth.

But if you're in touch with your workers, you'll know their personalities quite well and will be better equipped to gauge the trustworthiness and integrity of those involved. Like Gibbs on *NCIS*, listen to your gut.

Make a decision. You need to take action and make decisions about the matter, including imposing sanctions and issuing reprimands in certain cases. Depending on the severity of the breach of trust, employee dismissal may be the only option if the conflict cannot be resolved. It will be better in the long run to lose one bad apple than to spoil the whole bunch.

In matters of broken trust issues between coworkers, there are also things leadership should NEVER do, including:

Show favoritism. Never display favoritism or inconsistent rules and expectations within the team. This may ignite unhealthy competition or negative feelings.

Listen to rumors. Don't make rash decisions based on hearsay, rumors, or accusations that may or may not be true. Call HR or investigate the issues firsthand.

Lose your temper. If you deal with team problems with anger, snap judgments, or generic, across-the-board punishments, you'll only be adding fuel to the fire.

Take sides. Once a trust breach is evident, don't voice your allegiance to one party over the other before investigating and hearing all sides of the story. Do not side with one person or favor the underdog if the rest of the team is telling you there is an issue. Your workers are probably not "ganging up" on the person. Instead, they might be trying to tell you something.

Ignore the problem. The worst thing you can do is nothing. If you ignore the problem, it will inevitably escalate to a red-level, powder-keg situation. By sweeping the issues under the rug, you're sending a message that you don't care and can't be trusted as a competent leader.

Facing Personal Trust Issues

Let's face it. There are bound to be conflicts from time to time in any corporate culture. But when you're the WOW leader and a betrayal is committed against you, the way you deal with those issues can have a direct impact on your entire following. If you aren't proactive about repairing issues of personal trust against yourself, the very core of your team can be rocked and shaken so badly that it may never recover.

As the victim of a broken trust as well as the one in charge, you must take action immediately when issues arise or else run the risk of falling apart and taking the entire team down with you. You must face the problem head-on and attempt to rebuild, repair, and salvage a cooperative working relationship with the one who betrayed you.

Here's what you need to do when someone betrays your trust:

Be honest. Remain candid about your own role in the situation. Did you provoke the action in any way? Did you assume confidentiality in a matter without making it clear and then later feel betrayed? Were you not only the victim but the offender as well, participating in a mutual back-and-forth of rumors or backstabbing? Reflect on whether the issues are truly a one-sided breach of trust or a case of personality conflict.

Communicate. Have a transparent conversation with the problematic colleague or staff member, putting all the issues out on the table. Present your concerns, and then listen to the explanation without accusing or interrupting. If appropriate, ask for an apology or a formal retraction. Let the coworker know what you expect without making demands or issuing ultimatums.

Stay calm. Keep your cool, even when you've been wronged. Don't fly off the handle and publicly take aim at the colleague who broke your trust. You'll not only inflame an already tense situation, but you'll also cast a negative shadow over yourself and your character. As they say, take the high road—especially if the low road is already taken.

Be patient. Recognize that rebuilding trust is a process and it will not be repaired overnight. You may be able to move past the lapse in trust, especially if the offending colleague makes efforts to right the wrong, but it will take time to regain a solid, trusting relationship.

Issue sanctions. If a team member under your direct supervision committed the offense, there may need to be penalties for the insubordination. Once it's been clearly established that a staff member has broken your trust, you may need to issue sanctions, ranging from a write-up to a pink slip, depending on the scope and severity of the betrayal.

Appeal to a higher-up. If another leader in a lateral position committed the offense, you may need to protect your own interests by bringing the matter to the attention of someone with a higher authority than yourself. In cases of premeditated betrayals, rebuilding relationships may be next to impossible, especially if your character and integrity is being bashed or if your job is in jeopardy as a result. Be proactive in clearing your name and keeping your WOW status intact.

There are also a few things you should NOT do when someone betrays you at the office:

Point fingers. Don't publicly accuse a coworker of a breach of trust or spread rumors about the person's behavior. It only makes you look bad and inflames the situation.

Retaliate. Don't respond in kind to a broken trust. Retaliation or tit-for-tat actions will not solve the problem; they will only create more trouble.

Ignore or cower. Never ignore or overlook a breach of trust by a colleague. If you wait for the offender to approach you with an apology, you'll likely be waiting forever. Also, don't allow yourself to be bullied by cowering in a corner and pretending not to be hurt; this is not the definition of taking the high road. Stand up for yourself by initiating a healthy conversation that brings the problem out into the open.

Bend over backward. Do what you can to mend the relationship, but realize that your efforts may be met with resistance, denials, or outright lies that can make the situation irreparable. Don't go out of your way to make things right if your coworker won't even lean in with an apology.

Run or resign. Don't let someone run over your trust and ultimately run you out of a job. Face the issues head-on in a timely manner before you feel backed into a corner and unable to cope in a hostile work environment. Even if you can't repair the broken trust, don't let it break you.

Although I wouldn't recommend his methods per se, Don Draper, the slick adman from the period drama *Mad Men*, must deal with trust issues in the episode "Red in the Face." Don's boss, Roger Sterling, makes a drunken pass at Don's wife after having dinner at the Drapers' home. Don remains outwardly cool, never raising his voice or losing his temper, even after Roger "apologizes" by saying, "When a man gets to a point in his life when his name's on the building, he can get an unnatural sense of entitlement." However, Don has revenge on his mind.

The next day, with an important client (Nixon's campaign managers) on the docket, Don encourages his boss to join him in scarfing down oysters and booze during a lunch meeting. When they return to the office drunk, the elevator is conveniently broken, and they must climb twenty-three flights of stairs to reach the waiting clients. Being younger and in better shape, Don manages the trek with ease, but Roger doesn't fare as well. He greets Nixon's people sweaty, red-faced, and unable to speak. Instead, he vomits on the carpet.

Sure, Don's retaliation was probably justified, given the circumstances, but nothing was truly resolved by the exchange. Don may have felt temporarily better by exacting his revenge, but the relationship remains tarnished by the breach of trust. Keep in mind, too, that Don, although dapper and skilled at advertising, is a DUD himself: egotistical, self-serving, and a philanderer—making him a hypocrite to boot.

When trust is broken between colleagues, the road to repair can be long or never ending, but it must be traveled in an attempt to fix the potholes and roadblocks to success. Both parties must be cooperative and willing to move past the situation, with the guidance and intervention of higher-level leadership, if needed.

Trust is a fragile but vital component of any company's corporate culture. Once that trust is shaken, disastrous tremors of hostility and resentment can send aftershocks reeling through the team, causing cracks in the very foundation of the business. As a WOW leader, be sure your integrity is solid and never resort to breaking a trust. If you do fumble, own your mistake and go directly to your colleague to make things right. By demonstrating your honesty even when you err, you'll set yourself apart as a WOW leader worth following—trust me.

TV's Kiss of Death: Breaking the Viewer's Trust

There's more to a successful company than just the CEO at the helm—there's an army of WOW individuals making things happen on a daily basis. In much the same way, there's more to great TV than what's portrayed on our screens. Often, what makes or breaks a show is what goes on behind the scenes, in that place invisible to viewers but vital to the existence of the medium. The decisions made by producers, directors, studio executives, and others are largely irrelevant to us; we simply don't care as long as our show is reliably entertaining. But once our trust as viewers is broken, it can mean the end of our loyalty to the show.

For example, if our favorite TV show regularly airs on Thursday nights at 8:00 p.m., we expect to switch on the box and find it there to watch. We trust the schedule we've been promised, and if we're let down too many times, we're going to become frustrated and confused and eventually stop tuning in. That's what happened in the case of the once-popular series *Moonlighting*, starring Cybill Shepherd and then-relatively unknown Bruce Willis.

Moonlighting, a detective series recognized as the first so-called "dramedy," aired from 1985 to 1989 and is often heralded as a groundbreaking, innovative series. However, the complex scripts and filming techniques employed by the show often caused production delays, which, in turn, made *Moonlighting* notorious for airing reruns when new episodes were expected. Viewers, although enamored with the content and quality of the program, lost faith in it. They could no longer trust their show would deliver what it promised, which likely contributed to the show's ultimate decline in ratings and its eventual cancellation.

Integrity in the Face of Adversity

WOW leaders aren't always popular, they aren't always right, and they certainly aren't always perfect. But they maintain their integrity even when their decisions come under attack. In the face of adversity, WOW leaders must ignore the naysayers and focus on being authentic to their own goals, choices, and beliefs.

Admittedly, it isn't easy to maintain composure and stay on course when being attacked or encouraged to stray from your intended path. It's even harder when you feel your adversaries outnumber your supporters. But, that's when WOW leaders prove their mettle. That's how you separate the WOWs from the wannabes.

Here are a few tips to help you maintain your integrity in the face of adversity:

Keep your chin up. Don't let others dictate your level of confidence. Stand fast and firm in support of yourself, always displaying the self-assuredness you possess.

Stick to your principles. Regardless of outside pressures, negative opinions, or inferences of doubt, stay true to your core principles. Have an honest, truthful, frank internal conversation with yourself, evaluating who you are and what you stand for. Don't compromise on your belief system to please anyone else.

Be fearless. Don't let the fear of failing, being unpopular, or eliciting negative reactions prevent you from acting on your beliefs. When you're unafraid, nothing can hold you back—even adversity.

Don't be defensive. Be the bigger person. When you're under attack, your first instinct may be to fight back. Sure, you'll want to defend yourself, discredit your opposition, and point out the injustice of the attack. But stooping to the level of the attacker only makes you look bad. Plus, it shifts your focus toward justifying your goals and away from implementing and succeeding at them.

Lean on your supporters. Build a support network that keeps you grounded and secure. Instead of being discouraged by those who oppose you, focus instead on those who back you up and stand beside you no matter what.

Look forward, not behind. Keep moving forward, making decisions, and taking action to support your goals. Look toward the potential of what's to come, not backward at any missteps or mistakes you might have made along the way. Those who oppose you will be

quick to point out your past, but in the face of adversity, always turn
toward the future.

In the words of TV WOW leader Frank Reagan, the commish from
Blue Bloods, "Doing the right thing may be hard, but it sure as hell isn't
complicated." Leaders with integrity at their core maintain their WOW
factor in the face of adversity, never succumbing to the temptations of
those who oppose them.

Being honest and trustworthy is at the heart of WOW leadership
because you can't build a strong structure without a secure foundation.
Just as you can't create a hit TV show without the right mix of behind-
the-scenes factors—a capable crew, an exemplary cast, and a believable
script—you can't form a winning business team without first securing
a sense of trust. And to do that, you must be an honest leader whom
others trust enough to follow.

Chapter 2

WOW Leaders Are Humble and Respectful

"There is no respect for others without humility in one's self."
—*Henri-Frédéric Amiel*

The behind-the-scenes foundation of a WOW leader is built on trust but also has its roots in humility and respect. The greatness of WOW leaders lies not in what they say about themselves or in the accolades they receive, but in their ability to lead a team while acting with fairness, foresight, confidence, and understanding. Exceptional leaders conduct themselves not as if they are the most important link in the chain but rather the link responsible for connecting the rest; thus, they are consequently as strong or weak as the other members of the team. Truly great leaders acknowledge their decisions, even when they prove to be wrong. They do not divert their mistakes onto their subordinates in an effort to make themselves appear blameless.

By keeping the perspective and feelings of the entire team in mind, WOW leaders stay grounded in the realities around them. After all, a little understanding goes a long way. Outstanding leaders know the relevance of the team members' feelings and want them to have a voice in their own careers. Rather than having a "deal with it" attitude, they're empathetic to the stresses and hesitations the staff may be faced with on a daily basis.

Self-assuredness is essential to great leadership. WOW leaders have confidence in themselves and do not need their egos stroked. They invest in and support their teams and are secure enough in their leadership role to share in or even pass on the glory of their successes. They're also secure enough to absorb any blame from potential missteps. They will not push their team into the darkness while they stand alone in the sun.

WOW leaders are strong in their abilities but also respect the abilities of their employees. They do not operate with a hunt-or-be-hunted attitude. Instead, they create a cooperative, peaceful environment in which everyone on the team is empowered to succeed.

The fictional WOW leader Captain Frank Furillo, from the popular drama *Hill Street Blues*, bucked the cop-drama stereotype of the "hard as nails" lead officer. Furillo resonated as a more soft-spoken, quiet, yet focused leader who boosted his team's productivity and morale with patience and diplomacy. Rather than browbeating those under his command, he inspired the eclectic group of police officers, using techniques similar to business greats Peter Drucker and Warren Bennis. Using a softer, more understanding approach, he empathized with and related to his staff rather than employing fear tactics or trying to puff himself up as the alpha male. He established a trusting, cooperative work environment where his sometimes-dysfunctional officers could be themselves and, therefore, do their best work.

Unlike the patient and authentic Captain Furillo, those who are constantly stepping on others to boost themselves up higher are egoists, not leaders. DUD leaders' egos precede them; they're more focused on their titles than their actual jobs. They'll bend over backward to work their accomplishments into a conversation, and they'll be sure you know exactly how successful, important, and vital they are to the company. "Humble" is not in their vocabulary; they might even have a portrait of themselves hanging in the boardroom. Or, as in the case of Michael Scott, Dunder Mifflin branch manager on *The Office*, they may sport a self-purchased "World's Best Boss" coffee mug from which to sip their daily brew!

Remember, humility is not a weakness; it's a strength. Being a power-grabber who shows no concern for those around you weakens your character and sets you apart only as a first-class jerk. Showing you are humble and grateful for the opportunity to lead demonstrates that you are respectful of others and that you feel no sense of entitlement or superiority. WOW leaders do not need to point out or boast about their greatness . . . they simply are great.

R-E-S-P-E-C-T

Respect is the hallmark of any good business relationship. As the leader, you want your staff to respect your authority as well as your character and abilities. You also need your colleagues to respect you as an equal and your superiors to respect your decisions and ability to lead the team. But WOW leaders know that real respect is not given simply because they're in a position of power—it must be earned. And a large part of earning respect comes from giving it back. In other words, to be respected, you must also be respectful.

One TV boss who garnered little to no respect from his staff was Arthur Carlson, the underqualified, indecisive station manager from *WKRP in Cincinnati*. Mr. Carlson was given his title because his wealthy mother owned the station, not because he was qualified for the role. His ineffective, often backward managing style kept the station constantly underwater financially. Although his heart was typically in the right place and he wasn't an out-and-out DUD in terms of his motives, his actions—or lack of action—regularly held the team back from success. No one respected his authority, because he didn't have the skill set to lead.

While it's impossible to respect leaders who haven't earned the designation, it's even more difficult to respect leaders who use their titles only for their own advantage. DUD leaders are often tyrants, egomaniacs, and narcissists who operate in a bubble of their own authority: shielding themselves from blame, pointing the finger at those around them, and caring only for what they can personally gain. They have no respect for others, and it shows. Such DUDs are not respected; they're feared. WOWs, alternatively, focus on the team, the company, and the job at hand—not their own agenda. They don't demand respect; they give it—which leads to receiving it in return.

Here's how to be a WOW by dishing out respect to your team, coworkers, and colleagues . . . one letter at a time:

Reward. Give credit when credit is due. Reward privately as well as publicly for a job well done. Demonstrate your respect by showing your appreciation for those who put in effort, go the extra mile, and perform beyond expectations. In addition to positive reinforcement, offer career-based incentives like expanded responsibilities, promotions, or monetary raises when possible.

Empathize. Seek to understand and relate to the issues, problems, and concerns of others. When you care enough to acknowledge the perspectives of your staff and your colleagues, you give them the respect and attention their opinions deserve.

Share. Don't hog the limelight or the successes. Share best practices with colleagues, coworkers, and team members. It's disrespectful and selfish to hold others back while you soar ahead, deliberately hiding your knowledge of process or strategies—especially when you are benefitting from someone else's work. Show your respect through your transparency and willingness to openly share what is working with others who need to know.

Protect. When mistakes happen or things don't go exactly as planned, don't stab your coworkers and staff in the back . . . have their backs! Protect your team from the fallout of negativity when they've done their best and it just didn't pan out. Stand behind them and lift them up, rather than pushing them down, when the going gets tough. You can't be respected if you throw your team under the bus . . . especially if you're driving it!

Empower. Respectful leaders encourage and enable their employees to make decisions, take action, and have a voice within the team. Give your trusted workers the latitude to share, contribute, and act on their ideas. Help them utilize their skill sets and develop new ones by encouraging them to grow, change, and expand their abilities.

Communicate. Effective communication is the pinnacle of respect.

Making yourself clearly heard and understood is a given, but actively listening to the opinions, questions, and feedback of your staff is equally as vital. By encouraging a reciprocal, free exchange of ideas and overall communication, you're acknowledging the importance of those you lead. When you shut people down by not listening, not caring, or not enabling them to speak and share their thoughts, you destroy the relationship and lose all respect.

Trust. Just as your team members need to trust that you're moving them in the right direction and making the best possible decisions for the group, they also need to feel that you trust them to make it happen. Always operate with integrity and honesty, even when the choices you make are unpopular or go against the grain. Be authentic and truthful, and you'll be respected even when you must make tough decisions. In the same way, demonstrate your faith and trust in your people by teaching them to be their own best selves, not carbon copies of you or someone else. Value them as unique individuals with unique skills and perspectives—and respect their ability to WOW just as much as you respect your own.

When Aretha Franklin famously spelled out R-E-S-P-E-C-T in her iconic song, the whole world took notice and collectively nodded in agreement. After all, we all want to be respected, not taken for granted or treated with aloof disinterest or outright negativity. Great leaders know that they must earn the respect of their followers, and a big part of that comes from affording them the respect they deserve. When WOW leaders spell out R-E-S-P-E-C-T, they dish it out by Rewarding, Empathizing, Sharing, Protecting, Empowering, Communicating, and Trusting their people.

One of TV's most respected military leaders was Colonel Sherman T. Potter, who took over as head doc on *M*A*S*H* after Colonel Henry Blake's untimely departure. When the gang of misfits at the 4077th lost their beloved Colonel Blake, it seemed impossible that they could accept and ultimately embrace another leader. But after a week under Frank Burns's tyrannical temporary command, the doctors were pleasantly relieved when the experienced, take-charge Potter arrived in season four's "Change of Command." Colonel Potter was consistent, trustworthy, communicative, and inspirational. He brought the right mix of humility, authenticity, humor, skill, empathy, and above all, mutual respect needed to successfully meld with the team.

Emotional Intelligence

Being humble and respectful means being empathetic, caring, and cognizant of others' feelings and internal conflicts. Contrary to what people may think, the best leaders don't necessarily have a high IQ—but they almost invariably have a high EIQ. Emotional intelligence quotient (EIQ) is a much better indicator of future or current leadership success than raw intelligence After all, most of us have encountered really smart, attractive leaders who look great in a suit, are well-spoken and knowledgeable, yet who fail in the business world. Why don't they make it? Often, it's because they lack in the area of EIQ.

We often characterize people as either street-smart or book-smart, but with EIQ, it's all about being people-smart—not in the way a used-car salesman is smart about manipulating, controlling, and persuading people. It is more like the way a parent is sensitive to a child's emotions.

People with high emotional intelligence are in touch with their own emotions as well as those of their team members. They interact with others in a way that draws people in and makes them feel comfortable, secure, and understood. By relating to and engaging with people in a more meaningful way, those with a high EIQ form healthier relationships, achieve greater success at work, and lead a more fulfilling life.

If you have a high EIQ, you have:

Self-awareness. You understand your own emotions and how they affect your thoughts and behavior. You're self-confident; you know your strengths and you acknowledge your weaknesses.

Self-management. You're able to control your feelings and behaviors by managing those emotions in healthy, positive ways. You take initiative, follow through on commitments, and are adaptable and flexible to changing circumstances—all of which are critical skills for the future.

Social awareness. You seek to understand the emotions, needs, and concerns of other people. You're attentive and connected and are able to pick up on emotional cues and body-language indicators. You feel comfortable socially and recognize the power dynamics in a group or organization. In short—you care!

Relationship management. You know how to develop and maintain good relationships through dedication and commitment. You communicate clearly, inspire and influence others, work well in a team, and are able to effectively manage conflict.

Organizations are great only when their people work as hard for each other as they do for themselves. As a WOW leader, be sure your top-performing team includes those with a high EIQ who are willing and able to encourage the emotional growth of those who fall short in the EIQ area. Many people have the potential for a high EIQ, but don't know how to harness it or when to put it to use. Some people are conditioned to believe in an old-school culture of leadership, where a rock-solid, rigid exterior denotes power. They may be afraid to tap into their EIQ because they feel it is a weakness. WOW leaders demonstrate that a culture of caring is more productive, and a high EIQ is prized.

Of course, there are also people who aren't willing or capable of increasing their EIQs because teamwork is just not in their DNA. They do not play well with others and have no interest in doing so. In short, they're DUDs.

One TV character who epitomizes high IQ and low EIQ is Dr. Sheldon Cooper, PhD, the off-the-charts genius theoretical physicist on *The Big Bang Theory*. Sheldon may be mega-intelligent, but he's socially inept in the extreme. Not only does he have a laundry list of idiosyncrasies and OCD habits, he has no sense of tact, empathy, or conversational boundaries. While he has no sense of humor and doesn't understand sarcasm, he's often the source of both with his deadpan delivery and awkward, "friendly" interactions with others. He's direct and forthcoming to a fault, never quite getting how offensive or hurtful his words can be. His lack of emotional intelligence is displayed time and time again.

In the episode "The Cooper-Nowitzki Theorem," Leonard persuades a reluctant Sheldon to speak to a group of graduate-level physics students. "It's a waste of time," he says within earshot of the class. "I might as well explain the laws of thermodynamics to a bunch of labradoodles." After Leonard threatens to cancel their trip to the comic book store, however, Sheldon agrees to speak, but does so with disdain, arrogance, and absolutely no EIQ.

He begins by demeaning the group with a comparison to himself when he was a "lowly graduate student." He points out that he was only fourteen at the time and had already accomplished more than they, as adults, ever would. Next, Sheldon goes on to surmise that most of those in attendance do not have the qualifications or potential to make it as theoretical physicists.

"In short," he says, "anyone who told you that you would someday be able to make any significant contributions to physics played a cruel trick on you. A cruel trick indeed. Any questions? I weep for the future of science."

When recruiting people or assessing a new team dynamic, seek out those with high EIQs and steer clear of those on the low end of this scale. A low EIQ should be a deal-breaker as far as hiring, promoting, or retaining your employees. If you observe even one instance of hubris or self-importance, be wary. And if you notice people who refuse to work in teams, point fingers and call out others, or drain energy out of the system through self-promotion, that's an instant red flag to remove them from the team—fast!

WOW leaders have many exceptional traits, including high EIQs. Be sure to cultivate and use your emotional intelligence and align with those people who do the same.

Boost Your EIQ

WOW in Action

EIQ is about how well you process and react to emotions—yours and those of others. Unlike IQ, which you're born with and which remains more or less stable throughout your life, EIQ is not set in stone. It's a skill that can be developed, not a core trait that can't be altered. Although many people are innately more prone to having a higher EIQ than others, you can boost your EIQ factor if you recognize its importance and make the choice to enhance it.

So, how do you grow your emotional intelligence skills? Like any other skill, you need to know what good looks like, have the desire and motivation to change, and then, of course, practice. Here are some of the basics on improving your EIQ:

1. *Observation.* To get more in tune with your EIQ, try to become more observant of other people's reactions, feelings, and body language. Write down what you notice. Even if they weren't actually arguing or disagreeing, did their demeanor, tone of voice, or eye contact change at any point? Did your responses and reactions cause them to shut down, tune out, become uncomfortable, or get agitated? By jotting down your observations, you'll begin to formulate a recognizable pattern when it comes to social and emotional behaviors. You'll begin to understand the importance of paying attention to and responding to emotional cues. In the same way, try writing down how certain situations made you feel.

2. *Modeling.* Before you can change or improve a skill, you have to know what you're aiming for. When it comes to EIQ, you need to know what great looks like. How do those with a high EIQ behave? What are they doing that you aren't? Find a role model whom you recognize as having a high EIQ. Consider interviewing this person and asking questions that will help you fill in any gaps in your social awareness. Find out if your mentor has observed any of your behaviors that could be changed.

3. *Motivation.* A strong and sustainable motivation is often the most challenging part of change. Maintaining the drive to improve is what trips all of us up, because, too often, the daily grind gets in the way. So much energy goes into just keeping up that getting ahead and improving our skill set frequently gets pushed to the back burner or altogether forgotten. But determination to improve is what separates the WOWs from the rest. Make up your mind to invest in your own self-improvement, and

then put in the extra effort to make it so. To maintain motivation, try writing down a weekly or monthly goal for your EIQ behaviors and then, at the end of the period, evaluating how you did.

4. *Connection.* At the heart of emotional intelligence is being engaged and connected. To truly listen and focus on the moment isn't difficult, but it does take practice and discipline. There are moments when you must stop multitasking, turn off the TV, refrain from texting, resist the urge to check your emails . . . in short, tune out anything that is not relevant to the current interpersonal interaction. By really, actively listening and turning your full attention to those you're relating with, you're demonstrating an emotional connection that will improve your social awareness skills. To ensure your connection in an interaction, make it a habit to face the person you are speaking with and provide nonverbal feedback that assures the other person you are attending to what he or she is saying.

5. *Communication.* Listening is a great start, but being connected is about reciprocal communication. Be genuine and forthcoming about your point of view, but also acknowledge, respect, and try to understand the other side. Ask thoughtful, pertinent questions that show you care about what's being communicated to you. Inquire about the other person's feelings, thoughts, or comments on any given matter. Let it be a give-and-take exchange rather than a one-sided directive. By asking questions, listening, and engaging in meaningful conversations, you demonstrate your genuine interest in the other party or parties.

6. *Reinforcement.* Let's face it—people like those who like them. They respond better to those they get along with and can interact with on a comfortable level. It's hard to simply say, "be likeable," but having a high EIQ is tied, in part, to likeability. Think of it from the other person's point of view. If you're not listening to me, don't care about what I say, or have little interest in my feelings, I'm not going to like you. But if you demonstrate that you value my opinion and are invested in my feelings, I'll value and respect you in return. Positive reinforcement goes a long way. So, make it a practice to be generous with authentic praise and positive remarks regarding others. People will cling to a sincere compliment or statement of praise like a lifeline. However, a constant barrage of negative feedback will only drown their confidence and create hostility toward the one pushing them under.

WOW leaders are strong, confident, and self-assured, but that doesn't mean they're arrogant or uncaring. In fact, the greatest WOWs have the highest EIQs. Their elevated emotional intelligence factor enables them to be solidly in touch with themselves and those around them in ways that really matter. They're not merely concerned with performance based on results, numbers, and fact-based outcomes; they're connected to the individuals who drive those successes or failures. They are keenly aware that healthy, cooperative interpersonal relationships are what make or break the backbone of a team. If you want to be a great leader, you can't just focus on what's within you—you must care about what's within others. Only then can you develop and grow your EIQ and truly be a WOW.

I hate to dis him again, but Michael Scott, the fictional middle manager on *The Office*, is far from a WOW leader. In fact, he displays many DUD qualities, including being self-centered, egotistical, and odd. He once said, "Would I rather be feared or loved? Easy. Both. I want people to be afraid of how much they love me."

Although Michael tries to be "friends" with his staff, he fails miserably because he has an extremely low EIQ. This inept boss doesn't know how to relate to his coworkers or to see things from their perspective. Here's an example of his lack of empathy and tact: "Toby is in HR, which technically means he works for corporate. So he's really not part of our family. Also, he's divorced, so he's really not a part of his family." Really, Michael?

Michael sometimes tries to connect with his employees by injecting humor into the workplace, but because his comments are often inappropriate or offensive, it naturally backfires. Case in point: his go-to quip, "That's what she said!"

Lighten Up

If you have to ask someone, "Can't you take a joke?" he probably can't. But as a leader, you should be able to ask yourself the same question and, without hesitation, answer, "Yes, I can!" Why? Because leaders with confidence, self-assuredness, and humility know how to find humor in their own idiosyncrasies, and yes, even in their mistakes!

Comedy Central's Jeff Ross, known for his in-your-face approach, says that humor shows that you are "thick-skinned and very accomplished in your field." Leaders who can take a joke, poke fun at themselves, or make light of a serious situation have a much better and easier rapport with their colleagues and direct reports. And in turn, they see better work-related results.

William Makepeace Thackeray said, "People who do not know how to laugh are always pompous and self-conceited." If you're a leader who can't crack a smile, that's probably how your team will perceive you.

Having a sense of humor, even in the workplace, is a sign of maturity, wisdom, and good character, as long as you aren't doing a stand-up routine or making jokes of a crude or inappropriate nature. The key is being able to laugh at yourself, not to poke fun at others or constantly try to entertain the crowd.

When leaders take themselves too seriously, their fears get the best of them, and they run the risk of becoming consumed with giving the perception of superiority and infallibility. WOW leaders are well-rounded, confident, and secure individuals who, in spite of having serious business know-how and savvy, rein in their egos and don't take themselves too seriously.

Reverse a Bad First Impression

First impressions are often lasting, and if they're bad, they may be difficult or even impossible to recover from. DUD leaders may not care about the impressions they make, but WOW leaders should, especially if they've represented themselves in a less-than-favorable light. WOW leaders are not infallible, and they don't maintain a robotic, perfect level of WOW at all times. Like everyone else, they may have moments that they later regret, or at the very least, want to reverse. If an initial impression isn't ideal, WOW leaders are humble enough to admit the error of their ways and try to right the wrong.

Great leaders know the importance of building, maintaining, and fostering working relationships. It doesn't behoove anyone to create hostilities or set a negative tone at the onset of a meeting. But how can you dig yourself out of the hole of a negative first impression? What can you do to bring a damaged relationship out of the rough and smooth out the divot you created in the first place?

While there are no guarantees, relationships—especially those deemed important to your business—are worth the effort. Here are a few steps you can take to help reverse a bad first impression:

Admit it. Don't excuse your behavior or turn a blind eye to it. If you've made a bad first impression, be humble enough to admit it—not just to yourself, but to the parties you may have injured or offended in some way. Be transparent and open about acknowledging the error of your ways. Sincerely apologize and admit you may have made a bad first impression. Ask outright for another chance.

Reach out. Don't wait for a second meeting to undo a bad first one. Initiate further contact as soon as possible by making a call or arranging for another face-to-face interaction. By swiftly pursuing the chance to reverse your initial blunder rather than hiding or running from your mistake, you'll be seen in a more positive, forgiving light. And you'll give the other party less time to form a lasting negative opinion.

Keep it light. When attempting to reverse a bad first impression, don't go overboard and ultimately make things worse. If you swing too far in the other direction, you'll come off as disingenuous and insincere, which is not the second impression you want to create. Be yourself and keep things light—perhaps even injecting a bit of humor at your own expense. By all means, avoid overt self-deprecation or a rehearsed comedy routine. But lightheartedly rebuking your first-impression mistakes can go a long way in reversing a bad opinion.

Make it count. If you're given the chance to reverse a bad first impression, make the follow-up count. Ask yourself what you did wrong the first time around and make a conscious effort *not* to repeat it. After all, if you botch the second impression, your fate may be sealed. When attempting to reverse a bad first impression, slow down and be present in the moment. Respectfully focus on the person in front of you, turning all your attention to the relationship at hand. Maintain eye contact, and for goodness' sake, keep your eyes—and hands—off your smartphone! Make sure your tone of voice matches your intended impression. Were you too forceful, domineering, or off-putting on your first encounter, or were you too timid, distracted, or uncertain in your responses? Change your tone of voice this time around to change the impression.

Return the favor. You're not the only one who has bad days or gets off kilter from time to time. Be forgiving and reserve judgment when someone makes a bad first impression on *you*. Give others the chance to make relationships right if they take the time and exert the effort to reverse the situation. The more understanding, cooperative, and communicative you are, the more likely you'll be perceived as a WOW leader in general. That solid reputation, in turn, will only help your cause if you ever need to reverse a bad first impression yourself.

We've all had off days when we may have acted out of character or displayed a side of ourselves we had no intention of revealing. We may have been distracted, irritable, or disconnected at the time of an important interaction and needed to right the wrong. WOW leaders don't condemn themselves—or others—when a first impression goes sour. Instead, they humbly and respectfully aim to reverse the situation and move forward with a positive, more accurate representation of who they truly are and the relationships they want to build.

Tearing Others Down Doesn't Build You Up

In addition to making a great first impression or striving to remedy a bad one, WOW leaders must consistently build and maintain great relationships. They know that while it's easy to criticize, point fingers, and tear down the accomplishments of others, there's no value in it. It only fosters negativity, sabotages relationships, and makes you look petty and insecure. So why are so many people so quick to judge, gossip, and talk behind the backs of others—even their friends and family? Because they falsely believe that by pointing out the faults of others, they somehow look better; by tearing others down, they think they are raising themselves up.

In business, DUD leaders notoriously lay blame, pass the buck, and belittle those around them. They don't lift up the people they lead; they hold them back in a vain, self-serving effort to steal all the glory for themselves. DUDs are only concerned with their own success and are willing to trample on anyone to rise to or stay at the top. They'll point out the team member's shortcomings but never applaud their strengths. They'll shove the team into traffic, but never step out in the street themselves.

The feel-good comedy *Family Ties* is hardly a show you'd imagine featuring a DUD leader. But in the episode "Designing Women," Mallory Keaton comes face-to-face with someone more concerned with her own success than with honesty, integrity, or morals. When Mallory lands a prestigious internship with a big-name fashion designer, the woman assigned to be her mentor ends up stealing Mallory's designs and passing them off as her own. "How can you stand here and smile and take the credit for it?" a stunned Mallory asks. "How can someone pretend to be your friend and pretend to like you and then turn around and stab you in the back? Why did you do this to me?" The woman explains that she had lost her creative edge and needed to come up with something new to save her job. In fact, it's Mallory who turns out to be WOW in the end, choosing to let the desperate DUD have her moment and take all the credit. She keeps her integrity intact, taking the high road even though she's been so blatantly wronged. When the mentor finally comes clean and apologizes, Mallory doesn't berate her, she encourages her. "You don't need to steal. I've seen your work. It's incredible. Maybe you're in a slump right now, but you'll come out of it."

Part of the journey toward becoming a WOW leader is recognizing your own mistakes, shortcomings, and issues—and then having the strength and courage to learn from, grow, and change those behaviors. The only way to be a WOW is to be someone who inspires, motivates, and empowers others. If you speak negatively, spread rumors, and berate your coworkers or teammates, you're not a leader; you're a bully.

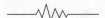

Whether you're an executive at a Fortune 500 company, a middle manager leading a small team, the foreman of a construction crew, or any kind of leader in between, your job is not to make yourself look better;

it's to elicit the best from your team. Tearing others down doesn't build you up; it weakens your reputation, damages your credibility, and deflates your leadership value. Exposing the weaknesses of others doesn't make you any stronger. Only by lifting others up can you lead with the strength of a WOW.

Chapter 3

WOW Leaders Are Dedicated to Self-Improvement

*"There is nothing noble about being superior to some other person.
The true nobility is in being superior to your previous self."*
—*Hindustani proverb*

In the same way TV shows with solid ratings must continually innovate to retain their viewers, WOW leaders must be dedicated to continuous self-improvement, regardless of the level of success they've already achieved. Knowing who you are, who you want to be, and what drives and motivates you to lead is the only way to stay tuned to the WOW within. If you're ever going to bring out the best in others, you need to constantly assess and reevaluate whether you're putting the best of yourself out there. Whatever your leadership title, it doesn't mean that you're above reproach or that you're innately prone to always making the right decisions; it means you're smart enough, wise enough, and experienced enough to constantly check and then double-check yourself to stay on the right leadership path.

Leading Is Learning

Leadership is about guiding, teaching, and mentoring—but above all, leading is learning.

Every day is a learning day for a leader: providing new opportunities to grow, change, and obtain new information, perspectives, and experiences. When leaders stop learning, they cease to WOW, because they're no longer open to the possibilities and viewpoints around them. If they've stifled themselves into the rigidity of stale, ineffective routines, refusing to entertain new ideas, they're not really leaders; they're just figureheads in positions of power.

Perhaps no one on TV does less as a leader than *Parks and Recreation*'s Ron Swanson, the fictional director of the parks and recreation department of Pawnee, Indiana. As a strict opponent of big government, Ron tries to buck the system by ducking duties on the job. He's content to let his second-in-command, Leslie Knope, do all the work while he unenthusiastically hides in his office. Set in his ways—which include heavy drinking and expressing as little emotion as possible— Ron has no interest in learning or changing as a leader. Although Ron demonstrates a soft spot for his workers on occasion, he's incompetent and ineffective at his job and has absolutely no interest in learning anything that might change that.

Unlike Ron, WOWs who embrace the notion that leading is learning create a reciprocal balance within the team and strengthen their own ability to motivate, guide, and inspire. Here are some ways you can learn to WOW on a daily basis:

Listen. A key to learning is listening to what others are saying. People in your charge and leaders above you have unique vantage points, opinions, and experiences that differ from your own. Actively listening to those voices gives you insight that helps you make decisions and formulate leadership strategies.

Ask. You'd be surprised how much you can learn if only you ask the right questions. Ask team members how a project is going, if they need any help, or whether there are any issues that need to be addressed. Chances are, your team members have a lot to say, but they may not be up front about offering their opinions . . . unless you ask!

Do. Another effective way to learn is through doing. You need to try new things, proceed with new strategies, and implement ideas and visions to find out if they will, in fact, be successful or not. Once you decide to do and not just talk about something, it becomes an active, living experience from which real-time lessons can be learned.

Fail. Getting something wrong or achieving results other than originally intended doesn't necessarily equate to a failure. Even the worst disaster or mishap can be a chance to learn, improve, change, and move in a new direction. The only true failure is not doing, not learning, and not moving forward.

Change. Sometimes the only way to learn from past mistakes or an ineffective current situation is to change it. Be willing to set a different course, take calculated risks, and venture into uncharted territories when the situation warrants it. Sticking to the straight line at any cost isn't going to help you learn as a leader . . . but being the catalyst of change certainly will.

WOW leaders accept that not every moment is going to be a WOW, not every day is going to be perfect, and not every decision is going to be "right." But within each new day is the opportunity to face new challenges that help you keep improving, growing, and of course, learning.

Those who reach WOW status have achieved a level of greatness to be revered and applauded. But there is no endgame to leadership. Once you're in the realm of WOW, you've got to work to stay there. That doesn't mean operating with a flawless record; instead, it means keeping the momentum of great leadership going even in the face of conflicts, failure, negativity, and personal challenges.

Aaron Spelling

Legendary TV producer, writer, and sometime actor Aaron Spelling was a mainstay on the small screen for decades, having been responsible for iconic shows like *Charlie's Angels*, *The Mod Squad*, *Starsky & Hutch*, *Dynasty*, *The Love Boat*, *Fantasy Island*, *Beverly Hills 90210*, *7th Heaven*, *Charmed*, *Melrose Place*, and others. But Spelling had to overcome tremendous obstacles before attaining his WOW career status.

Growing up Jewish in a rough part of Dallas, Texas, Spelling became the victim of anti-Semitic bullying at school. As a result of the constant torment, he lost the use of his legs at the age of eight, a psychosomatic response to the constant abuse. While confined to his bed, he reportedly immersed himself in reading, developing his love for imaginative storytelling.

As an adult, Spelling faced a rough entry into the Hollywood TV writing scene, often having his scripts and ideas rejected. Eventually, however, he triumphed. He rose above the challenges and obstacles he faced to become one of the most celebrated, famous, and successful TV producers in his genre. Rather than giving up, he learned from his experiences and became a WOW despite failures, setbacks, and negative situations.

Be Exceptional—Not the Exception

If you want to really be exceptional, don't think of yourself as the exception to every rule, policy, or expectation. In other words, don't hold yourself to a standard different from the one you apply to your employees. As a leader, you're not infallible or above reproach. You're not exempt from performing at the same level you expect from those you lead.

Hypocritical behavior is all too common in everyday life. Parents reprimand their kids for using foul language but think nothing of belting out expletives themselves. People (rightfully) chastise those driving under the influence but think they're "fine to drive" after three or four cocktails. Everyone knows it's dangerous to text and drive, but there are those who still believe they can do it safely. Think of how easy it is to give advice but how difficult it can be to take it.

In business, the same holds true. DUDs are known to preach one thing but do another. They often talk a big game but won't get their hands dirty. They arrogantly believe they deserve the glory and the success, even at the expense of those "beneath" them. If costs need to be cut, for example, DUDs won't hesitate to slash their workers' pay, but their own salaries certainly remain intact. In short, DUDs believe they are the exception—which is why they will never be exceptional.

On a 2009 episode of *The Mentalist*, "Carnelian, Inc.," a body literally drops from the sky at the feet of police during Carnelian Prime's team-building skydiving exercise. The death is no accident, of course, as the chute straps were sabotaged and the police were anonymously led to the very spot the tragedy occurred. Randall Faulk, the CEO of the firm, immediately comes off as arrogant, brash, and heartless, deciding to continue the company retreat despite his coworker's tragic demise.

When Patrick Jane (the mentalist) questions Faulk about his company's dealings, the cold CEO says he feels no remorse for having to lay off thousands of workers when his private-equity firm dismantles businesses. But obviously his own well-being and financial status is quite another matter. After a second murder is committed during a subsequent paint-ball exercise, Jane cracks the case, tricking the CEO into admitting that he was the mastermind behind the deaths. It turns out the first murder was a ruse to cover the motive of the second: to kill the female coworker suing him for sexual harassment, secretly negotiating with the competition, and driving down stock prices. In other words, the selfish, DUD leader believed he was the exception. It was fine with him when others lost their life savings, their jobs, or their lives, but he was too exceptional to fail or face losing his fortune and reputation. While murder and sabotage aren't usually the way leaders show their hypocrisy in the real-life world of business, the message is the same: DUDs hold themselves to a standard different from the one they hand down to the people they lead.

WOW leaders, in contrast, rise above the double standard. While they're motivated by their own success, they recognize that success as a leader is based on the success of the whole. They strive to build up their team members, not just themselves. WOWs aren't the exceptions; they're the examples. And through leading by example, they prove to be exceptional, bringing out the WOW within those they lead.

If you want to be exceptional, be sure your actions match your words. Follow through with what you say and back up your expectations with consistent action. And keep these leadership double standards in mind. DON'T:

- Demand punctuality while arriving late to your own meetings.
- Expect transparency while keeping everyone in the dark.
- Pretend your organization is a democracy while ruling as a dictator.
- Respond to hero worship or flattery while ignoring realistic feedback.

- Criticize others publicly while patting yourself on the back.
- Require results while resisting change.
- Make promises while delivering only excuses.
- Ignore the big picture while micromanaging the details.
- Bark out orders while refusing to listen.
- Protect your own interests while neglecting the interests of others.

It's easy to point fingers at others, but it's much more difficult to put yourself under the microscope and admit you're far from perfect. WOW leaders take ownership of their behaviors and choices, continuously striving to learn, grow, and improve—because they know that to be exceptional, they can't think of themselves as the exception.

Don't Expect Perfection

Although WOW leaders and WOW employees have an "it" quality that sets them apart (see chapter 4), that doesn't mean they're without flaws. In leadership, in business, in the workplace, and in life, there's no such thing as perfection. Those hung up on flawlessness inevitably end up attaining the exact opposite.

The negative ramifications of expecting perfection from yourself and others include:

- A tense, stressful work environment
- Second-guessing and immobility due to fear ("paralysis from analysis")
- Stifled creativity and innovation
- Decreased performance output
- Missed opportunities for growth and change
- Negative, defeatist attitudes

DUD leaders often demand perfection from their team and accept nothing less. This drive for spotless performance is usually rooted in egotism, insecurity, and a lack of vision.

Alternatively, WOW leaders embrace failure and imperfections as a means to success. They know that the right path is often revealed only through trial and error. There's a clear distinction between insisting on perfection and encouraging and helping others to perform and be their best.

The same applies to the standards you set for yourself as a leader. WOW leaders are people who grow, change, and learn from mistakes and imperfect experiences along the way—and they're not afraid to admit it. DUD leaders are narcissistic, and therefore will deflect any mistakes onto others, never owning up to their own role in or responsibility for imperfections.

One of the most outlandish and outspoken perfectionists on TV is celebrity chef Gordon Ramsay, host of the reality series *Hell's Kitchen*. The cooking competition begins with eighteen chefs vying for the approval of the hard-to-please Ramsay. As the hopefuls are put through the culinary wringer, the volatile, hotheaded judge and supposed mentor screams, throws tantrums, and belittles them. Although the potty-mouthed Scot is an award-winning, accomplished chef in his own right, he's opinionated, harsh, and beyond demanding to those he leads, rebuking anything less than perfect.

However, he himself is far from perfect. He's a DUD through and through—a narcissistic bully and self-admitted liar and manipulator. For TV audiences, watching this destructive boss in action is like being a gawker on the highway: You know it's gonna be bad, but you just have to look. It's a different story for the folks actually on the receiving end of one of Ramsay's tirades. For them, facing the brunt of the DUD's hellish wrath creates anger, self-doubt, and stress.

DUD leaders like Ramsay thrive on hogging the spotlight at any cost, often bringing others down as they rise to the top. Portraying yourself as a "perfect" leader or expecting perfection from yourself is actually detrimental to your leadership or career success. Striving to meet goals and attain best practices will keep you moving forward, but striving for absolute perfection can actually backfire and impede your growth and performance.

Here are a few tips to help you avoid the expectation of perfection:

- Admit mistakes
- Embrace change
- Take calculated risks
- Accept failures as opportunities for growth
- Learn to laugh at yourself
- Celebrate victories
- Shrug off defeat and move on
- Keep your ego in check

In business, it's essential that you strive to be your best and help elicit the best in others. But to be a WOW, you've also got to accept that there is no perfection in leadership.

Practice—Not Perfect

Perfection itself may be an illusion, but the quest toward being the "perfect" version of you is a vital part of WOW leadership. Exceptional leaders are never satisfied with being "at the top." They know that in leadership, even when they're sitting in the executive's chair, the top, like perfection, is only an illusion. When setting out to truly be a WOW, they're always aware of the need for continual growth, improvement, and learning, regardless of any status they've already achieved. WOW leaders never stop "practicing" the art of leadership.

Practice makes perfect—right? Although we know there's no such thing as perfection, it's hard to disagree completely with the expression, because, let's face it, practice does improve performance. The key, however, lies in how and what you're practicing. If you keep repeating the same error in your golf swing, for example, it doesn't matter how many hours you spend at the driving range; you'll still miss the mark.

Sheldon J. Plankton, the little, green, microscopic menace on the hit animated series *SpongeBob SquarePants*, is a prime example of misguided practice. With a single-minded vision of "stealing the Krabby Patty formula," the villain of Bikini Bottom devotes countless hours and untold amounts of money to devising elaborate schemes to pilfer the prized recipe. He's clearly a genius, although in a mad-scientist sort of way: capable of incredible feats like infiltrating SpongeBob's brain, converting himself into a gaseous form, and turning the Krusty Krab employees into infants. However, he keeps expending energy on the same old, tired goal, rather than using his apparent brilliance to make his own business venture profitable. When it comes to leadership, rather than focusing on perfection, enhance your WOW abilities by practicing and honing the right traits and skills that give you your edge.

Recognize and fix mistakes. If something isn't working, make a change. Don't hang on to old methods that clearly aren't effective.

Reinforce the positive. Make a daily effort to point out the positive traits and successes of your team. By reinforcing positivity, you'll help forge a stronger team bond and culture of cooperation.

Set a consistent example. Practice the art of honesty, integrity, and consistent fairness across the board. Leaders need to be role models of unquestionable character to earn trust and ultimately inspire and motivate the people they lead.

Invest in improvement. Seek out a mentor or adviser to help you continuously improve your leadership skills. Look for a teacher with a proven record of leadership effectiveness who can guide, assist, and challenge you to be your best.

If you repeatedly practice ineffective leadership traits like covering up mistakes, passing the buck, or berating your employees, you'll become a perfect DUD leader. But if you put your efforts into practicing in the right way, you'll learn how to continuously improve as a leader, and eventually you'll be the "perfect" version of your own brand of WOW.

Recognize Blind Spots

Every leader has leadership blind spots. WOW leaders may be able to elicit the best results from their team, but they're not omnipotent. They can't be in the know about everything. They're also not immune to natural human emotional reactions. Sometimes bias comes into play when team members are well liked and respected but deficient in other areas.

In *Elementary*, a modern-day Sherlock Holmes solves crimes using the same level of deductive and intuitive reasoning as his classic counterpart. But even the supersleuth encounters situations where blind spots come into play, throwing him slightly off his game. For instance, his love for his girlfriend Irene, whom he thought to be dead, blinds his ability to see her for who she really is when she finally resurfaces. In the end, Irene turns out to be his archenemy, criminal mastermind Moriarty. While Sherlock eventually deduces the truth, his personal feelings for Irene create blind spots that slow down his typically keen detective skills.

What WOW leaders don't see is often as telling, or perhaps even more telling, than what they are aware of within the team. Even when favorable performance is achieved, a team may not be functioning at its best level. There may be skill gaps or relationship issues that are causing quiet but very real problems. So what can be done about these leadership blind spots? Here are a few tips to help you recognize your blind spots and ultimately see each situation more clearly:

Be self-aware. If you want to deal with leadership blind spots, you've got to realize that you aren't an all-knowing, all-powerful, flawless superleader. The first step is admitting that blind spots could be an issue. The second step is trying to figure out where they are.

Be proactive. Never assume there's a status quo within the team that keeps everything functioning at peak performance. Be proactive by figuring that you're out of the loop in some way; presume you're missing something and start digging around. In other words, you have to check your blind spots!

Be present. It's hard to ascertain the true inner workings of a team dynamic by pressing your nose up against the glass and looking in from the outside. Insert yourself into the daily mix to get a clearer understanding of what is truly going on within the group.

Be communicative. In addition to observation, you must also be a clear, open communicator. Ask questions about areas that stand out as potentially problematic or seem unclear in some way. Encourage a free exchange by granting others permission to speak freely and by demonstrating that you're a fair and active listener.

Be responsive. When gaps are identified or problems pointed out within the team, take action on the issues. Share your observations with the team or with the "weak link." Verbalize your expectations and come up with a plan to resolve or improve the situation.

Be diligent. Follow up on blind-spot issues and keep looking for others that may sneak up from another angle. When driving, you don't merge or change lanes without checking your blind spots. And you can't just check your rearview mirror and assume it's all clear; you have to use side mirrors, over-the-shoulder glances, and then double-check everything. With leadership blind spots, you need to do the same. Be diligent and thorough by finding subtle ways to identify, fix, and keep tabs on weak areas within the team.

Having leadership blind spots doesn't make you an ineffective leader, but ignoring their existence or failing to manage them correctly could weaken your ability to WOW. Once you begin to regularly check your leadership blind spots, you'll begin to see much more clearly.

Choose the Right Culture

Successful self-improvement depends on self-awareness. You need to constantly reevaluate your performance, progress, and skill set as a leader to stay grounded in WOW territory. But to be aware of yourself, you also need to be aware of your surroundings.

Culture has a huge impact on how individuals develop as leaders, as it provides an informal road map on how to be successful within the organization. Corporate culture varies from job to job, so it's vital to know what qualities are valued where you are, and either tailor your leadership style accordingly or choose another path.

Over time, employing the Pygmalion effect—a situation in which the higher the expectation placed upon people, the better they will perform—will elicit improved performance. However, leadership styles take their shape based on culture. A culture thriving on WOW leadership can take average, perhaps more traditional leaders and turn them into modern, outstanding leaders. The same holds true for mediocre or substandard, DUD environments: Over time, the leaders will bend—or shrink—to fit the culture.

Ultimately, to be a WOW, you must choose to work in a culture where your ideals mesh with that of the organization. Ask yourself:

- What kind of leader are you naturally, without being influenced by culture?
- What leadership style do you want to represent?
- Does your style fit into your organization well?
- Are you authentic to yourself, or are you just trying to fit in?

On one hand, while the Pygmalion effect is something of a self-fulfilling prophecy in which you rise to meet desired expectations, it works to your benefit if you're in an environment that challenges you to be your best. On the other hand, if you're leading in a culture where cutthroat tactics are praised, you'll eventually learn to be the best at cutthroat tactics. In the latter situation, if you remain true to your own ideals and go against culture, you may find yourself out of a job, but you'll save yourself from the path of the DUD.

The Life/Work Combination

People who are truly committed to self-improvement know that success is a balancing act between work and home. If your attention and devotion leans only in one direction, the other side will suffer, sometimes beyond repair. But does there have to be a symmetrical balance, a 50/50 split between the two, in order to succeed?

Regardless of individual career or personal aspirations, everyone wants to be successful in his or her endeavors. But the definition of success varies from individual to individual. Some measure it in terms of position and title, others in dollars and cents, and some base it primarily on tangible accomplishments. And then there are those who only feel successful if they have it all . . . power and wealth in addition to a laundry list of accolades to brag about.

The life/work combination can be equated to the familiar expression "Live to work, or work to live?" How you formulate your life/work equation is up to you. What one considers too much work, another might think is just the tip of the iceberg. It all depends on your priorities, your perspective, and your personal goals.

For many people, working 50, 60, or even 80 hours a week is the norm and perhaps even enjoyable. Self-proclaimed workaholics not only put in excessive hours on the job, they crave it. They're satiated by accomplishing work-related milestones and gratified by challenging themselves to excel in their careers. For some people, money drives this ambition; a fat paycheck more than makes up for the extended time on the clock. While being with loved ones may be important to them, their life/work combination is heavily skewed in the direction of career, and it works for them and their family.

However, there are those who put in extra hours out of a sense of duty or for fear of losing their jobs, but they aren't necessarily enamored with spending half their lives in the office. For them, the life/work combination is off kilter, and sacrificing time with family and friends is a high price to pay. They may become burned out, overloaded, stressed out, and even resentful of their jobs. As a result, their performance and attitude may end up suffering, both at home and at the office.

Still another subset of individuals, which includes those in the millennial generation, has a different perspective on the life/work combination. Although they're hard workers, they put life first on the continuum of what makes them happy. They would rather have more time off than a pay raise. While they're willing to give 100 percent at the office, they also expect an ample amount of time away from it. Sacrificing time with family or personal free time is not a trade-off they're comfortable making. Career is vital for these individuals, as long as it's on their terms. Living life to the fullest is nonnegotiable and trumps the paycheck or career status.

The life/work combination might mean working a traditional and predictable 9-to-5 job for some, but others might thrive on a flex schedule or a work-from-home scenario. Some people work best when they put in twelve-hour workdays or are away with business travel for extended periods of time. The differences often depend on the culture or industry of your vocation. For example, a high-powered attorney who bills $595 per hour probably has different expectations and priorities than a Hawaiian surf shop owner who'll close down for an hour or two when the waves are up. Neither is right or wrong; it depends on what works for the individual. Asking the right questions, communicating with your loved ones, and doing an honest self-evaluation is key to figuring out your ideal life/work combination.

Perhaps no TV family balanced the life/work combination with more ease, style, humor, and grace than Dr. Cliff Huxtable and his attorney wife, Clair, of *The Cosby Show*. With five children and two successful careers to manage, the good doctor and his patient, loving spouse create a strong, mostly smooth-running family unit that thrives on communication, support, and team-based cooperation. In the memorable episode "You're Not a Mother Night," Cliff helps alleviate his wife's stress on the home front by whisking her away for a romantic staycation at a hotel. The Huxtables work hard to ensure they set the right combination for a harmonious lifestyle: one that balances success on the job with family values, fun, and togetherness.

Setting Your Combination

Countless factors come into play when managing the right life/work combination. Money, career passion, family responsibilities, extracurricular hobbies and interests, health, and more are all part of the mix. How do you find the balance that blends everything together into just the right formula for you and your family?

How did notorious crime boss Tony Soprano do it? Well, he didn't do it the legal way, that's for sure. The ongoing dilemma for the head mobster on the groundbreaking series *The Sopranos* was balancing a rocky family life with a stressful job as a mob boss. Tony's idea of setting the right life/work balance included sending out-of-line associates to "sleep with the fishes," repeatedly lying to his wife and kids, and providing his family with material wealth as a replacement for loving stability. Although the Mafia prince sought counsel for his depression and anger issues by seeing a therapist on a regular basis, his dark side always seemed to win the day, and he never achieved the balance he truly needed.

While the typical leader's work and family life is much less dramatic (and homicidal) than Tony Soprano's, the need for structure and balance is just as vital. Here are some ways to help set your ideal life/work combination:

Make realistic decisions. Decide what you want your combination to be in all key areas of your life, ensuring that it's a reasonable mix. Assign time for work, family, friends, and yourself. Be realistic—it can't add up to more hours than there are on the clock. Discuss things with your family so it's acceptable and doable for everyone.

Find your motivation. Understand what motivates you to choose a particular life/work combination. If you currently feel out of balance, is it due to stress? Health issues? Are you working for an unappreciative, DUD leader? Are you feeling the emotional tug of children longing for your attention? Ask yourself why—and whether—your life/work combination needs to be altered.

Set goals into action. Take action to make your life/work combination a reality. Don't just say, "This is how I want it to be"; take steps to make it so. Write weekly or monthly goals that realistically work toward achieving the balance you desire. It might take time to get there, and especially at first, you may face daily challenges. Depending on what you desire, you may need to consider changing jobs or even careers to attain the right life/work balance. Make sure you write down your goal, review it daily, and make adjustments as needed.

Be accountable. Hold yourself accountable for your decisions and actions. If possible, assign an accountability monitor to help keep you on task. This can apply both at work and at home. At home, have your spouse or older child remind you about what you've promised to do, and then be mindful of keeping true to your word. At the office, a direct report or coworker can take on a similar role.

Sharpen your skills. Assess your skills, including your strengths and weaknesses, and then develop strategies around them. You may find that you need better time management skills, improved organizational tools, or more consistent planning and preplanning techniques to more effectively manage your life/work combination. Work on enhancing those areas that seem to upset the balance you want to attain.

Trim the fat. Determine the "time wasters" in your schedule that don't align with the goals of your life/work combination. When something doesn't add value, provide enjoyment, or help create balance . . . get rid of it! Find a solution that works for your desired combination. It could be as simple as paying bills online or buying prechopped vegetables for your recipes. Find ways to buy back time for what's really important.

Find a role model. Although your life/work combination is unique, you can take cues from others who seem to be hitting the mark for themselves. When you find yourself wondering, "How does so-and-so make it look so easy?" or commenting that someone else seems to "have it all together," don't be afraid to ask that person how he or she does it. You might get some useful tips, a reassuring boost, or a much-needed reality check.

Cut yourself a break. If you're the go-to person, chances are those at the office depend on you to get things done. And while it may be in your nature to do it all, it might not fit into your life/work balance. Discuss your life/work combination goal with your boss or team members. Suggest training or cross-training someone else on the team to step into the go-to spotlight, taking some of the pressure off of you. At home, outsource what you can to free up your time for family and fun. For example, pay someone to cut the grass, help with the housework, or do household maintenance.

Nix negativity. Avoid negative people at all costs; they suck the life right out of you! Negativity zaps your energy and throws you off your game. You'll need a positive, motivated attitude to keep your life/work combination in check. You don't need naysayers, downers, and second-guessers telling you what can't be done, shouldn't be done, or is being done wrong! Have confidence in what's right for you, and move in the opposite direction of negative influences.

Setting your life/work combination is an individual endeavor, based on your own ideals, priorities, and goals. But getting your family, loved ones, and even your employers on board toward helping you achieve that balance is vital to its ultimate success.

Staying Positive

If you're trying to improve yourself, the first thing on your list should be improving your attitude or keeping it in check. Staying positive on a regular basis is something a WOW leader must learn to master. Some people seem naturally unshakeable, always displaying a bubbly, care-free personality. They make it look easy! But if you're not prone to an easygoing disposition, you'll have to remind yourself on a regular basis to kick the positivity into gear.

If you want to be awesome—be happy! Think about it: If you're a miserable, grumpy, angry person, how can you be viewed as a WOW leader? How can you be thought of as an amazing, inspiring voice of authority if you're always the picture of doom? How can you inspire and motivate yourself to be an effective leader if you're stuck in a rut of nega-tivity and unhappiness? So, if you're looking to WOW, try being happy.

Sure, being happy is easier said than done. But it is possible. To be happy, you must be content with what you have, who you are, and where you're headed. You need to redirect your thought process to steer away from negative responses and instead take a detour to a healthier frame of mind.

Happiness is not reserved for those who have everything or who never experience difficult times. Often, it's precisely those people who have the least or who are tested the most who somehow always man-age to find the silver lining. But how do they do it? They just do. They *decide* to be positive. They choose not to dwell in a counterproductive cycle of misery, self-pity, and blame. Instead, they put forth a conscious effort to appreciate what they can, forgive when they must, and put more emphasis on what's right than on what's wrong. They are coura-geous enough to allow themselves to be happy.

Most people are afraid to truly feel happiness. They somehow think being positive equates to being ineffective, as if it means you've settled and are no longer trying to make improvements or achieve more. But happiness is not a game-ender. Being happy doesn't mean you can no longer have more; it just means that you're satisfied, grateful, and posi-tive in the here and now, as well as hopeful, enthusiastic, and encour-aged about the possibilities the future may hold. Being happy isn't a weakness; it shows that you're confident, secure, and strong.

If you ask most people what makes them happy, work would prob-ably be low on the list of responses. Even those who are working in their chosen profession are faced with the daily stress, exhaustion, and demands that come with having a career. For many, work is challenging, rewarding, and fulfilling on many levels but wouldn't be described as a source of happiness. Still, it can be.

Remember the girl who could "turn the world on with her smile?" Who could "take a nothing day and suddenly make it all seem worthwhile?" Mary Richards, of course! The theme song for *The Mary Tyler Moore Show* reminded viewers at the start of each episode that Mary was a positive, happy person. As a career woman in the man's world of TV news, the kind, patient, and ever-cheerful Mary kept her spirits up, even when she was surrounded by the negative influence of her coworkers and boss, Mr. Grant.

In the episode "The Lars Affair," Mr. Grant is facing backlash from the station manager when his idea to have a cameraman ride along in a police car produces no newsworthy results. Mr. Grant naturally blames Mary for supporting him from the start. "I wouldn't be in this mess if you had said 'rotten,' but you said 'wonderful'!" Later, he wrestles with himself again over the viability of continuing the ride-alongs, considering the officers hadn't made an arrest in more than three weeks. "I know it's gonna work. Tell me, Mary, is it going to work?" he asks. She enthusiastically backs him up again, saying, "Oh, yes. It's a wonderful idea!" But Mr. Grant is still worried. "I gave you another chance to say 'rotten,' but you said 'wonderful'!" In the end, Mary's positive attitude proves correct when an armored car is robbed and their cameraman is on the scene with the police. Mr. Grant is thrilled, exclaiming, "I said it would work and it worked!" He never apologizes to Mary or thanks her for believing in him. But Mary doesn't expect or demand gratitude—she's just happy for Mr. Grant and the station.

The key to being happy at work lies in being authentic and true to yourself. Gandhi said, "Happiness is when what you think, what you say, and what you do are in harmony." Nowhere do those words ring more true than on the job. If you're a DUD leader who lets greed, selfishness, and power seeking rule your actions, you'll never be happy. And you'll never be awesome.

If you want to be happy on the job, you must have the courage to do what's right. If you do your best to make decisions and act with honesty, integrity, and self-respect, you'll be happy with yourself even when you err, because you'll be content with the purity of your intentions. People aren't inspired by those who always *get it* right, but rather, by those who always *do* right. Those who are bold enough to stand up for their beliefs will not only be happy with themselves, but will bring out the best in others. And *that* is awesome!

Instead of asking yourself, "Am I happy?" or wondering, "Should I be happy?" tell yourself, "I'm happy." And then allow yourself to be. Be happy, be awesome, and be a WOW!

Wake Up Your WOW Voice

We all know the saying "You must love yourself before you can love another." With leadership, the same holds true: You must lead yourself before you can lead others. Knowing your own path and guiding yourself toward continual improvement, growth, and success is even more important than leading others, because it's the foundation for building and sharing your WOW leader skills. Remember: You've got to WOW from the inside out.

This means that to champion your own leadership, you must listen to your inner voice. You know the one: that voice inside your head that speaks to you with complete honesty and without a filter. It can lift you up when you need a boost, but it can just as easily plant doubt in your mind. To succeed, you need to let your inner voice guide you. But before you do, you must train that voice to be a positive, encouraging, and insightful guide.

The queen of soul searching, self-reflection, and "living your best life" is also the queen of the talk show hosts herself, Oprah Winfrey. Over the course of *The Oprah Winfrey Show*'s 25-year tenure, Oprah not only inspired her audience to wake up their WOW voices, but she also shared her own story and demonstrated how her struggles, as well as her triumphs, helped her find and embrace her true self.

Oprah encouraged her viewers to follow her lead in a powerful journaling exercise. In her "Gratitude Journal," the billionaire celebrity keeps grounded to what really matters by writing down five things each day for which she is thankful. However, in her *O* magazine article, "What Oprah Knows for Sure About Gratitude," she admits that her journaling waned for a time when things became too hectic:

> I wondered why I no longer felt the joy of simple moments. Since 1996 I had accumulated more wealth, more responsibility, more possessions; everything, it seemed, had grown exponentially—except my happiness. How had I, with all my options and opportunities, become one of those people who never have time to feel delight? I was stretched in so many directions, I wasn't feeling much of anything. Too busy doing. But the truth is, I was busy in 1996, too. I just made gratitude a daily priority. I went through the day looking for things to be grateful for, and something always showed up. (*O, The Oprah Winfrey Magazine*, November 2012)

She went on to conclude, "I know for sure that appreciating whatever shows up for you in life changes your personal vibration. You radiate and generate more goodness for yourself when you're aware of all you have and not focusing on your have-nots." Oprah knew how to listen to and channel her inner voice in the right direction, and so can you. To take advantage of all the things you have to be grateful for, see the section in this chapter titled "At the End of the Night, Write the Right."

When you get up in the morning, you have a choice about how that inner voice will speak to you. Since you control the voice, you can literally decide to turn off the negative aspect: the part that discourages, blames, accuses, and doubts.

One of the greatest leaders of all time, Abraham Lincoln, said, "Most people are about as happy as they make up their mind to be." Make up your mind to be positive and self-affirming. The power of positive thinking, beginning first thing in the morning with an encouraging inner voice, will boost your leadership strength and keep it going throughout the day.

If you let your inner voice tell you things like "You'll probably blow it at the meeting today," or "Joe Salesguy is way better than you,"

you're going to crash and burn. But if you choose to think, "Today is going to be a great day. I'm going to make a positive impact in people's lives. I'm going to succeed," chances are, you will.

Challenge yourself to wrangle that inner voice, to grab hold of it like a cattle rustler and take control of it. Keep your grip firmly on the positive, never letting negativity slip out. Try starting the day with a renewed energy, realizing that you are leading the most important person you will ever lead: yourself. Start each day with a WOW attitude, and you'll be on your way to WOW leadership.

Start Your Day Strong

Start your day strong if you want to be strong all day! As a WOW leader, you're constantly challenged to give the best of yourself in order to bring out the best in others. You need to set the example for your team by exuding positivity, confidence, clarity, and motivation. As the leader, you set the tone. When you're strong, the team's going to be stronger. But when you're dejected, negative, and stressed, the people you're leading will reflect that too.

However, knowing it is much easier than doing it. You aren't always going to wake up fully engaged and eager to conquer the day. A million stresses, distractions, and doubts can creep into your psyche and weigh you down with fear, worry, or even anger. Or you might just feel out of sorts and disconnected, starting the day with a mild case of the blahs. It happens to everyone! The best WOWs know how to take hold of their emotions, channel their energies into good directions, and start each day with strength, honesty, and positivity.

Here are a few strategies to start your day strong:

Smile. Have you ever noticed that when someone around you yawns, you can suddenly become tired yourself? The same psychological trigger occurs with smiling. A smile can help you and those around you feel happier and more positive. When you wake up with the blues, put on a happy face, and your brain is more likely to follow suit.

Think thanks. When you get up in the morning, focus on what you're grateful for, not what you feel is lacking. Concentrating on what you're thankful for steers you in a positive direction and gives you a solid foundation from which to begin shaping your day.

Turn it up. The worst thing to do when you're in a rut is dig yourself into a deeper hole of gloom and doom. Stay away from depressing news reports, the stack of bills on your desk, or weepy love songs. Reenergize yourself by listening to your favorite upbeat, energetic tunes as you get ready for the day. Plug in your iPod or smartphone on the drive to the office and soak up the positive vibes! Try putting together an energetic mix for your phone or car, and turn it up to turn your mood around.

Say it differently. Challenge yourself to use different words today, steering clear of negative-speak like "can't" or "no" or even "yes, but . . . " Choose to say "yes," and then build on your own ideas or the ideas of others in a positive way. That doesn't mean it's a free-for-all in the office; it means you're deciding to be more open to a positive and creative flow of ideas. In addition, try communicating internally with more of a solutions-based "if, then" approach. Instead of telling yourself, "I don't think I'll deliver a great business review next week," say, "If I'm going to deliver a great business review next week, then I'll have to . . . "

Unplug and reflect. If the loud music approach isn't your style, maybe quiet reflection will do the trick. Instead of waking up and immediately checking potentially stressful emails and texts, start the day "unplugged" and disconnected from your electronics for a period of time. Try yoga, meditation, a morning walk, or just a warm, relaxing shower to clear your head and harness your own inner strength. Get yourself powered up mentally and physically prior to grabbing for the challenges facing you via your smartphone or computer.

Dress the part. When you look great, you feel great. Take the time to give yourself a fresh, strong, confident outer appearance as you start the day. Wear your favorite outfit, color, or accessories to give yourself that extra boost of self-assuredness. When you see the best version of yourself reflected back in the mirror, you'll exude that WOW throughout the day.

To start your day strong, don't step into the quicksand and start struggling to get free; you'll only make things worse. Try avoiding the stressful pitfalls and traps that can bury you in worry, doubt, and frustration. Relax, smile, be thankful, and look at yourself and your day in a more positive, upbeat way. Start your day strong and turn the next *blah* morning into a WOW one.

Dealing in the Day

Once you've settled into the day, even when you've started off on the right foot with a positive outlook, things tend to come at you fast and furious, testing your resolve to stay upbeat. Dealing with the pressures and demands at work can break even the brightest mindset if you're blindsided by a barrage of negative situations. That's why you need to be prepared in advance for what might go wrong throughout the day. And know that, despite inevitable challenges, you can handle it.

On *Gilligan's Island*, the seven passengers of the S.S. *Minnow*'s infamous "three-hour tour" face the harrowing, seemingly hopeless day-to-day pressures of trying to survive on a remote, uninhabited island. Not only must the eclectic group learn to coexist, but also they often need to work together to overcome a number of obstacles and problems. On top of that, they have to deal with the bumbling, often disastrous mishaps brought about by Gilligan's repeated efforts and schemes to get off the island.

Given the situation, most of the castaways handle things quite well and with each new episode are able to bring humor and lighthearted fun to the screen. But the standout among the group is the Skipper, who repeatedly demonstrates his ability to remain positive, even under the direst circumstances. The Skipper's positive attitude and quirky smile gives him the amazing ability to keep a desperate situation from reaching paralysis. Imagine how different the show would have been if he were portrayed as a depressed, angry, or cynical leader who constantly reminded everyone how bad they had it and how they might never see civilization again.

Beyond his overall positive demeanor and attitude, the Skipper displays positivity through his actions: Every time there's a remote possibility of devising a solution to get off the island, he excitedly gets behind the opportunity. He doesn't give up and he doesn't shoot down or belittle the suggestions and schemes from the team of islanders.

Exhibiting a fresh, hopeful attitude day in and day out, he deals with the pressures, problems, and setbacks of being marooned.

To be a WOW leader, a morning routine rounded out by an inner pep talk will provide a solid foundation of positivity to help you deal in the day. But to keep it going, try employing the following techniques when a difficult situation arises:

Think before you react. An instant, knee-jerk reaction to bad news or unfavorable reports usually leads to regret. Quick, snap judgments only heat up your mood and ignite a defensive, hostile attitude from those involved. Even if you retract your initial display of negativity, the damage is done. Instead, take a moment or two to absorb all the relevant information before you make any decisions to respond.

Count to five. If you're a parent, you know the drill. To help combat a reflex response to a bad situation, try mentally counting to five (or ten if you need it) before opening your mouth. Usually, that brief interlude provides enough distance from the negativity for you to get a grasp on your emotions and react with more control.

Go to your happy place. It might sound a bit preschoolish or yoga-esque, but it works. When blasts of discouragement attempt to usurp your cheery disposition, dodge those bullets of doom by mentally removing yourself from the line of fire. Immediately think of greener pastures, of better days, of something that makes you laugh—whatever it takes to prevent you from giving in to the dark side.

Seek out positives. There's nothing worse than sitting at your desk waiting for conflicts to come to you. Build up an arsenal of positivity by interfacing and checking in with your team on a regular basis, finding out what they are accomplishing and succeeding at but aren't always knocking on your door to announce. Having that background knowledge of what's being done right will give you some needed perspective when things go wrong.

Focus on the solution. When things go awry, don't focus on the worst-case scenario, even if it feels like the worst has just occurred. There's always another way to look at things if you concentrate on solution-based reactions. Shifting your energies away from the negative of failure and toward positive alternatives will allow you to use the bump to navigate unexplored roads and perhaps find new success.

At the End of the Night, Write the Right

Anyone who's ever been in a serious relationship knows the benefit of the maxim "Never go to bed angry." Those who don't settle their arguments by the close of the day run the risk of never settling them at all, letting the problems fester, grow, and become larger than they were to begin with. The same holds true for personal, internal issues and frustrations, especially those regarding your abilities and goals at work.

Your state of mind at the end of the night is just as important as beginning each day with a positive attitude. Even if you've made every effort to keep an even-keeled or happy-go-lucky mindset at work, there are times when you may be struggling with a setback, mistake, or unresolved decision. Whatever you do, don't go to bed with a negative outlook.

Unless you're an egotistical, DUD-type personality, you probably find yourself evaluating your work performance often: questioning choices you've made, rating your leadership performance, and reviewing your goals and aspirations. Self-reflection is a valuable, worthwhile tool—but not if you berate yourself on a nightly basis. Shift the focus of your personal analysis to solution-based next steps. Focus on what is right, not on what you think you've done wrong. At the end of the night, write the right, and bring your mindset back to the positive.

A recurring theme on the comedy *Everybody Loves Raymond* was the end-of-the-night bedtime banter between Raymond Barone and his wife, Debra. The hilarious but often squabbling duo typically closed out the challenges of each day with a long discussion, attempting to right the wrongs before turning in for the night. In most cases, a resolution of sorts was reached, and the dysfunctional but loving pair talked it out enough to kiss and make up . . . at least until the next argument set in.

Like the fictional Barones, try to set things right within yourself at the close of each day. Here's an exercise to keep you zeroed in on the bright side.

Staying Positive

1. Keep a "positivity" journal or notebook at your bedside.

2. Write down at least one thing you've done right that day.

3. Include one goal for the following day, focusing on what you want to do right tomorrow.

4. Make your entries simple, concise, and matter-of-fact, aiming for no more than one or two lines.

5. Avoid any negative statements.

6. Get in the habit of writing every night.

By forcing yourself to shine the spotlight on something positive before you turn out the light each night, you'll be reinforcing your value and worth instead of doubting your skills and abilities. Even on the worst of days, you're sure to find something good to focus on if you look hard enough. Never go to bed negative! Write the right and you'll wake up more self-assured and better equipped to harness the WOW voice within.

Change Your Can't-Do Attitude

Negativity often presents itself as a defeatist attitude. How many times have you given up because you think you "just *can't* do it"? Have you settled for less because you "can't possibly" attain your dream? Are you conditioned to think things "can't be done" and as a result, end up missing opportunities or squashing your potential to grow? If you're striving for self-improvement, maybe you need to ask yourself: Is it can't—or won't?

The consummate "can't" man on TV has to be the underachieving, unmotivated, neurotic, dishonest, and self-deprecating George Costanza from the WOW series *Seinfeld*. Not only does the odd little bald man rarely succeed, but he also actually revels in his own lack of ambition and work ethic. "I'm a great quitter. It's one of the few things I do well. I come from a long line of quitters. My father was a quitter;

my grandfather was a quitter. I was raised to give up," he says in the episode "The Old Man."

In another memorable scene from the episode "The Phone Message," he quips about not doing laundry. "Instead of doing wash, I just keep buying underwear. My goal is to have over 360 pair. That way I only have to do wash once a year."

And who could forget the episode "The Pitch," when Jerry and George try to persuade NBC TV executives to produce a show "about nothing"? George's lack of self-confidence and gumption is obvious once again. "I can't do this, I can't do it. I've tried, I'm here, it's impossible," he cries to Jerry at the meeting. "Hey, this was your idea," Jerry tells him. "What idea? I just said something," he says, panicked. "I didn't know you were gonna listen to me!"

For George Costanza, follow-through is always the biggest problem. He wants to be successful, but never thinks he can be, and therefore never wants to put in the effort to make it happen. He convinces himself he is incapable, and therefore, he doesn't bother trying.

Deciding that you can't do something is just that: a decision. It's a choice. There's no certainty that something can't be done unless the effort has been made to do it, and even then, there's probably more you can do to make it work. If you're not willing to put in the work to accomplish something, you must not have wanted it that much in the first place. Either that, or you're letting your fear of failure skew your perceptions. When you think something can't be done, you're actually deciding you won't do it because the risks are too great or the rewards are uncertain.

When a "can't-do" mindset holds you back from what you truly believe in, aspire to, or hope for, you're deciding that you won't invest in yourself—that you won't allow yourself to go after your goals. Changing a can't-do attitude might not be easy, but it can be done. Here are a few helpful suggestions:

Set your priorities. How important is the goal? If you want it, don't say you can't. Push forward and make it happen. Of course, there are times when it's wise to say you won't. You need to pick and choose your priorities, set moral standards, and establish personal and business boundaries. There's nothing wrong with putting your foot down and saying you "won't" do something illegal or you "won't" be able to take on additional tasks at the office. Saying no is often essential. The key is in the mindset—realizing that you're not saying no because you can't do it; you're saying no because you choose not to.

Stop making excuses. Don't use "can't" as a reason in and of itself. Chances are, you have the ability, just not the courage or the drive. Be honest about the why behind the can't. Once you realize what's holding you back, you'll stop automatically sabotaging yourself with a can't excuse.

Take baby steps. Instead of visualizing the complexity, vastness, or seeming inaccessibility of your endgame goals, break them down into smaller, more manageable steps. Thinking too big all at once often shuts down an idea with a "can't be done" attitude before it even has a chance to be tried. Start focusing on what you *can* do now, and establish a smaller goal. Then continue moving forward with what can be done next, and so on.

Turn it around. When you're faced with a decision, turn around your thought process by thinking of potential positive outcomes first, rather than immediately focusing on what could go wrong. Make the "what ifs" work for you, not against you. If you dwell on the negative possibilities, you'll convince yourself you can't do it. Instead, rally around the prospect of success, rewards, and accomplishment, and tell yourself you can.

WOW leaders aren't successful because they can do everything; they are successful because they do what they know they can. Be authentic about your talents, skills, and goals, and stop using can't as a reason to continuously play it safe. Realize that while there are things you decide you won't do, there are things you simply can and should do. Then think positively, and do it.

The Benefits of a Reboot

In addition to keeping a positive frame of mind, we all need to reboot ourselves every now and then to stay charged and refocus our energies.

In business, this is especially true because we are constantly challenged to reinvent ourselves and strategize new methodologies for success.

Of course, daily struggles in our career often take a toll on our forward momentum. Our energies and inspirations can be drained by a thousand distracting details, and our idealistic approaches can be halted or interrupted by any number of corporate roadblocks. It's not surprising that we often experience frustration and even paralysis that freezes us up, much like an overworked computer. During those times when our battery power is dangerously low or when we have basically ceased all effective operation, we need to reboot ourselves.

Self-Imposed Shutdown

When you're stuck in a rut of immobility, unable to muster the creative or motivational juices to inject life and productivity into your daily work routine, you may need to force a temporary shutdown and recharge your battery. During those times, you may be stressed out, unhappy, lost, or simply overloaded. You may find yourself wondering why you don't have the enthusiasm or spark you once possessed. You may question if you're the leader you want to be and if those reporting to you perceive you as an inspirational, effective leader or as a floundering, ineffective manager. Perhaps your weakened state has left you hovering somewhere in the limbo between greatness and utter failure.

When you reflect with an honest self-evaluation—scanning your internal hard drive, so to speak—you may discover some undetected viruses or blind spots in your usual steadfast progression. Now is the time for a reboot.

So, where do you begin? Unlike students, who are able to ease the mental exhaustion of school by recharging with an annual summer break, those in the unyielding world of corporate America are not afforded the luxury of a lengthy sabbatical or extended summer vacation. However, you can enact your own self-imposed time of reflection that allows you to take a break from the enormous pressures you may feel are crushing your motivations and creativity.

Taking a break or rebooting doesn't have to mean escaping your job for a trip or an extended leave of absence. While taking a few days to recharge by embarking on an excursion with your family or friends can be a great way to refresh and reenergize yourself, it only works if you use the time to reflect and strategize. If sitting on a beach or basking poolside is merely a means of escape, you'll find the same problems waiting on your desk when you return to work.

However, if you take the time to formulate a strategic plan to breathe new life into your leadership abilities, whether on vacation or simply sitting in your office on a Tuesday afternoon, you'll begin the rebooting process that will get you on track to a fresh start.

One of the most powerful, poignant episodes of *Star Trek: The Next Generation* has to be "The Inner Light," in which Captain Picard experiences the ultimate reboot. While his journey is not a self-imposed shutdown, Picard is able to live out an entire lifetime as a completely different individual. When an alien space probe locks onto him, he becomes catatonic and immobilized on board the *Enterprise* for a mere twenty-five minutes. However, during that brief shutdown, the captain is somehow transported to a now-dead planet called Kataan, where he is known as an iron weaver named Kamin.

Thinking he has emerged from a feverish illness and has dreamed of being a starship captain, he immerses himself completely into the new life. As Kamin, he marries, has children and grandchildren, and lives into his eighties. Through it all, he experiences the simple yet complex ups and downs of familial love, something that has eluded him as a career military explorer.

Eventually, the doomed planet begins dying, and a weakened, elderly Kamin attends a rocket launch with his family. The launch is the very probe that had held him in his "shutdown" mode. It had been designed, he learns, as a sort of living time capsule that would hopefully be "opened" by someone in the future: someone who would then be able to preserve the memories of the species. "Oh, it's me," he finally realizes. "I'm the someone it finds." Now fully aware of what has transpired, he awakens aboard the *Enterprise* as Picard again, carrying with him the experiences, memories, and perspectives of Kamin.

Although a life-altering, otherworldly experience of the sci-fi kind may not be possible, you can choose to step back from your current situation and look at things from a fresh new angle. When you hit the "CTRL-ALT-DELETE" of your own career, beginning the process of a temporary shutdown, you are actually taking a step toward improving your self-confidence, boosting your attitude, and sharpening your leadership skills. Those who aren't courageous enough to reboot in times of corporate crisis or personal insecurity inevitably impose that stress and self-doubt on those around them. They create an unhealthy atmosphere where a lack of guidance and direction spins their team into a vortex of doubts, fears, and inaction.

Leaders with the fortitude to reflect on their own personal goals and aspirations and to take honest stock of their abilities, weaknesses, and strengths will be able to keep their low battery power from draining into a complete shutdown mode.

Refresh and Refocus

Even the most successful and forward-moving leaders need to impose a shutdown or take a break every now and then. In fact, the most successful WOWs aren't afraid to reboot when they recognize they are overloaded, underperforming, or operating on dangerously low battery power. Those who take the time to reenergize, reflect on their goals, and strategize a plan or direction will be able to better determine their aspirations and return to work with a renewed and recharged attitude and perspective.

Once a temporary shutdown has been imposed, it's time to take inventory of current situations, structure a game plan, and assuage any fears you may have regarding action. If you're the boss in your office, this may mean figuring out ways to redirect your team, deciding on new motivational techniques, or determining whether your leadership style needs to be revamped or improved.

To make the most of this self-imposed "refresh" mode, you'll have to have an honest internal conversation in which you face the reality of your own leadership performance. Ask yourself how you are being perceived as the boss; ask yourself if you are investing in your team and making the most of their core competencies; ask yourself if you are leading with integrity and courage.

Honest self-reflection is the best way to refocus your leadership and refresh your energy and passion for success. Once you identify the glitches or bugs that may be clogging up your internal hard drive, you can make the move to purge your system and clean up your desktop, so to speak.

If you're not the boss, but rather a valued team player looking to hone the WOW leader within, a temporary reboot is just as beneficial and in some cases could be pivotal to your success on the job. You, too, will need to dig deep to explore and take inventory of your skills, attitude, and output.

Rather than focusing on what needs to be changed in your industry or within your department or team, and instead of externalizing the blame on forces outside of your control, you'll need to learn how to accept the new or changing culture you are immersed in and devise a plan to be your best within the scope of that reality.

When embarking on a refresh and refocus mission, you'll need to ask yourself if the skills you are projecting to your direct reports are the ones that are valued and rewarded within the organization. Are you putting forth a cooperative team attitude and adjusting your methodologies and strategies to support the overall success of your department or organization? In these ever-evolving, shaky economic times, are you accepting that the new norm within the corporate world may mean a bumpy and anything-but-normal atmosphere of change, chaos, and uncertainty? Can you learn to operate at your best and most productive within the confines of what can sometimes be confusing and often unfair new restraints?

Whether you're the boss or a player on the team, communication with your superiors or those you lead can be just as important as a frank self-examination. As a WOW leader, you can incorporate feedback from your trusted employees as to what is and what is not resonating and succeeding within the ranks of the organization. You can be open to and even invite complaints, suggestions, and questions from your team so that you are aware of any problems that are or may be brewing. Knowing and being receptive to how your team is responding to you, your policies, and your methodologies is a valuable measure of your leadership effectiveness. If you're willing to use that knowledge as a springboard to change, you can use those tools to help you reboot.

Those weaving their way through the corporate maze can seek the advice and feedback of a valued WOW leader. Gaining the true and honest opinions and evaluation of a courageous and supportive superior can provide you with the guidance and motivation you need to get your mind and actions refocused on a winning strategy.

Learning to identify and come to terms with the realities of your career and corporate mission will enable you to adjust your way of thinking and operating within that environment. By initiating this reboot, you'll be able to brainstorm the path to your success, and then begin taking steps along that road.

Power Up for Success

Once you've committed to initiating a shutdown and refreshing your game plan, you're already well on your way to succeeding. But after the thinking and planning phase is complete, you still need to power back up and put the plan into action.

Perhaps the hardest part of the reboot process is the restart, where you'll actually implement the changes that need to be addressed. Some of those epiphanies you achieved during your shutdown may be easy to incorporate into your daily routine, while others may prove more challenging. The trick is to stick to your guns and have confidence in this journey of self-improvement. If you keep moving forward, you'll ultimately reach your goal.

That's exactly what happened in the case of Dr. Frasier Crane, the fictional psychiatrist who was first introduced on the sitcom *Cheers* and then became the focus of the self-titled hit series *Frasier*. The premise of the spin-off is the pompous doctor's personal and career reboot. When the bar closes in Boston, so to speak, Frasier finds himself newly divorced and ready to start fresh in Seattle. He begins a career reboot, utilizing his psychiatry skills in a whole new way as a phone-in radio show personality with the tag line, "I'm listening . . . " No longer working in a private practice with long-term clients, Frasier must let go of his previous paradigm and find happiness and success after his reboot.

When you initiate your own reboot, be sure to communicate your revised strategies to those who need to be involved. Even if the plan seems to be more personal in nature, such as a change to your leadership tone or style, it's a good idea to hold a meeting or send an email to explain the new tactic. Needless to say, if a revised set of team initiatives comes into play, verbalizing those measures and being open to suggestions and feedback is imperative to the success of the strategy. It also helps keep you accountable for the behavioral changes. At times, when a reboot occurs, you may decide on a more extreme course of action for your career future. The shutdown you impose may enlighten you in such a way that you realize the only chance for your ultimate improvement and growth is by restarting in a new position or in another industry altogether. When you make a commitment to self-awareness and honestly assessing your current situation, you may ultimately conclude that life is too short to remain where you are.

Perhaps the corporate culture in your company is no longer in line with your own personal philosophies or beliefs. Maybe there's a disconnect between the politics and ideals of the organization you work for and the leader you strive to be. Or perhaps you are surrounded by individuals who are anything but WOW leaders. If that's the case, it may be best to move forward in a completely new direction.

As a strong and committed WOW leader, you have the tools and wherewithal to execute the changes you need to succeed and grow. It's up to you to make the most of your restart by proceeding with passion, fearlessness, focus, and determination.

Reboots On and Off the Screen

The benefits of a self-imposed shutdown and reboot are found in the world of television, too. Remember back when contestants on *Wheel of Fortune* had to use their winnings to "shop" in various rooms stocked with merchandise and prizes? They'd have to make purchases quickly on air and would invariably end up with something completely useless or hideous, like a ceramic monkey or a set of table tennis paddles. Somewhere along the line, executives decided to reboot that formula and reinvent the prize portion of the game. Thankfully, the shopping was discarded in favor of keeping the actual cash. While the show was still popular and thriving at the time of the switch, having the foresight to make changes and move forward in a new direction enabled it to remain fresh and relevant for years to come.

Another reboot example is one that didn't happen on-screen, but rather behind the scenes. Ron Howard began his TV career in front of the camera as a child actor on *The Andy Griffith Show*. Later, as a young adult, he starred as Richie Cunningham in the hit series *Happy Days*. He also enjoyed some success in big-screen movies like *American Graffiti* and *The Music Man*. However, rather than continue as an actor, he followed his passion and reinvented himself, eventually becoming one of our generation's most accomplished producers and directors. While there's no doubt Ron Howard had the acting chops to maintain a successful and lucrative career in that profession, he instead chose to impose a reboot and succeed in another direction.

As a WOW leader, don't be afraid to step back and reevaluate your circumstances, imposing a shutdown and reboot to keep moving forward.

From Tired to Inspired

If you're not able to go full force into reboot mode but you've reached that place of mental exhaustion that results from being overworked, overwhelmed, and overextended, you need to go from tired to inspired. You need to tap into the potential within and get motivated to change your attitude, move in a new direction, or reenergize your stagnant efforts to begin working toward your goals.

If any TV show epitomizes the phrase "from tired to inspired," it would have to be the weight-loss program *The Biggest Loser*. The long-running series begins each season with a fresh batch of overweight individuals who have come to "The Ranch" to slim down and compete for a large cash prize. Inevitably, as the road to weight loss begins, the out-of-shape contestants can barely finish a light workout. They struggle with fatigue, injuries, and finding the motivation to push forward. But little by little, with the help of the trainers, the encouragement of their team members, the positive results on the scale, and the monetary incentive always in the background, they ultimately succeed.

In actuality, the *Biggest Loser* competitors have already made the decision to make a change before "officially" starting on the series. They've become inspired to improve their current situation and begin making positive life changes. Choosing to make the show the vehicle by which they accomplish their goals is the first step. Then, as the pounds are shed during the course of the game, they build on the momentum of that initial inspiration, and we watch as they become slimmer, stronger, and increasingly more confident. What we see on camera and what happens off-screen during the course of their journey becomes inspiring to us as viewers as well. Watching the dedication and motivation of the contestants helps us see that it is truly possible to go from tired to inspired.

Here are some things to consider when you need to refresh, recharge, and become inspired once again:

Say no. If you're already feeling overwhelmed, don't take on more projects, more responsibilities, and in general more than you can handle. Be willing to stop, take a break, and get your bearings before adding more to your plate.

Clear your head. Write down what's bothering or overwhelming you. Keep a journal, take out a sheet of paper, or key it into your iPad . . . use whatever is at your disposal. Make a list of rants, jot down a goal sheet, or write a manifesto: anything to clear your head and put your feelings into words.

Change your perspective. Step away from what's overwhelming you. Take a walk, go to the mall, play with the dog, spend an hour in the garden. If possible, schedule a vacation and relax. Whatever you do, just do—and think about—something else.

Step out of your comfort zone. Do something that scares you or thrills you in a way that is wonderfully unexpected. Pick up a new hobby, take a cooking class, enroll in Pilates, or try your hand at painting. Take a chance . . . don't think, just do!

Laugh. A good, hearty chuckle may be the last thing on your mind when you're at your wits' end, but in reality, it's the best medicine for what ails you. Allow yourself a night of release by scheduling an evening out with friends, playing a game with family, or revisiting old home movies (hint: Nothing is more humorous than watching people dance at a wedding).

Compliment someone. Inject some positive energy into the world. Give someone else a boost by acknowledging a job well done or by complimenting his or her efforts and achievements. You'll naturally feel better by making someone else's day, keeping in mind that what you put out into the world is usually reflected back.

Seek out inspiration. If it's motivation you need, don't slink into a corner and retreat—unless you go there with a good book in hand. Find inspiration via a great leadership manuscript or even an uplifting movie, novel, or TV show focused on overcoming obstacles.

Pay it forward. Nothing inspires like giving back. Release some of the weight that's holding you down by sharing what you have with others. Spend a few hours at a homeless shelter, nursing home, or children's hospital, and you'll begin to see your issues in a whole new light.

Being a WOW leader doesn't mean you're always "on." Even the best of the best get thrown off course and need to regroup and reinvent themselves in order to succeed. During those times when you're feeling tired and lost, wake yourself up with a fresh approach to the everyday . . . and become inspired to be the best you can be.

Mentoring Yourself

Another way to keep your self-improvement goals in check is to be a mentor to yourself. No, that doesn't mean simply giving yourself a glorified ego stroking or a self-inflicted pat on the back. It doesn't mean channeling the fictional self-help guru Stuart Smalley of *Saturday Night Live* fame. Remember his Daily Affirmations mantra? "I'm good enough, I'm smart enough, and doggone it, people like me!" Mentoring yourself can be a constructive and productive way of self-evaluation and motivation. But you have to do it with the right attitude and with an honest commitment to self-reflection.

When formal mentorships are not available in the workplace, you should seek out informal relationships with experienced, respected individuals. However, that kind of arrangement is dependent on the other party's availability, schedule, and willingness to participate. When a trusted adviser isn't on hand, mentoring yourself can be an effective and worthwhile alternative. Here are some tips, techniques, and strategies for mentoring yourself.

Self-Mentoring

1. Role play. Have a conversation with yourself, playing the part of "you" and the part of "mentor" in reversing roles. Actually speaking and engaging out loud, rather than just thinking about your situation, can truly bring about new epiphanies and different perspectives. It forces you to confront things at all angles and respond to questions in a more truthful and honest manner. Plus, in the mentor role, you're stepping out of yourself and looking back from the outside, which will help you shed some light on how you might be perceived by others.

2. Write a letter. Sit down and write yourself a letter that outlines your goals, your struggles, and your personal observations. Include a detailed self-evaluation that honestly critiques your performance, objectives, strengths, and weaknesses. Tell yourself what changes you could make, where your passions lie, and how you can go about achieving future aspirations. Putting your feelings and thoughts into words on paper sometimes helps to make them more real and more valuable.

3. Embrace affirmations. Positive quotes, sayings, and mantras can be a leader's best friend. Visual reminders and affirmations, printed out and displayed in prominent places, can give you a daily boost and serve as a friendly reminder to keep moving in the right direction. Scan Pinterest, business websites, or simply Google "success quotes" to draw inspiration. Better yet, come up with your own positive mantra that speaks directly to your own needs. An uplifting affirmation is akin to having your own personal mentor, providing encouragement and motivation when you need it.

4. Schedule a review. Make it a habit to schedule monthly, bimonthly, or even weekly self-reviews. Take the time to go over your accomplishments and setbacks as well as establish new goals or review your progress with ongoing goals. Identify issues, problem areas, or questions and make a plan to implement changes where needed.

If possible, seek out a trusted, respected mentor to serve as a role model and guide. But for those times when mentors are unavailable, or when you need a quick attitude pick-me-up, look to the person you trust the most, and try mentoring yourself.

Investing in Yourself

Investing in your own self-improvement isn't always a top priority, but for WOW leaders, it should be. Let's face it: Life as we know it is a jam-packed, chaotic juggling act, to say the least. Personal development often gets pushed down and buried at the bottom of a seemingly endless to-do list. Between keeping up at work, managing the home, taking care of the kids, attempting a bit of a social life, and trying to squeeze in a few hours of sleep, how are you supposed to focus on investing in yourself? Unless you can add hours to a day, how can you carve out time for your own personal development?

Although investing in yourself on a regular basis may seem impossible, it's actually quite doable in small doses. Early on, my father taught me about the value of saving money, and he gave me a strategy to build on. He told me to write my first check (no matter how small) to my savings account, then pay the rest of the bills. Over time, of course, the seemingly meager dollars invested began to add up. The same concept can be applied to your own personal development.

Investing in yourself by doing something small each day (even for five or ten minutes) can make a huge difference. Like anything else—including the bank account that grows with small deposits—you need to have a plan, commitment, and the wherewithal to get it done. Studies have proven that a new habit can be created in seventeen days. So, a routine of investing in yourself can be achieved in just over two weeks with a modicum of stick-to-it-iveness!

Success in any endeavor is possible only when there is a level of passion for attaining the goal. There must be a mission and a desire to complete the mission. In other words, you have to want it. If investing in yourself by expanding your personal development is a priority, then make it a priority! When the passion and the drive is there, you'll find ways to work your goals into your busy day. Think about where there may be small openings or gaps in your schedule. Even if your first reaction is that there are no minutes to spare, I guarantee you'll find them if you want it badly enough.

Here are some ways to prioritize investing in yourself:

Schedule it. Schedule short but consistent blocks of time in your calendar. Carve out daily or weekly minutes that are dedicated to the one specific target you're aiming to achieve. Treat those appointments as commitments that can't be broken. When it comes to investing in yourself, it's okay to be a little selfish!

Communicate it. Discuss your new priorities with your boss and/or family, making them aware of your intentions. Communicate your dedication to learning the new skill or achieving the desired goal by seeking their buy-in and commitment. When the people important to you know and understand your passions and drive, chances are they will support and encourage you, making it easier to instill small changes and handle schedule conflicts along the way.

Share it. Go a step beyond talking about your plans and actually involve those closest to you. Ask your family and loved ones to not only understand your commitment to personal development, but also to share in the experience. They may have an interest in improving or developing themselves in a similar way, or they may have ideas to help you with your process. Investing in yourself with the help of others can expand your learning potential—plus, it can be fun!

Believe it. Investing in yourself often requires a change in your mindset. You must believe that you're an important asset worthy of investment. You must reinforce your commitment to bettering yourself and meeting the goals that matter to you—without feeling guilty about it! Believe that you are a priority, or believe me, you'll always end up last on the list.

Stick to it. There is no endgame to investing in yourself. It's an ongoing process that will help you grow your skill set, improve your WOW abilities, and make you more marketable, versatile, confident, and content. If you're continually investing in yourself, you'll never wonder what could have been or what you might have done "if you'd only had the time." Make the time now and stick to it!

When it comes to investing in yourself, you have to be passionate, driven, and creative enough to find room in your already busy schedule. Try replacing a dreaded chore—a housekeeping or home maintenance task—with a personal-development activity. Delegate the busy work to someone else—a family member or hired helper—and invest the time you've gained in yourself.

As a leader, you're a commodity in your own right. What you bring to the table in terms of skills, attributes, and experiences is what makes you valuable in your current position and what sells you to a potential employer. If you're not investing in yourself and making personal development a priority, you're selling yourself short. Start making those small daily deposits today, and begin building up your personal WOW account!

WOW leadership isn't achieved by being named to a position of great power; you accomplish it by doing great things and working hard to maintain and surpass that level of greatness. Only through a tireless dedication to self improvement and avoidance of autopilot leadership can you become better than you were yesterday. When you strive to live up to the position you're in—rather than relying on others to hold you up—you're committed to WOW leadership. And through that example, you'll be able to bring out the WOW in those you lead.

Chapter 4

WOW Leaders Are Authentic

*"Be what you are. This is the first step toward
becoming better than you are."*
—*Julius Charles Hare*

Authenticity is the fundamental core of WOW leadership. When you choose to be an original and not a weak spin-off of someone else's success, you're representing yourself in a truthful, genuine manner.

The awkward but lovable and hardworking Betty Suarez from the comedy *Ugly Betty* is a true original. In addition to being young, naive, and inexperienced, Betty has absolutely no sense of fashion or style, frequently wearing bold colors, mismatched patterns, and overall quirky ensembles, all while trying to succeed in the cutthroat world of high fashion. When the owner of fashion magazine *Mode* hires Betty to be his womanizing son's personal assistant, it's because, as the show title suggests, she's unattractive and won't be a temptation or distraction. But Betty proves herself to be more than what she was hired to be. Not only is she a positive, motivational force, but also her unique, offbeat, and wacky ways are a breath of fresh air in the stale, stagnant world of corporate coldness. Throughout the course of the series, Betty is always trying to improve herself, better her skills, and grow her career, but she never changes her core self. She doesn't change her wardrobe, style, or her ideals to blend in. Instead, she remains authentic, and by doing so, she stands out.

If you're a WOW leader, your authenticity is all the more visible because there's nothing phony or suspect about your character. Alternatively, those who talk a big game or lay it on too thick seem disingenuous and suspicious. Refrain from name-dropping, using hollow buzzwords, or making unrealistic promises. Don't brag about your exploits, and more important, never fabricate, exaggerate, or misrepresent your accomplishments. Don't pretend to be someone you're not. Instead, keep it real so you'll be respected as the real deal.

Authentic leaders transcend position, status, and perceptions. Whether they are über-wealthy CEOs or financially challenged middle managers, they lead from the heart.

Take Deputy U.S. Marshall Raylan Givens, the flawed but dedicated lawman on the hit series *Justified*. While not perfect, Deputy Givens is authentic and true to himself and his own gut instincts and beliefs. He's got a unique swagger and personality, punctuated by his out-of-place "Old West" style—complete with cowboy boots and a Stetson-type hat. What makes the character likeable—and more believable—are the imperfections and originality that go beyond a typecast of a modern-day sheriff.

No quality defines a WOW leader more than authenticity. Being an authentic leader means being honest, trustworthy, and willing to make and own up to mistakes. Authentic leaders possess integrity, character, and a self-assuredness that guides them and shapes their decisions and actions.

DUD leaders, contrastingly, can be slippery and fake, portraying an outward image of perfection while leading for all the wrong reasons and in all the wrong ways. Since DUDs are primarily focused on bettering their careers and making themselves look superior, they don't lead from the heart . . . they lead without heart.

Here's how to be the real deal by displaying the qualities of an authentic leader:

Rein in the rhetoric. Communicate transparently and fairly with your team and colleagues. Be clear with your instructions and expectations. Invite questions and reciprocal dialogue. Don't lead with cryptic rhetoric that's nonspecific, confusing, or one-sided. Using big words and CEO-speak doesn't make you a leader; finding the right words to inspire, motivate, and direct your team does.

Do what's right, not what's popular. Integrity and honesty are the hallmarks of WOW leadership. When making leadership decisions, go with your gut and do what you feel is right, not what others are demanding or expecting. If you turn away from your own principles and instincts, you're turning away from yourself, and you're not being authentic to the leader within.

Turn off the power. Leadership is not about the glory of achieving power and prestige; it's about lighting the way for others to shine. To be an authentic WOW, it's important to lift up and inspire the people you lead, not use them as catalysts for your own personal success. When team victories are earned, turn off your own power and share the credit with those who deserve it.

Eat some humble pie. Being genuine as a leader means remembering your roots and not acting like you're omnipotent, better, or more important than those coming up behind you. Keep your humility intact by admitting when you make mistakes, praising and encouraging those you lead, and being open to suggestions and changes.

Expect initiative, not perfection. Keep your team focused on innovation, not perfection. Authentic leaders encourage their staff members to try new techniques and show initiative with fresh ideas, free from the fear of reprimands when mistakes or failures result. Show you're the real deal by guiding those in your charge toward taking calculated risks based on sensible, informed decisions. And then help lift them up—don't push them down—if the risk doesn't pay off.

There is no perfection in leadership. But for WOWs, there is authenticity, and that can make all the difference. Stay true to yourself, and whether you do everything right or not, you can't go wrong.

Canned Laughter

When TV first began gracing the homes of the American people, most sitcoms used a single-camera filming technique, which made it impossible to shoot before a live studio audience. But radio shows had conditioned people to expect the sound of laughter during programming. Thus, the laugh track, or prerecorded audience laughter, was utilized to enhance and enliven the viewing experience.

Studio engineer Charley Douglass developed the laugh track, which he also used to "sweeten" or "de-sweeten" the inconsistent laughter of studio audiences during live shows. While controversy and criticism has consistently been a part of the laugh-track device's existence, it has been used in various degrees and formats since the 1950s.

Not surprisingly, with the advent of canned laughter, some people argued against the need to "prompt" the viewing audience to recognize the show's humorous parts. Many believed that removing the public's choice was something of an insult to the viewership and as a result, detracted from the program's overall quality. Others, however, believed that the standard had been set and it had come to be expected by the American people. Reliance on canned laughter has been a mixed bag ever since, with some shows opting to remain silent and others still filling the voids with piped-in chuckles.

But what does canned laughter have to do with leadership? Does "being an original" and "keeping it real" mean you can't use proven and already established leadership techniques to achieve your own successes? Or does it mean using any and all tactics (within the realm of honesty and fairness) to go about attaining your unique goals? Like using or not using artificial laughs, the choice is up to you.

As a WOW leader, you set your own path and establish what works and does not work within the scope of your leadership environment. If you've carved out your own niche and want to try your hand at something unheard of, by all means, set the bar yourself: Go it alone, without the canned laughter. But it doesn't make you any less of a WOW if you draw from the experiences and practices of the people who came before you, provided you're using those examples in your own original way: Use the canned laughter, but only to enhance a quality program. You make the call; there's no right or wrong as long as you're engaging and inspiring your audience of followers.

Stick to Your Style

WOW leaders are authentic, self-aware, and won't change their leadership style in order to align more perfectly with their company's culture. They'll seek the culture that aligns with them or set the culture themselves when possible. In terms of leadership styles, the range runs the gamut. Some WOWs are linear leaders, while others are nonlinear. Some lead with modern style, while others lean toward traditional tactics. Perhaps the most controversial comparison when it comes to leadership style is masculine versus feminine.

Even in today's equality-conscious society, there are still many who are wary of female leadership. The thinking still exists that leading "like a woman" means either being too soft or overcompensating and being a stereotypical "boardroom bitch." But are male or female leadership styles really any different?

Is there any reason we should categorically believe that men are better leaders than women or that women are superior to men? To do so would be succumbing to age-old stereotypes and preconceptions that have no place in the modern business world. We are all striving to achieve our best leadership results and to succeed in today's corporate landscape with traits pulled from both modern and traditional styles of leading. Leadership ability doesn't depend on the leader's gender; it depends on the leader, period.

Your leadership style is your own and should not be dictated by "rules" or expectations based on gender. For a woman, it may be hard to be soft, but if that's your style, be an effective leader with a "softer" personality; don't turn on the bitchiness in an attempt to be perceived in a more acceptable, "masculine" light. Likewise, as a male with a gentler approach, be secure enough with your own style to lead without traditional and stereotypical "tough-guy" tactics.

The only way to be a WOW is to be YOU . . . traditional, modern, or anywhere in between. Be authentic and you'll be successful.

Surprisingly, perhaps no one said it more eloquently than the TV character Jax, outlaw biker on *Sons of Anarchy*. In the opening scene of the season six premiere, "Straw," the president of the motorcycle club is in his infant son's nursery, writing in a journal. "I feel like my life has taken a turn. I'm heading down a road I've never been down before. Nothing is familiar. The signs don't make sense. Do I get off the road, or do I keep riding? Do I go alone, or take others with me? Who do I trust for the journey?"

Leaders don't always have all the answers or know which path is the right one to take. But when they lead with authenticity, their decisions are guided by where they want to go. As Jax struggles with his journey and the way in which he wants to lead his crew, he realizes that his own truth is his best guidance. "The only advice I can give you," Jax writes to his sons, "is to examine who you are as men, figure out what's important to you, know yourselves, know what's in your heart. Don't be swayed by fear or history or the opinions of outsiders. Find your own truth. It will lead you to the things you love."

Strong Characters

In the landscape of TV culture today, there are strong male leads as well as strong female leads. But it took awhile to get here. One of the most empowered females of her time, Lucille Ball, broke ground in the industry with her iconic show *I Love Lucy*. Not only did the show revolve around a strong comedic female lead, but also she was married to a Cuban nightclub singer (shocking!) and was depicted as pregnant on the series. Lucy's strong character presence resonated with audiences at the time and still does today in syndication.

Over the years, strong female characters continued to emerge: Mary Tyler Moore, Maude, Samantha from *Bewitched*, Roseanne, Clair Huxtable from *The Cosby Show*, and Buffy the vampire slayer, to name a few. Today, strong women are omnipresent on the small screen: *The Good Wife*'s Alicia Florrick, *The Americans*' Elizabeth Jennings, *Modern Family*'s Gloria, and more. Many crime dramas, like the *CSI* franchises or the *Law & Order* shows, pair males and females together as equally influential and capable performers.

TV portrays a slew of WOW and DUD characters, some male and some female. Gender doesn't determine strength in the fictional world of television, nor should it be a measure of WOW in leadership.

Harness the Superhero Within

Although TV, comic book, and movie superheroes are larger-than-life legends with powers beyond the norm, they're not just childhood fodder; they're inspirations to harness the superhero within each of us. In our life, career, and society, many of us have become comfortable with the norm and content with complacency. We shrug our shoulders and accept that we can't have it all. Much too easily, we move on with our mundane, ordinary, and often unfulfilling existence. However, it doesn't have to be that way. If you think like a superhero, anything is possible.

Everyone has the potential to become a superhero in his or her own right. Just as with the fictional crime fighters we all know and love, reaching superhero status takes courage, determination, and above all, the will and desire to use the powers and skills we've been given. All the extraordinary characters in the superhero genre face their own demons when it comes to using, accepting, or harnessing their own strengths. And none of them are without flaws or weaknesses. Their stories are only interesting and inspirational because our beloved superheroes triumph despite their shortcomings.

Superman may be the Man of Steel, but he is rendered powerless by kryptonite. Batman is wealthy, super-intelligent, and beyond dedicated to his superhero quest, but he is, after all, only human. His mortality and his many idiosyncrasies are weaknesses that his nemeses readily use against him. Would we still admire, revere, and want to emulate superheroes if they were gods without flaws—if they never had to overcome the potential for failure? If power is absolute and guaranteed, what's so super about that?

The TV series *Heroes* featured an extensive lineup of characters with superhuman abilities. Each had unique powers, including mind reading, regeneration, time travel, invisibility, super strength, flying, electronic "clairvoyance," and passing through inanimate objects. However, the so-called heroes were just ordinary folks living in modern times with families, careers, high school classes, and all the rest. For some, the powers were more curse than gift, conflicting with the normal progression of their lives. Living with and mastering the control of their extraordinary characteristics was not only a challenge but also sometimes resulted in disaster for the hero or others. The characters who successfully blended their "special" talents with their lifestyle and core inner beliefs became WOW heroes on the side of good, but those whose gifts overpowered them drifted to the dark side and became evil. Ultimately it's not just our skill sets or special talents that make us WOWs; it's what we do with them, how we incorporate those abilities into our everyday routines, and how we overcome our shortcomings and mistakes to keep doing what's right. That's what makes us "super."

As kids, we put on our capes and dreamed of being able to fly. As adults, we still want to wear those capes, but now our perspective has changed into a more realistic vision of flying. Now, we want to be the superheroes not of the universe, but of our own lives. We want to soar and excel in our careers, our goals, and our dreams. And we can do it, as long as we don't succumb to the fear of the kryptonite that can stop us.

Here are a few tips on how to harness your superhero self:

- Never give up; even when the odds aren't in your favor.
- Understand your weaknesses, but focus on your strengths.
- Refuse to let your enemies get the best of you.
- Work toward a greater good, acting with integrity and honor.
- Use, and don't suppress, the talents, powers, and skills you've been given.
- Wear a mask of humility, never seeking praise for your achievements.
- Be the hero you were meant to be (Spiderman doesn't try to be the Hulk).

If you want to WOW—as a leader or a person—harness the potential within yourself to be the superhero you know you can be.

Reality Isn't Always Real

It didn't take long for people to conclude that reality TV wasn't quite the frank, open, and "real" portrayal of ordinary lives that it often claims to be. Obviously, the editing and massaging of footage on any show enables it to be displayed in out-of-sequence and unnatural ways to add more drama. Important information can be easily omitted and conversations can be spliced together to create more interesting or shocking scenarios.

On shows like *The Bachelor*, the show's producers arrange over-the-top dates in one-of-a-kind locales, so the fairy-tale romance that puts "regular guys" to shame is not quite a fair depiction of dating reality. When the show wraps and mountain-top picnics are no longer possible—surprise, surprise—the winning couple's relationship inevitably begins to fall apart off-camera. In "real" life, when the two gorgeous daters are left to their own devices and must navigate their courtship while getting back to their jobs, their families, and their daily responsibilities, things don't always work out. Hard to believe, isn't it?

Besides the unrealistic dating rituals on *The Bachelor*, the viewers hardly get an accurate look at what really goes down during the show's filming, especially during the infamous rose ceremony. The rose ceremony is portrayed as a five-minute segment where the sought-after single man chooses and eliminates from the group of potential "brides," handing out rose after rose until the "final rose" is given and those left flowerless go home in tears. But it's been rumored that the order in which the roses are given out is predetermined, and the filming of the event takes hours, not minutes, to accomplish.

There has been no shortage of controversy, opinions, assumptions, and rumors about the possibility that the show is rigged, scripted, or at the very least, edited in an inaccurate way to create more interesting story lines. Similar accusations have cropped up in reference to numerous other popular reality shows, including *Storage Wars*, *House Hunters*, and *The Real Housewives*.

On *House Hunters*, a former participant on the show came forth claiming her experiences of shopping for new homes were prearranged and that much of the show is reenacted and does not happen as organically as it seems. The same holds true for the storage-locker auctions held on the popular *Storage Wars* series. A former cast member, Dave Hester, was fired from the show and then made allegations that producers "plant" treasures in units to create a more interesting outcome.

Even reality shows that aren't necessarily fake portray at best a slanted view of reality. Sure, the stars of *The Real Housewives* are "real" people, but how many of their interactions with each other were organized and massaged by the producers? In yet another example, *Dog the Bounty Hunter* portrayed the exploits of real-life, legitimate bounty hunters Dog and Beth Chapman. While it's never been proven that the "hunts" were anything but real, it was rumored that much of the show was scripted and that the production crew obtained approval from families involved prior to filming.

Reality TV may or may not be a microcosm of society as a whole, but it does provide insight into the importance of honesty. As TV viewers, we may not really mind all that much if a reality show is faked, since after all, it's only entertainment. By and large, we're not personally affected one way or another when something happens on TV. But when it comes to our leaders, truth and reality are a primary and vital requirement. If we're led down the primrose path by *The Bachelor*, so what? But it's a completely different story if our boss bamboozles us.

Keep it real as a WOW leader and your faithful followers will know that, unlike the questionable "reality" programming offered on the small screen, they can trust what you're all about. They'll know that what's behind the scenes is the same as what's in front, and they'll keep tuning in for more.

The "It" Factor

WOWs are honest and trustworthy, humble and respectful, dedicated to self-improvement, and authentic. But they also have something else: an "it" factor that sets them apart from others, distinguishing them among an army of would-be leaders.

Great leaders resonate because they have a certain presence: a way about them that exudes excellence and self-assuredness, without being boastful or arrogant. There's just something about them that makes you want to believe in them. The same holds true when it comes to TV. Our favorite characters are the ones that ring true as believable, realistic, and authentic—not the one-note clichés or caricatures that fail to resonate. Standout characters bring something extra to the screen that can't always be defined but clearly sets them apart. It's often those "it" characters that make or break a series. After all, what would *The Sopranos* be without James Gandolfini's Tony? What would *Game of Thrones* be without Peter Dinklage's Tyrion Lannister? What would *The Big Bang Theory* be without Jim Parson's Sheldon? What would *I Love Lucy* be without . . . you get the idea.

On TV, characters can have a positive "it" factor even if they themselves are negative. Even a DUD character can WOW in the world of entertainment. But in the real world, a DUD's "it" quality causes people to withdraw and recoil. DUDs can be quirky, off balance, and make rash and unpopular decisions. They're usually so full of themselves that they have blinders on in regard to how they are perceived by their peers and their staff . . . or they just don't care.

What does it take to differentiate yourself as a WOW leader with an "it" factor—to stand out from the ho-hum, mediocre, or outright ineffective leadership we see in offices everywhere? Is there one kind of leader that excels at WOW leadership? Masculine or feminine? Traditional or modern? Linear or nonlinear? Controversial or conservative? Top-tier executive or mid-level manager? What kind of leader should you try to be? The answer is as simple as it is complex: To be a WOW, you've got to be YOU.

WOW leaders are not only great at what they do, they have something above and beyond the leader next door. While it's nearly impossible to quantify or define the "it" factor that makes a WOW stand out, it's deeply rooted in being authentic. In other words, you can't be "it" without being "you."

On *American Idol*, industry professionals judge the vocal talent and star-quality of aspiring singers in a competition-style format. In the audition phase of the season thirteen installment, celebrity judge Harry

Connick Jr. tells a contestant that his decisions on who progresses in the contest are largely based on "believability." Fellow judge Keith Urban agrees, explaining that it takes a "nanosecond" to gauge a person's authenticity. "It's an indescribable thing," he says. "Sometimes you just start singing and the way you look when you sing, and the way you move your mouth, and all that stuff, and you immediately go, *oh, born singer.*" Later, he reiterates the point with another contestant. "It's real," he states. In other words, it's not someone trying to imitate another artist or attempting to create an image—it's someone who owns and displays individuality and projects a unique style that rings true and is therefore trusted to deliver.

Anyone worth associating with in life, especially in business, will be able to spot a poser or false personality a mile away. Nothing is more off-putting than a leader who puts on airs, tries to emulate a certain type of persona, or comes off as disingenuous. You'll never succeed or earn respect as a WOW if you're trying to be someone you're not. You can only be "it" if you're confident, self-aware, and secure in your own ideals and values. By presenting yourself in the genuine light of your own truth, you'll shine the spotlight on what makes you unique and worth following.

Why was the Detective Andy Sipowicz character such a success on the groundbreaking cop show *NYPD Blue*? Besides (or in spite of) the fact that he dropped his drawers on prime time more often than censors (or viewers) would have liked, Andy had an "it" factor that audiences responded to. Yes, he was grumpy, hard-edged, and not altogether an appealing personality. He had numerous personal demons, didn't always play well with others, and made more than his share of mistakes. But he did his job with conviction, dedication, and authority. When push came to shove, Andy was there for his partners and did what was right. Sipowicz wasn't perfect, but he was a WOW in many ways. Warts and all, you had to love the balding, middle-aged detective for being real, authentic, and true to himself.

Shows That Have "It"

Since the beginnings of television, there have been countless shows aired—some hits and even more misses. Of those hits, many resonate with an enduring WOW factor that sets them apart from the others. Those series not only enjoyed a steady and loyal viewership in their prime but also were imitated, loved, and remembered long past their final episodes. Like the WOW "it" factor, it's hard to pinpoint exactly what puts certain shows into this elite category, but there's no disputing their rightful place among the best of the best.

To name a few, in no particular order: *I Love Lucy*, *The Honeymooners*, *Dallas*, *Gunsmoke*, *Friends*, *M*A*S*H*, *Seinfeld*, *ER*, *Cheers*, *The Simpsons*, *Lost*, *The Cosby Show*, *Sex & the City*, *The Office*, *Roseanne*, *Saturday Night Live*, *NYPD Blue*, *The Sopranos*, *Taxi*, *All in the Family*, *The Mary Tyler Moore Show*, and *Law & Order*.

There are several more current series that also possess an "it" factor, although their longevity has yet to be determined. Hits like *The Big Bang Theory*, *Mad Men*, *Modern Family*, *Family Guy*, *Breaking Bad*, *Game of Thrones*, *Dexter*, and *Glee* come to mind. In the game show category, those long-running series like *Jeopardy!*, *Wheel of Fortune*, and *The Price Is Right* no doubt have an "it" quality that have kept audiences tuning in for decades.

The "it" factor cannot be manufactured in the formulaic sense. There is no perfect, exact recipe for the ideal TV show any more than there is an exact set of qualities that makes a WOW leader shine. There are certainly elements that must come into play in order for leaders—or TV shows—to succeed. But to elevate beyond "success" and into the realm of WOW takes originality, courage, and self-assuredness that can't be forced or faked. That lack of genuine substance is why so many copycat shows are ultimately doomed to mediocrity or failure. Shows that have "it" are authentic, real, and true only to themselves, which, despite the occasional bad episode or poorly received critique, enable them to stand out among the crowd.

Be an Original

In your quest to become and continue to be a great leader, and throughout your career as you endeavor to remain a WOW, be an original. The best and most inspirational innovators emerge and survive because they have the courage to be themselves. If we were all carbon copies of each other, we'd never advance and grow as a society. The same holds true in business, where leaders with new ideas and fresh perspectives inspire and drive the people they lead, while those who are afraid to be authentic are stifled by inaction and repetition of the same old thing.

However, being unique doesn't mean you can't benefit from the example of others. Seeking out and learning from a mentor is a wise and beneficial route to take when striving to be a WOW. A mentor can be a voice of encouragement and experience as well as a positive role model. Draw inspiration from others—but be you.

It's one thing to admire the accomplishments of someone successful—say, Steve Jobs—and set out to achieve the same level of accomplishments through your own set of visions, goals, and aspirations. It's quite another to say, "I want to be the next Steve Jobs," and then attempt to eat only fruit, go barefoot, and wear nothing but turtlenecks.

You can be your own original self while having been influenced by other WOW examples, but you can't be unique if you plagiarize other people's ideas, choices, and experiences to write a story for yourself. Imitators are never as good as the original; they can never deliver or achieve the same results as the person they are aspiring to be.

Copycats not only fail to inspire, but they also lose the qualities within themselves that make them special, unique, and valuable. By attempting to be someone else, imitators stifle their own potential; they kill their inner WOW.

When TV producers decided to revive the popular detective drama *Hawaii Five-O*, which ran from 1968 to 1980, the new version's creators were tasked with modernizing the show to jibe well in the present day. While the overall concept and story lines still had impact, a lot had to be altered to align with the expectations of current audiences—especially the personalities of its top characters. Instead of simply inserting a new actor into the old role of Steve McGarrett, for example, a new take on an old favorite was created.

What worked well in the '70s with Jack Lord's portrayal of the "it" character McGarrett wouldn't necessarily stand out as "it" today. In the original depiction, McGarrett had an egotistical and smug charisma, operating as a more traditional leader. The team existed to make the boss look good, putting him at the center of every case and crediting him as the source for all successes.

In the contemporary iteration, however, McGarrett, played by Alex O'Loughlin, shares the spotlight with his team. He leads by supporting and uplifting his fellow officers and support staff, not by standing on a pedestal above them. The revamped head honcho still has the "it" factor, but in his own unique way and with a leadership style more in line with today's modern culture.

Just as the new McGarrett wouldn't succeed as a direct imitation of the old, you won't succeed if you're not totally you. To reach the status of WOW, you must believe in your own passions and in your ability to bring them to fruition. Trust that your individualism is the most valuable part of your leadership skill set, and stay authentic and original. Only then can you WOW with what's naturally within you to achieve.

Originals

The most inspirational WOW leaders have an "it" factor that make them stand out among the crowd. They're confident in what they have to offer, even if it differs from the perceived norm or the safe bet. In the same way, the most remembered, beloved, and admired TV shows of all time were originals that broke the mold, or created a new one. These groundbreaking series succeeded despite commonly accepted standards on TV and persevered in the face of controversy and critical doubt. As a WOW leader, you must do the same.

Here's a look at some of TV's most original, groundbreaking shows:

- *I Love Lucy* (1951–1957) not only was the first comedy to be filmed before a live studio audience, it also tested new waters with its focus on a strong comedic female lead.
- *The Mary Tyler Moore Show* (1970–1977) broke tradition by portraying a strong, intelligent, unmarried, and likeable career-oriented woman as the main character.
- *All in the Family* (1971–1979) touched on sensitive, dramatic topics within its comedic scope, which was previously unheard of. Portraying frank, inappropriate language and racial epithets, it was the first show to feature the sound of a toilet being flushed—scandalous!
- *Soap* (1977–1981) was the first show to feature an openly gay central character.
- *Three's Company* (1977–1984) raised eyebrows with its sexually oriented humor and innuendos.
- *The Cosby Show* (1984–1992) opened the door for shows based on a stand-up comedian's humor but also stood out for its characterization of a successful, loving, tight-knit, African American family.
- *Moonlighting* (1985–1989) was recognized as the first series to provide an equal mix of drama and comedy, thus giving birth to the "dramedy" genre.
- *Golden Girls* (1985–1992) proved that age doesn't matter. The show often shocked audiences by portraying geriatric ladies as real women dealing with modern issues, including sexuality.
- *Roseanne* (1988–1997) was credited for its honest, realistic take on the blue-collar family; for its tackling of hard-hitting topics like abuse, infidelity, and teen sexuality; for its reliance on a strong female matriarch who was not sugar-coated or meant to be "likeable"; and for featuring two overweight leads without using their weight as a source of comedy or a prominent part of the plotline.
- *Life Goes On* (1989–1993) included a main character with Down syndrome, portraying him in a realistic light as a person beyond his "disability."
- *Seinfeld* (1989–1998) was self-proclaimed as a show "about nothing." *Seinfeld* followed the ordinary happenings of four single adults with less-than-stellar, often despicable personalities, prov-

ing that we don't have to "like" the characters to relate.

- *The Simpsons* (1989–?) is America's longest-running sitcom, achieving its prime-time, longstanding success using adult-style humor that parodies the working middle class.
- *Friends* (1994–2004) shifted culture by depicting a lifestyle in which young singles lived and succeeded on their own and only needed their friends.
- *Lost* (2004–2010) changed the landscape of dramas by introducing a complex, intriguing story line based in science fiction and mystery.
- *The Office* (U.S. version, 2005–2013) became the innovator of the mockumentary genre of comedies by delivering a stinging, hilarious take on office life.

Subscription series like *Six Feet Under*, *The Sopranos*, *Dexter*, *Homeland*, *Game of Thrones*, *Breaking Bad*, *Boardwalk Empire*, *The Americans*, *True Blood*, *Walking Dead*, and others feature unique concepts mixed with controversy and without the censorship of prime-time TV, enabling a whole new level of honest, sometimes graphic portrayals.

Nothing resonates with audiences like an original, innovative TV show that moves us to laugh, cry, think in a new way, or scratch our heads in utter disbelief. We want to be entertained, but we also want to be taken in new directions and challenged to address difficult, sensitive, or offbeat topics. While we sometimes give in to the "guilty pleasure" viewing of less-than-quality programming, we're most loyal to the shows that provide us with substance, value, and originality.

In much the same way, people prefer to follow leaders who challenge them, draw out the best from them, and provide them with value beyond the ordinary. Be a WOW, and strive to be your own original self.

Spin-offs

In the age of the reality show, TV originality seems to be a dying art. Once a successful formula is hit upon, a slew of knock-offs quickly emerge, some with a bit of a twist or a slightly different format, but all with the same basic idea. How many variations on the cooking-contest theme are out there or have been out there? *Top Chef*, *Cupcake Wars*, *Hell's Kitchen*, *Iron Chef America*, *The Chopping Block*, *Food Network Star*, *MasterChef*, *Chopped*, and *Kitchen Nightmares* are just a few.

And let's not forget the spin-offs to some of the more successful franchises: *Iron Chef America* is itself a spin-off of the Japanese version, and *The Next Iron Chef* was born from the American hit, while the *Top Chef* dynasty sprouted to include *Top Chef: Masters*, *Top Chef: Just Desserts*, and *Top Chef: Junior*.

And how about *Real Housewives*? It began with *The Real Housewives of Orange County* and grew tentacles to include *The Real Housewives* versions from New York City, Atlanta, New Jersey, DC, Beverly Hills, and Miami. The Beverly Hills version of the franchise further spun into *Vanderpump Rules*, a show chronicling the exploits of Lisa Vanderpump's SUR restaurant staff.

Apart from the reality genre, spin-offs have long been a part of TV culture, with varying degrees of success and longevity. Think of the variety of crime dramas that serve as mothers to a series of offspring shows. *Law & Order* became a franchise that included *Law & Order: Special Victims Unit*, *Law & Order: Criminal Intent*, *Law & Order: LA,* and *Law & Order: Trial by Jury*. Another show, *CSI: Crime Scene Investigation* expanded its scope to feature *CSI: Miami*, *CSI: NY*, and *CSI: Las Vegas*. Adding a military twist to the crime drama, the long-running series *JAG* was spun-off into hit show *NCIS*, which itself became a parent to *NCIS: Los Angeles*. In these instances, the spin-offs have generally fared well and have been hits in their own rights.

Spin-off shows only have a chance if they are unique enough to stand on their own without relying on the success of the original. But uniqueness isn't the only qualification for audience acceptance. Factors such as casting, timing, and of course, writing quality, also come into play, making spin-offs a gamble at best.

Shows like *Frasier* (spun from *Cheers*); *Knots Landing* (spun from *Dallas*); *The Jeffersons* (spun from *All in the Family*); *Private Practice* (spun from *Grey's Anatomy*); *Laverne & Shirley* and *Mork & Mindy* (both spun from *Happy Days*); *Benson* (spun from *Soap*), and *Trapper John, M.D.* (spun from *M*A*S*H*), were all hits, while other spin-offs, some from the same parent shows, tanked quickly.

While *Cheers* parented one success (*Frasier*), it also gave birth to the failed and forgotten show *The Tortellis*. *Happy Days* inspired two hit spin-offs (*Laverne & Shirley* and *Mork & Mindy*), but didn't strike a chord with *Joanie Loves Chachi*. Although *Trapper John, M.D.* was technically spun from the film that preceded the popular *M*A*S*H* TV show and became a popular series in its day, another character spin-off, this one featuring the post–Korean War life of Corporal "Radar" O'Reilly and set to be titled *W*A*L*T*E*R*, never made it past the pilot stage.

Other spin-offs that didn't make the grade include *The Apprentice: Martha Stewart* (parent: *The Apprentice*); *Joey* (parent: *Friends*); *The Ropers* (parent: *Three's Company*); *Three's a Crowd* (parent: *Three's Company*); *Top of the Heap* (parent: *Married . . . with Children*); and *Vinnie & Bobby* (parent: *Married . . . with Children*).

The idea behind a spin-off isn't necessarily a bad one; why not take a good idea and run with it? In business, it's done all the time. And, as in the TV world, sometimes it's a hit, while other times it's a miss. The premise behind reprising the roles of beloved characters or expanding the scope of interesting but underdeveloped characters on hit shows is fundamentally sound. What makes or breaks the success of the off-spring is execution.

If you want to be a Bill Gates spin-off—great! But be sure you're a unique take on what Bill Gates has already accomplished and that you execute the steps of your own path with passion and confidence.

Copycats

Generally speaking, copycat shows aren't as well received as spin-offs, because where spin-offs draw from one idea to create a new one or embellish and expand on the original, copycats imitate and regurgitate the same old thing. Here's a list of a few hit TV shows and the copycat shows that followed:

Original	Copycat
Mad Men	*The Playboy Club*
Project Runway	*The Fashion Show*
Top Model	*Make Me a Supermodel*
Sex & the City	*Cashmere Mafia*
Diff'rent Strokes	*Webster*
Wife Swap	*Trading Spouses*
Hoarders	*Hoarding: Buried Alive*
ER	*Chicago Hope*
The View	*The Talk*
What Not to Wear	*How Do I Look?*
Survivor	*I'm a Celebrity . . . Get Me Out of Here!*

This list represents just a small sampling of the many TV series whose original ideas were "borrowed" by others. Remember the original *The People's Court* with Judge Wapner? Think of the slew of "judge" shows that followed that formula. Aren't they all virtually interchangeable, with the exception of the person holding the gavel? What makes Judge Judy any different from Judge Alex or Judge Mathis? Answer: the "it" factor of the show's star! In the case of the copycat or the spin-off, there must be another originality factor that makes it stand out from the group. That is why Judge Judy reportedly earned $47 million between 2012 and 2013.

Strive to be your own best version of yourself and not a knock-off version of someone else. By bringing something real to the table, you'll exude the authentic "it" factor that makes a WOW leader worthy of following.

Part II

In Production—
WOW in Action

Chapter 5

WOW Leaders Are Goal-Driven Visionaries

"Visionary people face the same problems everyone else faces; but
rather than get paralyzed by their problems, visionaries
immediately commit themselves to finding a solution."
—*Bill Hybels*

L eaders must have vision. WOW leaders are confident in their ability
to lead effectively and trust that they are capable of moving their
team in the right direction. Of course, there is a huge difference
between being confident and being arrogant. WOWs are self-assured and
strong in their convictions, but not overtly so. They may have a clear, set
vision, but they don't become blinded by it in such a way that they no
longer accept input or constructive criticism from others.

WOWs have the ability to rise above mistakes they've made along
the way. They believe in themselves, but care about others. They have
a vision, but they are not blinded by it. And they possess the skills to
guide others even as they are learning from them.

Alternatively, DUD leaders lack vision and passion. They're not
motivated or driven to succeed, because they already think they've
achieved personal success. Their inability to inspire others is a direct
result of their own inaction, static leadership style, and lack of inspiration. DUDs are typically content to just sit back and rest on their laurels
while others do the work and make them look good. Their vision is
limited to short-term, immediate gains, especially any that work in their

favor. They commonly put long-term strategies and goals of a visionary nature on the back burner or forget about them entirely.

Being a confident visionary means being forward thinking and appreciating a larger, overall picture. Leaders who make decisions based solely on short-term rewards or financial gains will suffer in the long run. Forward-thinkers can look past today's results by anticipating the steps and outcomes of a long-term view. They facilitate creative thinking and encourage the free exchange and development of new ideas. Visionary leaders implement plans for a company's future goals and achievements. They strategize and prepare well in advance in order to move their teams in the direction of success.

Case in point is Don Draper, TV's favorite retro adman from the hit series *Mad Men*. As the creative director at Sterling Cooper, and then founding member of its offspring, Sterling Cooper Draper Pryce, no one can match Don's visionary approach to pitching advertising copy. In one memorable scene from the season one episode "The Wheel," Don develops a masterfully creative concept for Kodak's new slide-presentation device. He doesn't simply have an idea; he has a vision.

"Nostalgia—it's delicate, but potent," his pitch begins. "Teddy told me that in Greek, nostalgia literally means 'the pain from an old wound.' It's a twinge in your heart far more powerful than memory alone. This device isn't a spaceship, it's a time machine. It goes backwards and forwards . . . it takes us to a place where we ache to go again. It's not called the 'wheel,' it's called the 'carousel.' It lets us travel the way a child travels—around and around, and back home again, to a place where we know we are loved." Don's brilliance as an advertiser lies in his vision and creativity: his ability to think beyond the boundaries set before him and move his ideas to a place of action. With his passion and confident vision, he does more than sell a wheel, he reinvents it as a carousel.

Vision to Revive

The hit TV series *JAG* ran for more than nine seasons and enjoyed a steady audience and impressive ratings. However, if it weren't for the visionary executives at

CBS, the popular military legal drama would have faded forever into the background like so many canceled and forgotten series (and the spin-off *NCIS* franchise might never have been born). *JAG* originally aired on NBC but, due to poor ratings, was canceled before concluding its first season. As can often happen with TV shows, however, the ratings lag was most likely due to an error in scheduling or insufficient promotion and not because the show lacked substance or didn't resonate with audiences. CBS had the foresight and vision to resuscitate the dying show and help make it the success it eventually became.

Marrying Vision and Implementation

In business, we always face the age-old question: "Which is more important: strategy or implementation?" Those on the R&D side of the equation would argue that without developing, planning, and strategizing new ideas, implementation would be impossible. But people who carry out the ideas and implement the plans assert that the doing matters most, since without follow-through, strategy is nothing more than a concept. The truth is that without implementation, strategy ceases to exist, and vice versa. It's not a contest; it's a partnership.

The marriage of strategy and implementation is vital to the success of any business. However, many companies, teams, and leaders fail or lag behind when they put too much emphasis on the merits of strategy to the neglect of implementation. While it's true that technological advancements, new ideas, and cutting-edge innovations drive the industry, having a theoretical breakthrough won't pay the bills. Making the concepts a reality through implementation is what truly brings home the bacon.

Although a bus driver by trade, obnoxious but endearing Ralph Kramden of the classic TV show *The Honeymooners* was a visionary when it came to getting ahead and hitting it big. The problem was, he never succeeded at implementation. Ralphie Boy notoriously fell for and dreamed up numerous get-rich-quick schemes, but he failed miserably in the planning and execution. Remember KramMar's Delicious Mystery Appetizer from the episode "A Dog's Life"? When Ralph stumbles upon a delectable dish that he assumes his wife Alice has prepared, he instantly races off to his boss to give him a taste and proposes a business venture selling the dip. But, par for the course, Ralph doesn't do his due diligence by finding out what he's actually trying to sell, and his dreams are quickly dashed when his "breakthrough product" turns out to be dog food.

In another episode, "Better Living Through TV," Ralph invests a hefty sum into a cheesy kitchen gadget, even after Alice nixes the idea. Ralph the visionary has lofty dreams of buying so many of the "Handy House-wife Helpers" that he monopolizes the market in the area. However, the whole plan is doomed from the start, since there's no real demand for the item. Things only get worse when Ralph and friend Ed Norton book a spot on late-night TV to advertise the product, infomercial-style. The pair of bumbling "businessmen" haphazardly fumble through the spot as all sorts of mishaps occur, including props that don't work, sets fall-ing down, and Ralph getting stage fright. It's one thing to have a vision, but you also have to have the capability and drive to strategize and implement it so that your vision moves to completion.

Clearly, anything you do, whether on a business or personal level, begins with a thought or an idea. That spark of innovation and that mindset to achieve or accomplish something is like starting your engine. WOW leaders have vision and foster vision within the team, but if you do nothing more than idle in park, relishing the idea—thinking about it but never moving—where do you go? Nowhere. You've got to put the idea into gear, hit the gas, and actually drive toward your destination to get anywhere.

Strategy, however, isn't just about setting things in motion. It plays a role throughout the implementation process by insuring adjustments to the plan, troubleshooting when needed, and adjusting the original idea along the way. But none of those advanced levels of strategizing is possible—or necessary—without actually doing what's been developed. Strategy relies on implementation to make it viable and valuable.

While brainstorming new ideas and strategizing new options and directions for your team can be a restorative and morale-boosting exer-cise, it's little more than a game or meaningless fodder for speculation if nothing is implemented as a result. Strategy for the sake of strategy is worthless. If the ideas are cut off at the root and never put into place, or if they are never given the proper attention or necessary resources to make implementation possible, you're just leading your team or company into a brick wall.

How many times have you had an idea but haven't had the drive, motivation, or means to implement that idea? Has a product come onto the market or an invention or business been introduced that you had previously thought of yourself? Did you kick yourself for not following through with the idea when you had it? Did you recognize that while you did not implement your idea, someone else did? If you're only thinking, only planning, and only dreaming, you're not making anything happen . . . so nothing will.

WOW leaders who succeed embrace the partnership between vision and implementation. And they put the right amount of emphasis on each part of the equation. They look to the innovators and idea-generators to kick-start the action but know when to move the cerebral into the realm of doing. They don't celebrate the strategy so much that they can't let go and take it to the next level. Strategy is a catalyst for action, but implementation is the driver of success. WOW leaders are visionaries who take their ideas past the dream and into the reality of achieving it through implementation.

Creativity

WOW leaders facilitate the development and completion of new and established goals by allowing and supporting creativity in the workplace. Albert Einstein said, "Creativity is intelligence having fun." A confident visionary knows that creative influence is often the catalyst for greatness and therefore supports and nurtures it.

Imagine a world without creative influence. Not only would it be a world without art, music, and theater (which would be bleak, indeed)—but it would also be a world without the creativity needed to drive all innovation. Without creative thinkers and dreamers, we'd have no computers, iPads, or smartphones . . . heck, we'd have no electricity, safe drinking water, indoor plumbing, cars, roadways, appliances, or much of anything else. Everything worth having ultimately began with a creative spark.

As a leader, being a creative thinker and encouraging the creative process within your team is vital to your growth on both a business and a personal level. Here are just a few of the benefits of cultivating creativity in yourself and your team:

Creativity encourages movement. Being creative means being progressive and forward moving.

Creativity increases motivation. When the creative juices are flowing, people are inspired by the possibilities. Dreams drive motivation, because they provide new perspectives on exciting, uncharted paths.

Creativity improves performance. People work harder when they are motivated. When the team becomes invested in creative, inspired ideas—especially those they've helped initiate—they are encouraged by the potential for success, and hence, put forth their best efforts.

Creativity provides options and solutions. Being creative opens the door to finding solutions when problems arise. It also helps provide options and alternatives to current paths when roadblocks inevitably occur.

Creativity brings the team together. An atmosphere that encourages and invests in creativity strengthens the trust, communication, and cooperation within the team. When group members have the freedom to be creative, they have the freedom to bring an important part of themselves to the table. By fostering and championing that individuality, each link in the team chain becomes as strong as the next, forming a solid, powerful bond.

Cultivate Creativity

Creativity is an essential tool for all WOW leaders. By embracing the benefits of creative thinking, you're opening the doors to innovation, forward movement, and limitless growth potential. In order to foster and cultivate your team member's creative energy, you need to establish the right environment for their visionary thought processes. Here are some tips on fostering an environment of creativity:

Take the time. Recognize that creativity is a process, not an endgame. Allow time for developing and advancing the ideas within each team member. Carve out specific periods within the daily or weekly schedule to encourage creative growth and innovative thinking.

Communicate. Creativity within a team dynamic is useless if it's not shared. Encourage an open, unhindered, nonrestrictive policy of cooperative communication in which ideas and opinions can be voiced freely. As the leader, be an active listener in addition to consistently vocalizing your thoughts and reactions to creative input.

Reserve judgment. Keeping an open mind and not being reactive or judgmental about new ideas are crucial to maintaining a safe haven for creative breakthroughs. Each member of the team must be supportive and encouraging of each other's creative inspirations and resist the urge to instantly shoot down, poke fun at, or dismiss potential ideas.

Allow mistakes. Mistakes or missteps often give way to success. Only through trial—and sometimes error—can you find your way to the best solution. When the team operates in a controlled, perfection-focused environment where mistakes are met with punishment and reprisals, the creative process is often feared. By learning to accept mistakes as part of the creative learning cycle, you'll be allowing the free flow of ideas without the limitations, restrictions, and fears that often stifle innovation.

Reward creativity. In addition to accepting and moving past unforeseen mistakes, the best way to foster creativity is to reward it. Positive encouragement, praise, and supportive feedback go a long way toward bringing out the best in your team. If those who follow you know you value creative, new approaches, they will continue to deliver winning ideas.

Jumping the Shark

The phrase "jumping the shark" was coined in the 1970s, in reference to the turning point in a TV show when it goes from great to has-been. The terminology was born from the *Happy Days* episode in which the waterskiing Fonzie famously leaps over a shark while vacationing in California. Most critics will agree that while the stunt was meant to prove the leather-jacket-clad mechanic's coolness, it instead marked the end of the show's coolness factor.

Unfortunately, many long-running series, especially comedies, end up jumping the shark, eventually running out of fresh, creative material to keep audiences tuned in. Similarly, many WOW companies run out of steam or lag behind when they fail to move with the times, introduce new innovations, or inject fresh strategies into the mix.

As a WOW leader, motivate and inspire your team members to keep their creativity, ideas, and fresh perspectives at the forefront so you won't end up jumping the shark and succumbing to mediocrity.

Spark Creativity

There are many ways to help ignite the creative energy within your team so the ideas keep flowing. Try the following exercises.

Jump-Starting Creativity

1. Brainstorm. Schedule daily, weekly, or monthly brainstorming sessions—whatever works best for your group. Encourage the free flow of information and idea sharing.

2. Exercise the mind. When brainstorming lags, try a few creative exercises to draw out those light-bulb moments. Playing word association games with key words in rapid-fire succession often triggers ideas and solutions that may have been hovering right beneath the surface. Another game that can help open the mind is placing an ordinary object on the table and directing the group to generate as many uses for it as they can. Items like a simple building brick, a shoe, or an empty water bottle work well, but the options are endless.

3. Scan the headlines. Browse the Internet or go old school and flip through a magazine to spark ideas or new directions.

4. Get out there. Attend conventions, seminars, and trade shows that display and discuss the latest and greatest in your field. By drawing inspiration from what's been done, and even more important, identifying what hasn't been done, the next great idea just might be conceived. In addition, spending time with customers and asking them questions about their needs can help generate solution-based ideas.

5. Change the perspective. Why not move the meeting outdoors, if weather permits? Provide some munchies for a picnic break, or do a group walk-and-talk if your office is in an area where an easy stroll is feasible. Sometimes a change in scenery is all it takes to look at things in a new way and conjure up fresh ideas.

6. Organize a charity event. If budget and time allow, plan a charitable event that not only allows you to do good as a company but also helps you foster a spirit of companionship and camaraderie as a team. Nothing encourages creativity more than having fun, de-stressing, and coming together to help make a difference.

7. Get in the game. If a charity event isn't doable, organize some playtime on a smaller scale: maybe a company softball game, family barbecue, golf outing, or even an interoffice Scrabble tournament. By encouraging time to laugh, play, and socialize with each other, you'll not only be injecting creative energy into the workplace, but you'll also be helping to forge a team bond that strengthens the foundation for a cooperative creative environment.

Choose the Creative Path

Once creativity is embraced, encouraged, and enacted, you and your team will likely be inundated with scores of great ideas. Nothing wrong with that! But now you've got to narrow down your choices and decide on the next logical steps. Some of the ideas will be worth pursuing, some should be forgotten, and others can be shelved and revisited at another time.

In the *30 Rock* episode "The Head and the Hair," boss Jack Donaghy helps "lowly" page Kenneth pitch his TV show idea to NBC. Although supporting his employee's creative vision is commendable, Jack fails to recognize the show's fatal flaw and helps bring an obvious DUD idea to fruition. The show, called *Gold Case*, is a game-show format in which contestants must guess which case (being held by models) contains gold bricks. However, due to the weight of the bricks, it's painfully obvious which model is tasked with lugging the loaded case. Every contestant wins, and the show naturally fails. As Jack learned the hard way, not every creative idea is a winner. Here are a few ways to choose the right creative path and avoid the creative wrong turns:

Oust the obvious. Throw out any propositions that simply can't be accomplished due to serious roadblocks like legal issues, financial impossibilities, or outlandish time constraints.

Cut the controversial. When there's too much controversy and the team just can't agree on the viability of an idea, forget about it! Arguments or dissent among the ranks at the onset of the visionary stage are sure signs it's probably not the plan to pursue.

Stick to the standouts. Narrow the field by selecting the most standout ideas, setting aside the less impressive or less memorable proposals for backup consideration.

Pick your passions. Zero in on the ideas that you and the team are most passionate about. Don't force a connection to a creative inspiration; instead, choose what naturally attracts and inspires you.

Compare and contrast. Write out the pros and cons of each idea, including a side-by-side comparison that focuses on the steps involved with carrying each dream through to reality. Narrow down your choices by keying in to the plans with the most positives.

Think it through. When it comes down to it, success is the ultimate goal. Honestly assess which ideas would be the most feasible to accomplish while at the same time reaping the most rewards. Don't choose the easiest path that may only be a mild improvement, but at the same time, don't go for broke with the most grandiose idea that may be next to impossible to achieve. Think it through carefully to strike the right balance.

Commit to a choice. After weighing all the options, go with the idea that you're most passionate about and that has the greatest chance for success. Once you commit to a choice, make a plan, stick to it, and go the distance with that idea.

Save the seconds. Keep viable creative ideas that were among your secondary choices on the back burner for use at a later time.

Implement Creativity

Creativity is a process that begins with brainstorming and selection. The creative process is essential along every step of the journey to success—beginning with vision, moving into strategy, and continuing through implementation.

The Vision Phase

The visionary stage of any solution, goal, or innovation is where the creative process begins. Brainstorming, imagining, thinking, dreaming, hypothesizing, and turning the wheels of "what if" inside your brain . . . all great eventualities are born in the vision phase. A vision needs to be inspirational but also simple and clearly defined in order for the team to understand it and get behind it. But while creativity is the catalyst to the forward progression of ideas, it is perhaps even more essential as you go beyond vision and begin planning and strategizing how to move those ideas into action.

The Strategy Phase

Once the end goal is envisioned, you'll need to utilize your creative mojo to formulate next steps. Creativity, brainstorming, and idea formulation are just as important in the strategy phase as they are during the visionary process—maybe even more so. Planning how to make the vision a reality takes flexible options, varied solutions, and strategic outlining that only an open and imaginative mind can achieve. Define a clear course of action using creative approaches and well-thought-out scenarios, and then begin implementing the plan.

The Implementation Phase

The creative process isn't done once the meat of the plan is in place and you begin taking steps toward achieving the goal. Getting things done is all about resourcefulness, gumption, assertiveness, and confidence, all of which are supported and fueled by a creative, imaginative mind. In addition, as implementation occurs, there are always unforeseen hiccups, snags, or detours along the road to completion. To navigate successfully through the uncharted waters of your strategic vision, you'll need to creatively make adjustments and alterations where needed.

A vision, mission statement, or goal, once thought up, is only one small part of the creative process. The heart of creativity lies in HOW you achieve the goal. Unfortunately, while an open and creative approach solidifies the chance for success, it does not guarantee that your goal will be met.

While it's essential to growth, creativity is imperfect and can stall for any number of reasons. The key is finding ways to deal with those snags. Consider the following examples.

SNAG	SOLUTION
Corporate Culture: The corporate culture of a busy, cutthroat business often makes for a negative, demanding environment that ultimately chokes out or pushes aside creativity. Frequently, the fast-paced, quota-driven schedules of overworked team members just don't allow time or energy for creative opportunities.	**Coax the Culture**: When stuck in a negative, creativity-squashing atmosphere of corporate pressures and hostilities, inject positivity into the culture and do your best to coax change through your own motivation and drive.
Insecurity: If you don't believe in your ability to bring the vision to fruition, your lack of confidence will inevitably snuff out the creative spark.	**Believe It**: Insecurity can freeze you in your tracks, but believing in yourself and trusting in your vision gives you the power to plow through any bouts of self-doubt. The phrase "If you believe it, you can achieve it" may be overused to the point of seeming trite, but there's value and truth in the statement. Confidence will help you carry your creativity as far as you want to take it.

SNAG	SOLUTION
Outside Attacks: When others shoot down your idea, disagree with your line of thinking, or otherwise attack your creative vision, you may cave under the pressure and scrap your plans.	**Defend It**: When the naysayers or doubters attack your creative vision, don't lie down and let it die. Shield yourself and your ideas from outside harm by sticking to your guns and defending what you set out to do. Consider constructive, helpful suggestions aimed at helping you achieve your goal, but ignore negative comments that criticize without offering solutions.
Overzealousness: Although it's always advisable to find a way to make your dreams and creative ideas a reality, sometimes being too gung-ho shuts the process down before it even begins. If the goal is too wild and far-reaching, you'll have a hard time knowing where to begin and an even more difficult time framing feasible next steps.	**Be Realistic**: There's nothing wrong with going all out when the situation warrants it, but if you set your goals too far out of reach, you'll peter out before you even get started. "Dream goals" that are lofty and large scale are certainly achievable, but you need to approach them with realistic, manageable, smaller steps.
Too Many Ideas: When too many ideas flood the strategy and implementation phases, you'll be pulled in so many directions that you'll eventually burn out and give up entirely.	**Be Selective**: Don't get overwhelmed by addressing too many ideas at once. Be selective about which path to pursue, and then stay the course without wandering in the direction of other creative tangents.
Generalization: If your ideas are too broad and generic, the vision becomes unrealistic, unclear, and unachievable.	**Be Specific**: Concentrate on specific, clearly defined goals and then follow up with a specific, clearly defined strategy.
Finances: Ah, money! Creative ideas are free . . . but making them a reality doesn't always come cheap. Lack of funding can shut down even the best creative ideas.	**Invest in It**: Money is always an issue, but if the creative idea is the right one at the right time, don't let finances hold you back. If the funds aren't readily available, get creative. Seek out investors, take out a loan, liquidate some assets. The point is, if the goal is worth achieving, it's worth investing in.

SNAG	SOLUTION
Motivation: Like New Year's resolutions gone by the wayside, eagerly sought-after creative ideas and solutions sometimes lose steam when the work involved to make them happen becomes a factor. Motivation often wanes when the strategy is outlined and implementation needs to begin. If you aren't willing to put in the effort required to help your creative vision come alive, it will ultimately fall apart.	**Stay Motivated**: This is sometimes easier said than done, but a positive attitude and a drive to succeed is key to keeping the process actively moving forward. Celebrate small victories along the way, inwardly rewarding yourself and outwardly praising the team for implementing key strategic steps.

Creativity can breathe new life into any company, team, or entrepreneur. But corporations don't always support or encourage a culture of creativity, because there is too much "busy work" and status positioning mucking up the works. Too often, the best-intentioned creative visions, strategies, and plans never get off the ground.

Leaders who embrace the benefits of creativity know that great ideas are like springboards to success. But you can't dive into an empty pool and expect to land safely. You need to fill the pool, so to speak, to protect those epiphanies and creative breakthroughs as you move into strategy and implementation.

Allowing, encouraging, and investing in creativity will catapult you to the success you desire. Imagine how many brilliant ideas fall to the floor each day only to be swept away because creativity is stifled or discouraged. Keep your ideas flowing, and as a leader, recognize and support the viability of creativity. WOW leaders don't suppress the free expression of ideas; they support and encourage it to inspire, motivate, and empower themselves and their team.

TV: Creativity Personified

Television, as a medium, is creativity personified. Besides the creative and technological genius behind the process of transmitting and projecting television across the world, the script writers, actors, directors, lighting experts, sound engineers . . . in fact, everyone involved in the production of a television show is drawing on creative influences to get the job done. Without creative vision, we'd never see progress or change in the area of TV programming. We'd still be watching live, single-shot broadcasts in black-and-white.

Creativity is the undeniable backbone of the television industry. But in today's landscape of cutting-edge technology, controversial subject matter, and reality formatting, has everything become so innovative that nothing seems new anymore? Has it all been done before? Are the shows we watch today nothing more than regurgitated versions of the "same old, same old" formulaic approach? While some people may see it that way, even copycat shows require new story lines, new scripts, and new ideas to attract and hold a steady audience.

Eventually, however, even the most successful shows may run their course when creativity wanes and the well of ideas has all but run dry. The best of the best, however, have sustained their ratings success by continuously challenging themselves with new and interesting plot twists, character development, or provocative episode styling.

One of the most acclaimed and popular series of all time, *Seinfeld*, was innovative and groundbreaking in many ways. Self-proclaimed as a "show about nothing," the comedy held our interest with the unlikable, and therefore relatable and weirdly lovable, core cast of four New Yorkers. The show enjoyed steady, high ratings throughout its tenure, continuously attempting to top itself by not only keeping its audience members laughing, but also keeping them guessing.

One of the most unique and creative single episodes in the history of television was "The Betrayal," often referred to as "The Backwards Episode," which utilized the technique of reverse chronology to weave its tale. While some have criticized the season nine episode for its use of gimmicky gags and shtick to make the reverse telling humorous, others have hailed it as creative genius—which, in fact, is the point. Television shows are a matter of taste, but when they're creative and different, their relevancy and importance can't be denied. Reverse chronology certainly had been used as a plot device prior to "The Betrayal," but *Seinfeld*'s brand of storytelling had not been done before.

Use your creative strength to tell your own story in your own way . . . to deliver the WOW message that you and you alone have to tell.

Be a Goal-Getter

Visionary leaders have goals and aspirations and, even more important, set a course to achieve them. Goals are carefully thought-out mission statements with a clear and achievable process to back them up. Goal setting is the best way to build a road map to future personal and business achievements. Once the goals are established, however, it's imperative to stay on course toward reaching those goals.

Setting Personal Goals

Writing a goal sheet is one of the simplest and most effective ways to determine, outline, and ultimately achieve your goals. But don't confuse a goal sheet with a bucket list. The trendy term "bucket list" is an overused phrase with a morbid twist that has been kicked around long enough. The Oxford Dictionary defines bucket list as "a number of experiences or achievements that a person hopes to have or accomplish during their lifetime"—in other words, things to do before you die. Rather than thinking in terms of kicking the bucket, look toward a more positive, living future when setting your goals. Take the time to write down your aspirations, both short- and long-term, with approximate or even exact dates attached to each goal.

Too often, with an open-ended bucket-list philosophy, the lofty set of objectives is continuously put off for later, because, after all, we have our whole lives to get there! But as Gandhi said, "The problem is, you think you have time." None of us knows when our number will be up, and most of us like to think in terms of a long, old-age scenario for our final days. So, we wrongly believe we have plenty of time to complete the generic bucket list.

With a goal sheet, however, we list what we aspire to do and when we hope to achieve it, building on that momentum and moving toward the next goal. It's not an endgame list, it's a game-play list. Identifying your goals and then cementing them in writing is like putting a key into a lock and readying it to open your dreams.

When drafting your goal sheet, remember that realistic goals are the key to future success. If your goal is to be a millionaire by the age of thirty, great! But there must also be an achievable set of steps to get you there. Winning the lottery is not a goal; it's a wish. Goals are much more powerful than wishes, because you have the tools to make them happen. Goals work when you work to achieve them, while wishes are completely up to chance.

Whether making business goals, financial goals, or personal goals, don't leave your dreams to chance. Kick over the bucket list, draft a goal sheet, and turn your vision into an achievable reality.

Drafting Your Goal Sheet

1. Define the goal. Decide what you want to accomplish or work toward.

2. List the steps. Write out how to get what you want. Make a step-by-step plan, complete with what you need to do and what you must NOT do in order to stay on task.

3. Think ahead. Consider where bumps in the road may occur, and think about alternate plans or ways to work around setbacks.

4. Set a timeline. Give yourself an achievable, realistic completion date and set a timeframe for hitting minitargets along the way.

5. Celebrate victories. Don't fall apart or give up completely when you veer slightly off track. Reward your successes as you go, noting that each small step achieved is moving you that much closer to the ultimate success.

Here's how to keep going:

6. Keep your eyes on the prize. Post your goal sheet in a place of honor, where it will be seen on a daily basis and therefore cannot be overlooked.

7. Stay organized. Keep your work space clean and clear; don't let things pile up that will become a distraction or overwhelm your aspirations.

8. Check your attitude. Stay upbeat and focused on positive achievements.

9. Open up. Talk to your colleagues, team members, and family about how they might help you in meeting your goals.

10. Take action. Do at least one thing daily to move closer to your goal.

11. Keep moving. Don't give up if you mess up. Keep moving forward, making improvements, and learning from your missteps along the way.

12. Take ownership. Stop pointing fingers or making excuses for why you haven't met certain goals or why you've made mistakes in the past.

13. Update as needed. Every now and then, conduct an internal review to assess if any of your goals have changed.

14. Find a mentor. The best way to be your best is to learn from the best. Align with a respected and trusted adviser.

15. Educate yourself. Stay aware of new developments in your industry, school yourself in the latest technologies, stock your library with inspirational books. By learning and absorbing more, you'll be more likely to find new and creative ways to meet your goals.

16. Enjoy the journey. The process of working toward your goals should be challenging but also enjoyable and self-motivating. Getting what you want shouldn't be an unwanted chore; it should be an exciting and rewarding journey.

In the season three opener of *Ugly Betty*, "The Manhattan Project," Betty has returned from a month of travel and is ready to begin working toward a new life plan. With a positive attitude and an "idea binder" filled with creative possibilities, she jumps headlong into fulfilling her three-pronged list of goals. On her list are: 1.) Take on more responsibility at work to get a promotion; 2.) No more romantic entanglements; and 3.) Get an apartment in Manhattan (she lives in Queens with her family). Unfortunately, while Betty's on the right track, her goal sheet is a bit underdeveloped. While she knows what she wants, there's no "how" to the list—no steps to complete the dreams. As often happens in sitcom situations, mayhem ensues as she sets out to haphazardly reach her goals. While things don't go exactly as planned, Betty is a goal-getter. Even if she doesn't get things right the first time around, she learns along the way and keeps building her skills.

If you want to be a WOW, you too need to be a goal-getter. Every day is a new chance to take positive steps toward becoming a better version of the great leader already within you. By writing a goal sheet and staying focused on working toward your aspirations, you're taking control of your future success.

Setting Goals for Others

In addition to your own goals, you must also set goals for your team of followers and help them stay on target to meet those directives. The same methodology of goal-sheet writing applies to carving out goals for others. You still need to define the goal, draft the steps, consider alternatives, establish a realistic timeline, and celebrate victories along the way. But as the overseer of the process, you'll also need to be the motivating force that ensures everyone in the group is doing his or her part.

When you set goals, you are putting vision into action. In TV terms, you need to fine-tune your vision so that from simple black-and-white, it moves to color, advances to Technicolor, and eventually expands to provide the clarity of 3D-HDTV.

On the show *Undercover Boss*, real-world, high-ranking business executives voluntarily and secretly immerse themselves into the actual workforce of their company. As "regular" employees, the leaders in disguise hope to gain insight into the inner workings of the business, thereby enhancing their vision and sharpening their ability to make informed, logical decisions.

An unfocused, unclear, or ill-defined vision, or one that is lackluster, dull, or without dimension, will create an uninspired reaction from your team and will prevent the goal from being attained. To move toward that coveted 3D-HDTV vision, here's how to create a vibrant, focused, multidimensional picture of your leadership goals.

Developing Your Leadership Goals

1. **Write it.** Nothing helps bring a fuzzy, incomplete, or underdeveloped picture into focus better than writing it out. By putting your vision into words, you'll be better able to gauge where any holes or inconsistencies exist. In addition, crafting your vision into a plan will give it life and substance that will take it from black-and-white to color.

2. **Share it.** Verbalize your vision with your team. If your ideas remain locked in your head or stay only on the paper you wrote them on, your vision ends there. To move forward, you must share it, explain it, and build on it with the help and involvement of your team. Once the group is on board and can reiterate and even expand on your ideas, you have moved your vision from color to Technicolor.

3. **Repeat it.** Don't let your vision die or fade into the background. Keep

repeating and reinforcing the goal so your team and others involved will stay on track. Repeating your ideas over and over—until you think you sound like a broken record—is essential to keeping the vision alive. To keep the momentum going, use words that excite and reenergize the team. Through the constant repetition and reinforcement that breathes new life into your plans, your Technicolor vision enters the realm of High Definition.

4. Do it. Making the vision tactile may be the hardest step of all. In some cases, the goal is intangible and cannot be quantified easily in a concrete way. However, making the vision a reality, getting out there and doing it, is bringing the vision full circle.

To successfully make your vision or goals tactile, you need to help your team move to the doing stage. Using the following techniques, you'll be able to facilitate the achievement of 3D, crystal-clear, HDTV results:

Assign roles. Once a goal has been established, carefully marry the correct team member with the correct task. As a WOW leader, you should be well aware of the strengths and weaknesses of your staff members. Be sure to assign specific aspects of the goal to the individuals with the right skill sets to make it happen.

Define expectations. Obviously, the expectation is that the goals will be achieved. But you'll need to establish definitive boundaries, intermediate deadlines, and parameters to support the progression of the mission.

Outline setback procedures. Set expectations high, but be careful not to rule based on fear. Create an atmosphere of cooperation and mutual respect by outlining procedures in advance for the inevitable setback or error. The team needs to feel comfortable bringing problems, and not just successes, to your attention. If they don't, the missteps can become huge stumbles that lead to the goal's demise.

Communicate. In addition to being open and available to answer questions and help with problems along the way, be a diligent and clear communicator in all aspects of the goal plan. Check and double-check that each member of the team is aware of the end-result goals and knows what his or her exact role is in achieving them. Don't assume you're being clear . . . clarify it even more.

Hold meetings. As a supplement to one-on-one communication, hold regular group meetings to discuss goal-oriented progress in an open forum. This not only keeps everyone in the loop about any new developments or setbacks but also ensures accountability.

Be involved. You're the one who dictated the goal, but that doesn't mean you should rule like a dictator. Rather than issuing demands and expecting them to be carried out while you hide out in your office, take an active part in the follow-through of the plan. Be visible and involved every step of the way.

Make changes. Keep a close eye on the advancement of your goal strategy, and be ready to make changes and adjustments if needed. Flexibility is key; if you're too rigid to allow for maneuverability, you may never attain the desired end result.

Offer incentives. Make achieving the common goal a challenge worth pursuing by issuing performance-based rewards. Get creative! Depending on what's at your disposal, you could offer gift certificates for massages, monetary bonuses, theater or sporting event tickets, or vacation days as tangible pats on the back.

Motivating a group or team to meet company-issued goals can be a difficult undertaking, but with a WOW leader's positive attitude, communication skills, drive to succeed, and forward-thinking decision making, you'll be up to the challenge. When your vision is clearly outlined, shared, and repeatedly reinforced, you and your team are more likely to move the experience to the tactile level, where you ultimately bring the vision to life and achieve your goals.

Reality Goal-Getters

Reality TV is deeply entrenched as the new medium on TV. One of the most popular formats for the genre is the reality competition series, in which "real-world" noncelebrities compete to win prizes, attain fame, and be named the "best" among their peers. What we tend to love about these shows is their relatability and human factor—even if the settings and situations for the programs are far from realistic. It's the "ordinary" person's journey that captivates us and keeps us watching.

With the reality competition show, we are witness to the goal-setting and goal-getting process of regular people. We relish each step along the way, whether they succeed or fail in their ultimate quest. Shows like *Project Runway, Top Chef, Survivor, The Voice, American Idol, America's Got Talent, So You Think You Can Dance?, Top Model, Biggest Loser,* and others all have one thing in common: Each contestant has set a personal goal, and they are working, in front of the camera, to achieve that dream.

Even though we're not fashion designers or vocal prodigies, we can relate to the desire to become the best at what we're passionate about—leadership. While most of us aren't going to compete on national TV to achieve our goals, we can take a cue from the hopefuls on these shows and embark on our own personal journey to become the best version of ourselves.

Past, Present, and Future Vision

The past, present, and future are like friends living on different continents; they are forever linked, but they can never actually touch. We recognize and appreciate the importance of each, but we understand that these moments in time must each stand alone and occupy a unique spot in our lives.

Great leaders must be solidly grounded in the present but also need to understand the past and have a vision for the future. They must be able to merge the layers into a big-picture scenario of success.

The Past

The past is a teacher, providing a real-world example of what worked, what didn't work, and how it was done. History is more powerful than theory, because there are tangible results to study. We can understand and pinpoint the variables and factors that affected certain outcomes. Ignoring or forgetting about what came before is like disregarding education. The more leaders understand the past, the better they will be able to perform in the present, and the more equipped they will be to project future endeavors.

The Present

The present is like a treadmill, constantly moving at a rapid pace. You must keep up or else fall off entirely. But unlike the treadmill, which takes you nowhere, today is the foundation of tomorrow, and the present is ever evolving into the future. Effective leaders are able to keep pace on the treadmill as it spins while understanding that it is a means to an end. They must be headed in a tangible direction. They are grounded in the present but always moving forward.

The Future

The future cannot be left to chance; it must be imagined and created. Leaders must visualize what is to come and use the present as a springboard to catapult them to that place. Being grounded in the present but stuck on the treadmill due to indecision, fear, and myopia denies the progression of a successful future. WOW leaders can imagine the future of their career and their life, so they set a plan in motion to get there.

Setting and writing down goals for long- and short-term plans is one of the best ways to enhance your vision for the future. The goal-drafting process is as effective as drawing the blueprints for a home or structure that will soon be built. When put to paper by an architect, what is imagined becomes real.

The next time you're meandering around a museum, flipping through an old photo album, or watching a documentary, reflect on the past and take a moment to learn from your own history. Use every moment that exists so fleetingly in the present to study, grow, and make plans for the future. Take care to avoid the complacency that stifles so many leaders in a loop of repetitive treadmill walking. Don't make the future a carbon copy of today with just a bit more dust and a few new wrinkles. While the old adage is true that "Tomorrow never comes," don't let that trick you into believing the future is always far away—because in reality, each tomorrow becomes today, and then it vanishes into yesterday. Make your moments count; make your future a history to remember.

To be a WOW leader, you must be a goal-driven visionary. While you have to have vision and encourage creative thoughts and ideas, those inspirations must be backed up by solidly formulated goals. Visionaries are just dreamers unless they attach strategy and, more important, implementation, to their epiphanies. As a WOW leader, you need to enact the vision and lead others to do the same. After all, it's doing, not dreaming, that yields WOW results.

Chapter 6

WOW Leaders Are Effective Communicators

"How can you galvanize, inspire or guide others if you don't communicate in a clear, credible, authentic way?"
—*Susan Tardanico*, Forbes, *November 2012*

Without communication, everything else that follows breaks down. However, it's important to remember that communication is a two-way street. This sounds logical and reasonable, but many people in authoritative roles tend to forget about the oncoming traffic; their communication goes only one way—from them to their subordinates. Naturally, a collision of sorts is inevitable in this scenario. Those trying to get their ideas across to a single-minded, closed-off leader will ultimately veer off the road, creating a standstill in the forward momentum of the team.

One of the all-time greatest fictional TV leaders is Captain Jean-Luc Picard from the long-running sci-fi series *Star Trek: The Next Generation*. By rank, Picard is the highest authority on the U.S.S. *Enterprise*, the futuristic spacecraft that serves as the primary setting for the series. But it's not his title that makes him stand out as an accomplished leader. Picard possesses and displays all the fundamental components of WOW leadership—most notably, he's an effective communicator.

Picard is the consummate professional, operating with integrity and military formality when in command of his ship. But he doesn't dole out orders blindly or with the arrogance of a dictator or DUD. He respects and regularly consults with his crew. Picard doesn't just issue commands or shout out orders, he gathers the facts, asks for the input of his team, formulates a plan, and explains his reasoning. As a highly intellectual, skillful diplomat, he draws upon reason, justness, practicality, and humanity to make decisions and get his message across.

Unlike the Picards of the world, who are effective and approachable communicators, DUD leaders are poor communicators who are perpetually inaccessible and unapproachable. While they may have certain expectations of or make demands on their team, these inefficient leaders do not adequately explain or outline their strategies. They don't make themselves available for interfacing or feedback. They communicate only to condemn, and they are visible and present only when there is an opportunity to gain something for themselves. When stuff is hitting the fan, you can bet the DUD leaders are nowhere to be found. But if accolades are being dished out and backs are being patted, you know those DUDs will be first in line for the rewards.

Communication is certainly not the strong point of Monty Burns, the quintessential DUD boss on the animated comedy *The Simpsons*. The reclusive billionaire oversees the work at his nuclear power plant via closed-circuit TV and can't be bothered with remembering the names of his employees. He leads like an evil tyrant with absolutely no concern for the safety, well-being, or success of anyone but himself. In the episode "American History X-Cellent," Mr. Burns announces the company's new annual Fourth of July picnic, to resounding cheers. "I'm afraid you misunderstand," he explains to his workers. "The picnic is for me. You will all be spending your Independence Day slaving away in the hot summer sun with no pay, lotion, or gratitude."

Listen Up

Leaders who drive along the road of success with their team, enabling them to express their ideas, voice their concerns, and even question procedures or practices, will not only benefit from a cooperative work environment but will also gain the respect of their followers, keeping everyone focused and on track.

It's important to understand that being open to communication doesn't mean agreeing with every idea voiced. Instead, it's about allowing each voice to be heard. It means having an open door and an open mind to accept fresh perspectives and innovative thinking. If you trust your team members and empower them to speak up when inspiration strikes, you will reinforce your position as a smart, forward-thinking leader. But if you shut down every idea that is not your own, you will shut down the productivity and respect of your team, which is completely contrary to the success of a WOW leader.

Speak Up

Listening isn't the only mark of a WOW leader. Clear, transparent verbal communication is vital. Great leaders take the time to invest in one-on-one interfacing or phone contact with their team, making sure that all messages and instructions are received and understood as intended. Too many times, communication breaks down because leaders do not clearly convey their needs.

WOW leaders should trust their team with all the information at their disposal so that everyone is equally informed about the "why" behind decisions. Voicing concerns, explaining expectations, sharing news, and even admitting mistakes is imperative to gain respect and keep the lines of communication flowing.

Equally, or maybe more important, is giving praise and accolades when a job is done well or when a goal has been met. Leaders who only communicate with their team members to condemn them or point out faults will quickly create an atmosphere of isolation and resentment. Those who also remember to lift their team up will keep the attitude positive and the successes will continue to soar.

The Message and the Method

Communication is the backbone of any good relationship, whether personal or business. WOW leaders impart information clearly, accurately, and decisively while simultaneously being receptive and responsive to incoming questions, comments, and feedback. Great leaders know that effective communication is always bidirectional; however, maintaining an effective flow depends on the method used to get the message across.

Keeping in touch is easy these days; almost all people carry a cell phone and have Internet access, making them reachable 24/7. But with email, Twitter, Facebook, texting, and even Skyping, does that mean we're communicating better as a result? Not necessarily. Being heard is not just a matter of putting our words out there; it's also about using the right communication tools to ensure the most meaningful exchange.

When to Text

Traditional texting, with its often-abbreviated informality, may at first seem inappropriate for business, but it's actually quite useful in certain situations. The trick is not relying too heavily on this shorthand method. Group texting can also be beneficial when you have two or more parties involved with the same project or issue. But be careful not to revisit the group texting string at a later time and include someone you hadn't intended to communicate with.

Group texting is what gets Mitchell and Phil into trouble with their significant others in the *Modern Family* episode "Diamond in the Rough." Claire and Cameron want to invest in a home and flip it for profit, but Mitchell and Phil aren't convinced they are up to the challenge. Neither wants to be the bad guy, so Mitchell and Phil each blame the other and pretend to be supportive themselves. Eventually, they end up hashing it out via texts, with both men demanding the other come clean and set things straight. What they don't realize, of course, is that they've been texting on a group string, and Claire and Cameron have been in on the digital conversation all along. Oops.

Here's when texting is handy, helpful, and apropos:

- **When an immediate yes or no response is required:** "Did you finish the report?"
- **To clarify or facilitate logistics:** "Meeting in 10" or "Call you in 5."

- **For simple reminders:** "I'm out of the office till 3."
- **To reach out or touch base:** "Great talking with you today."

When to Email

Emailing is an invaluable business tool for a variety of reasons. It's more formal than a text, more controlled than a phone call, and enables you to reach a wider audience with clarity and ease. Plus, receipts can even be requested so you'll know if and when your message was received. Email is best in the following situations:

- **When attaching documents:** Forms, contracts, forwarded emails, links, and more are easily distributed. Be sure to mark sensitive documents as confidential and clarify with a DO NOT FORWARD indication.

- **For multiple recipients:** Conveying information to several people at once via email makes the task easier, but it also ensures that everyone is getting the same message.

- **As a follow-up to a follow-up:** After you've touched base verbally, it's nice to follow up with a simple email to express your dedication or reiterate key points if necessary.

- **For CYA situations:** When it's important to cover your ass, put it in writing. An email is clear, traceable proof that you transmitted the proper information. If you've ever watched *Judge Mathis*, *The People's Court*, or the like, you know that proof in writing, including emails, can make or break a litigant's case.

When to Call

There are times when the somewhat impersonal-feeling modes of digital communication are simply not effective. In certain situations, it is best to skip the text, stop typing that email, and just pick up the phone for an old-school conversation. If you're tech-savvy, Skyping is the modern-day phone call that takes it even one step further.

Here's when to punch in those digits and make an actual call:

- **When forming a new relationship:** In business, building trust requires personal attention and the real-time exchange of words and ideas.

- **When the message is complex:** If there are multiple variables, steps, or points involved that could be easily confused or open to interpretation, you'll need the feedback of a phone call rather than an open-ended text or email.

- **When understanding is critical:** Anything of a high-risk nature needs to be personally communicated. When the outcome of that understanding is critical, take the extra step and make the call.

- **When it's not public knowledge:** Although emails can be marked confidential, there's no guarantee they will remain private. In matters of sensitive internal communications that are not meant for public ears, keep the conversation away from the forwarding-friendly world of texting and emailing.

When to Meet

With so many communication options, face-to-face, one-on-one interfacing often takes a backseat in the world of business. But there are certain instances when across-the-desk meetings are not only beneficial but also absolutely vital.

Schedule a meeting in the following situations:

- **For pivotal conversations:** When jobs are on the line, key information is in question, detailed explanations are required, or some kind of turning point has been reached, you need to communicate visually as well as verbally. Body language, reactions, and tone can be as telling as words.

- **To brainstorm:** It's hard to brainstorm over the phone and difficult for some people to do via text or email. Bring people together when you need to generate ideas and formulate solutions as a team.

- **When giving reviews:** Feedback should be given regularly and frequently and can be done via text, email, or phone calls. But formal reviews need to be conducted in person to ensure clarity and out of respect for the employee.
- **When the topic is touchy:** Sensitive issues need to be hashed out face-to-face in order to clarify all points and achieve the most total level of understanding.

When to Tweet

While social media offers loads of opportunity for marketing (either yourself or your company's products), it has little value in terms of effective business communication. However, for inspirational and motivational messaging, avenues like blogging, Facebooking, or Tweeting can be a fun, informal secondary form of communication. Never use these formats to transmit important, vital information that must be heard.

The bottom line is that open, effective communication is the hallmark of a WOW leader. To get it right, be sure you match the message with the appropriate method.

The Heidi Game

In 1968, the methods of communication available to the general public did not include texting, tweeting, or emailing. If you needed to get to in touch, you met, made a phone call, or sent a letter or memo. Had cell phones been invented, the debacle that became known as the NFL "*Heidi* Game" would probably not have occurred.

On November 17, 1968, NBC televised an intense matchup between the Oakland Raiders and the New York Jets. The eventful football game, which included an inordinate number of penalties and timeouts, ran longer than its allotted three hours of airtime. The network's schedule had the highly anticipated, made-for-TV movie *Heidi* slotted for 7:00 p.m. Eastern time, but more than a minute of playing time remained in the live-action game. With the home team Raiders down 32–29 following a 26-yard Jets field goal, the network cut to commercial and never returned to the game. Instead, they began airing *Heidi*. Enraged fans never got to see what happened next: a thrilling turnaround that included two Oakland touchdowns within nine seconds, resulting in a 43–32 Raiders victory.

History tells us that a failure in communication was the driving factor behind the fateful *Heidi* Game decision. When it became obvious that the game would run long, a choice had to be made. NBC executives had previously discussed such a scenario and had reportedly decided to follow regularly scheduled programming in the event a game ran overtime. However, with the intensity and fervor of the current contest, execs reportedly had a change of heart. An elaborate game of phone tag reportedly ensued, with one executive calling the other and attempting to get approvals and pass on messages—but the phone lines were clogged by frantic viewers trying to reach the station. With the switchboard jammed, the last-minute Hail Mary didn't get through to broadcast operations in time, and the studio had no choice but to follow protocol and run *Heidi* as planned.

The *Heidi* Game incident, brought about by a missing link in the chain of communication, led to a major change in the way professional football games are aired on TV. The NFL put it in writing, generating new contracts that required networks to run games to completion. NBC also made changes, including installation of a "Heidi phone" with its own switchboard and exchange to expedite and facilitate more direct communication in times of critical decision making. (Remember the red Batphone that Commissioner Gordon used as his direct line to the Caped Crusader in the 1966–1968 *Batman* series?)

Clear, direct, and timely communication is paramount to the successful operation of any business, team, or partnership. WOW leaders speak clearly, listen effectively, and match the right form of communication to each unique situation—ensuring that they're never faced with their own *Heidi* Game.

Attitude Is Everything

Just as important as getting your message across is the tone and attitude with which you deliver it. The nature of leadership in business is guiding your team toward goals that yield improvements, innovations, and most of all, results. But it takes finesse, patience, trial and error, and encouragement to guide and motivate a group to succeed. And while WOWs have the ability to keep the positive energy flowing, all too often, leaders resort to negative reinforcement.

Unfortunately, negativity is a commonplace, knee-jerk reaction to stressful, seemingly dire situations. When leaders impose their own frustrations and worries onto their team, the team, in turn, becomes frustrated and worried, creating an environment ill suited for success.

Phrases and comments that point toward failure are not likely to result in positive outcomes. Leaders who bombard their team with negative rants aren't inspiring greatness. Words like, "I don't see how we can possibly make our deadline," or "This is the worst group I've ever worked with," or "If things don't improve around here, heads will roll" will only elicit resentment, hostility, and doubt. Negativity begets more negativity, which then begets poor performance and, ultimately, failure.

If you're working in an atmosphere of negative hostility, you're probably not operating at your peak efficiency. More than likely, you're questioning your abilities and second-guessing your every move. The rest of your team or those within your office are likewise experiencing this same debilitating level of fear, resentment, or doubt.

On the goofball medical comedy *Scrubs*, many of the laughs are provided by DUD boss Dr. Perry Cox. But what might be funny in a sitcom's nonrealistic work environment would be disastrous and detrimental in an actual workplace. Not only does Dr. Cox repeatedly call his (male) underling Dr. John Dorian (J. D.) by random girl names, he's negative, demeaning, and downright nasty about 95 percent of the time to everyone on the staff.

In the episode "My Clean Break," Dr. Cox reams out an entire group of residents, saying, "I am accountable for the continuous, crashing, undeniable amateurism that you people drag into this hospital, day in and day out. And believe you me when I tell you that the next time one of you perpetual disappointments doesn't even have the common decency to try and do better at something you supposedly do, I will go ahead and toss your sorry ass outta here in about ten seconds, and then I will forget you forever in the next five."

In the episode "My Lucky Day," Dr. Cox cuts J. D. down even when he has made a correct medical diagnosis. "You know, Eunice, you never even woulda made that catch if you weren't such an all-purpose nerd, sitting home alone on a Saturday night, watching some medical special on TV!" While Dr. Cox's antics and persona are an over-the-top fictionalization, real-world DUDs can be just as harsh, negative, and off-putting in their own way, breeding an atmosphere of paranoia, angst, and self-doubt.

The best way to overcome negativity is through positive reactions. But that's easier said than done. Often, a negative-think environment grows over time and becomes stronger as more and more negativity is added to the mix. Sometimes the problem goes unnoticed or is overlooked or underestimated until it has grown to huge, unmanageable proportions. The negativity beast cannot be easily tamed once it is let loose to terrorize a team.

Some managers may argue that threatening and belittling their employees scares them into submission, forcing them to rise to the challenge, or else. But while short-term results may be gained, negativity will ultimately grow, stacking burden after burden on top of itself until the weight becomes too much to bear. Eventually, it all comes crashing down.

TV is chock full of negative characters, some who serve as foils to the central "good guy" and others who lead the series with their often-exaggerated DUD behavior. Archie Bunker, the patriarch of *All in the Family*, is an example of the latter. The notorious bigot and all-around crude, rude, and self-centered Archie is a classic TV DUD; he's flawed to the point of perfection. He's the guy everyone loves to hate, which works well for its entertainment value, but wouldn't be quite as funny if you had to deal with him in the workplace as a real-life boss. He's negative and berating to the point of being completely inappropriate, especially when it comes to his wife, Edith, or to anyone with an ethnicity differing from his own. Archie rarely cracks a smile or offers a compliment. In fact, he'll go out of his way to demean or insult someone.

Another DUD character, who serves as the comic rival of SpongeBob SquarePants, is the egotistical and narcissistic Squidward. The animated

Krusty Krab cashier and neighbor to the lovable SpongeBob is nothing if not negative. When it comes to interacting with others, Squidward is rude, condescending, and outright mean. Thankfully, Bikini Bottom's lovable fry cook, SpongeBob, is positive to a fault and is therefore rarely affected by his coworker's deplorable demeanor.

Like leadership DUDs, these and other negative TV characters are often disrespectful, hostile bullies who care more about themselves than those around them. If at all possible, steer clear of the Archie Bunkers, Squidwards, and DUD bosses of the world, and if you find yourself the victim of their negativity, hold your head up high and never stoop to their level of behavior.

Combating Negativity

As a leader, you must recognize the disastrous effect of negativity and the importance of fostering a positive work environment through encouragement, praise, and inspirational leadership. And although it may take discipline and practice to resist the temptation to demean, discourage, or threaten, the rewards will be not only a happy, productive team, but also a better bottom line.

Unfortunately, the antithesis of positivity in the workplace brings us back to the show *Scrubs*. Dr. Bob Kelso, chief of staff at Sacred Heart Hospital, thrives on watching his staff squirm. He delights in embarrassing them and calling them out with criticisms and put-downs. In fact, he actually strives to create a hostile, uncomfortable workplace where the staff is miserable and crestfallen. "Supportive" and "uplifting" are not in his vocabulary.

In "My Common Enemy," Dr. Kelso and his equally abrasive counterpart Dr. Perry Cox discuss their tactics for trying to destroy a cheery coworker's morale. Dr. Cox says, "When I crush a person's spirit, I like to use a combination of intimidation and degradation." Dr. Kelso rebuts, "I prefer to create an environment in which the subjects end up crushing themselves!"

While the fictionalized Sacred Heart Hospital leaders prefer a dejected staff they can control through fear and negativity, WOWs favor an environment teeming with positive reinforcement and encouragement. Unfortunately, even when the intentions are good, it's not always easy to remain upbeat and keep aggravations in check. One reason is that because WOWs often have a driven, goal-oriented nature, they tend to put a lot of pressure on themselves to do better, achieve more, and work harder. All this stress, however, can lead to a hostile, negative office atmosphere if emotions aren't kept in check.

WOWs can employ these techniques to help combat negativity in the workplace:

Identify the source. When the mood is bad in the office, you may not even realize you're operating in a negative environment. Too often, we just get used to the daily grind and aren't really aware there's a problem to fix. Once you zero in on the primary source of the negativity, you'll be able to face it head-on and ultimately defeat it. Is it one bad apple spoiling the bushel, or is it a particular set of circumstances that sets off a chain reaction of doom and gloom? Pay close attention to your team's behaviors, then try to step in and steer things in a positive direction when things start to sour. Also, try not to take negativity personally; keep your cool and don't get frustrated.

Check yourself. As the leader, if you're complaining, whining, joining in on gossip, making snap judgments, or commiserating with your team, you're part of the problem! If you want to work in a positive environment, you can't be negative yourself. Even WOW leaders have bad days, but it's imperative that you shield your staff from any fallout, or you might end up having to deal with the snowball effects of spiraling negativity.

Confront with caution. Don't sweep negativity under the rug—it doesn't go away, it just hides and festers. When you witness negative behaviors, communicate your concerns. But proceed with caution. The last thing you want to do is create more conflict in an already tense situation. Try to redirect the issue toward yourself. Say something like, "I wish I knew how to deal with all this negativity. How do you think we can make things more upbeat around here?" Whatever you do, don't accuse, lay blame, or point fingers. Exercise the compassion and understanding that you already possess as a WOW leader to address the negativity with a gentle touch.

Be the change. Gandhi said, "Be the change you wish to see in the world." The same holds true in an office environment. Focus on positive thinking, no matter what the situation. Encourage, uplift, praise, and suggest ideas that promote favorable outcomes. The power of your own upbeat attitude may even be contagious. Seek out the silver lining in every situation, focusing on achievements rather than mistakes. Try celebrating small successes and brushing off minor setbacks.

Find out why. There's often a legitimate reason for the negativity within a team. Sometimes it goes beyond the cliché complaints like "Too much work, not enough pay" or "Someone's not pulling their weight." Ask questions and voice concerns to get to the root of the problem. There could be a simple solution that, once addressed, will quickly change attitudes in the right direction.

Channel the negative energy. Not all negativity is bad. It just needs to be focused in the right direction. Channel your team's negativity to work together against a common outside "enemy," for example, the competition. Use it to work toward positive goals like breaking a sales record or winning an industry award. When an extreme defeatist mood exists, turn it around by emphasizing the underdog philosophy: When there's nothing to lose, there's everything to gain.

Align with a mentor. Look for role models who have successfully proven themselves in the workplace. Find out their strategies for dealing with negativity, brainstorm solutions, and model your behaviors after their positive approaches. Turning to a trusted mentor when you need guidance, advice, and feedback will help you navigate through negative waters. In addition, associating with a positive influence will keep you grounded in the positive. Just as negativity begets more negative thinking, being guided and surrounded by positivity begets more positivity.

Don't be a pushover. Just because you're trying not to be negative doesn't mean you can never say no or that you should overlook mistakes. Keep your expectations high and consistent, with any missteps discussed in a positive, strategy-based manner. Praise and compliment when warranted, but don't be a doormat for lackluster performance, shoddy results, or negative behaviors.

Pick your battles. Unless you're the owner or CEO of the company, there's only so much you can do. Focus on initiating changes, but don't

stir the pot if it's a huge, commercial kettle and you only have a tea-
spoon. Your own positivism can have a major effect on the attitudes
within a tight team environment but may have little strength against
larger corporate issues. Pick your battles, focusing most on your little
corner of the work world.

Leslie Knope, the central character of the TV show *Parks and
Recreation*, personifies positivity in a negative workplace. As the fictional deputy parks director of the parks and recreation department
in Pawnee, Indiana, Knope is friendly, motivated, driven, and perpetually looking on the bright side. Even when faced with negativity from
coworkers, her boss, or town residents, Leslie has the tendency to put
a positive spin on the situation. She never gives up or wavers from her
devotion to serving the government honestly and to the best of her ability. Although not always successful in her endeavors, she's the picture of
good intentions, ethical strength, and authentic positivity.

Similarly, Liz Lemon, Tina Fey's character on *30 Rock*, stays positive on the job despite having to deal with DUD boss Jack Donaghy as
well as the antics and stresses of her staff and coworkers. Even when
her personal life seems to be unraveling or taking a negative turn, she
continues to put on a happy face around those she leads.

The Nocebo Effect: Negative Suggestions

Unfortunately, you may be fostering negativity without even knowing
it. *Nocebo*, Latin for "I harm," is related to the familiar term placebo,
but it has the opposite effect.

In medical situations, if you give group A members an aspirin for
their headaches and give group B a "fake" aspirin—a placebo—many
in the placebo group are "cured" simply because they are told they've
been given the remedy. With a placebo, the power of suggestion has
been proven to have a healing effect.

With a nocebo, the converse can also be true. In the October 13,
2009, *Time* magazine article "The Flip Side of Placebos: The Nocebo
Effect," John Cloud reported on the nocebo response, stating, "When
doctors tell patients that a medical procedure will be extremely painful,

for example, they tend to experience significantly more pain than patients who weren't similarly warned."

The negative feedback focused on at the doctor's office or hospital does not have to be direct or outright negativity. It can be as simple as the use of the word "may" in reference to outcomes or side effects. When it is suggested that use of a certain medication or following a particular protocol "may cause you to XYZ," that suggestion can be imprinted in the subconscious, in effect causing XYZ to occur.

Although a nocebo is theoretically innocuous and should have no effect, it does. It causes harm by eliciting a negative reaction. While numerous studies have been conducted on nocebos in the medical arena, there isn't much extensive research on their impact outside of health care. But it's clear that the nocebo effect extends well beyond the boundaries of medicine.

Imagine a coach's pep talk to his players. Will they stand a chance of winning the game if he tells them, "You may lose," "You might not score again," or "This game may not be winnable." He's already planted doubt in their minds. They will focus on defeat and will probably lose.

Even for adults, the 1977 film *The Many Adventures of Winnie the Pooh* often holds a special place in the heart. Who could forget Pooh, Piglet, Tigger, and the lovable little pessimist Eeyore? In the business world, poor Eeyore would have had no chance of instilling motivation or driving a culture of enthusiasm. The lackluster, ho-hum donkey is sweet but never looks on the bright side. Even to a simple "good morning" greeting, he responds with negativity: "If it is a good morning, which I doubt." And he is forever setting himself up for failure, especially when it comes to losing his tail. "No matter. Most likely lose it again anyway."

This little purplish pessimist of children's TV programming is akin to those who lead without a confident, self-assured voice of authority. A negative tone or attitude, warnings or ultimatums, or even suggestions of doubt such as "We may never meet our quota" or "This may be impossible" can all but ensure failure within a corporation or team. It's a combination of the nocebo effect and the psychological pattern of the self-fulfilling prophecy.

The nocebo effect in the workplace, especially when repeated over time, creates an atmosphere of negativity within the group that is hard to repair. The results of negative reinforcement on business teams, even with the more subtle negativity of nocebo commentary, include:

- Drops in performance levels
- Decreased desire to improve productivity
- Increased visualizations of negative results
- Surges in health-related problems
- Overall increases in defeatist attitude and feelings of despair
- Patterns of negativity, begetting more negativity
- Eventual failures or repeated outcomes of limited success

As a leader, you set the tone in the workplace. Are you creating an atmosphere ripe for success, where cooperation, encouragement, and guidance are given through positive reinforcement? Or are you sabotaging your team by pointing out every flaw, stressing the difficulty of each task, and hinting at the possibility of failure? If so, you may be too negative, contributing to the ineffectiveness of your own strategies through the nocebo effect.

I'm not going to say that regularly keeping things upbeat in the office is a challenging undertaking. I'm not going to tell you that it might sometimes be hard to keep yourself focused on the positive. And I wouldn't dream of suggesting that many leaders find it difficult to praise their subordinates. Because if I did, you'd be focused on the negative. You'd be doubting your ability to lead in a positive manner.

What I will stress is the importance of attitude to your own leadership strength as well as to the success of your team. Only through a winning attitude will you win. Only through a sustained and direct approach to positivity can you foster a positive outcome. As a WOW leader, if you tell them they can, they usually will. But if you tell them you think they can't, they certainly won't!

Keeping positive in a negative environment can be challenging. But if you inject a positive attitude into everything you do, positive things will come your way, and you'll most likely improve the collective mood of those around you as a result. When you and your staff are happier, less stressed, and more approachable, you're better equipped as a team to focus on, meet, and even exceed your goals.

In the 2013 remake of *Ironside*, the wheelchair-bound detective Robert Ironside continues police work after an on-the-job shooting renders him paraplegic. However, the tough, determined Ironside focuses on his abilities rather than his disabilities. In the pilot episode, the physically challenged cop finds a murder weapon that other officers overlooked. Using his "unique perspective" from the wheelchair to his advantage, Ironside turns a seemingly negative situation into a positive, proving that attitude, not circumstance, is what matters most.

Positive Reinforcement

You've heard it before: If you don't have anything nice to say, don't say anything at all. However, doing so is usually easier said than done. Many people, whether in business or personal relationships, feel a certain vulnerability when it comes to openly praising and commending others but can be quick to issue a reprimand or react in anger or frustration with a negative rant.

Those with tendencies towards knee-jerk criticisms may feel a temporary release through "venting," but once the harsh words are spoken, the damage is done. Overt public criticism is humiliating for the recipients and will put them on the defensive. They'll feel demoralized, exposed, and attacked rather than guided and corrected. Even controlled, calm, and seemingly constructive negative critiques can be destructive, especially when issued in a public setting.

Keep your criticisms, negative comments, or reprimands in check until they can be dealt with privately in a one-on-one setting. In that way, you'll be productively addressing a problem, suggesting a change, or pointing out a mistake without simultaneously disrespecting or damaging a relationship that should be built on trust and cooperation.

One of the most offensive, inappropriate reality shows to hit the small screen revolves around a hypercritical DUD who berates and belittles the people she leads. And the worst part is, all the yelling, ranting, and public humiliation is aimed at children. In *Dance Moms*, studio owner Abby Lee Miller expects perfection from the young dancers in her charge and uses negativity, hostility, and fear to elicit better performance. She'll call out girls in front of their peers, criticize their bodies and looks, and publicly humiliate them by ranking them from best to worst. Rather than complimenting and encouraging her young students to improve, she regularly threatens and condemns. In fact, one of her favorite reprimands is "Everyone's replaceable."

The moms themselves are no better: They are driven to outdo each other vicariously through their kids. Not only do they choose to subject their daughters to the negativity of Ms. Miller, they actually pay her to do it! The catty, backstabbing moms push their kids into an unhealthy level of competition using verbally abusive tactics, taking all the fun and joy out of dancing. A show like this perpetuates what's fundamentally wrong with the DUD's approach to communication. DUDs bully and berate rather than discuss and praise. Thankfully, "everyone's replaceable," and eventually, DUDs usually get their due.

WOW leaders know that it's best to criticize privately and reward publicly. When it comes to complimenting a job well done, a private pat-on-the-back is nice, but a public acknowledgment has the added effect of boosting morale, instilling pride, injecting positivity, and encouraging continued exceptional performance.

On the flip side, WOW leaders NEVER:

- Post staff criticisms online
- Discuss personnel negatively around the water cooler
- Call out individuals in a group setting
- Jump quickly to hostile reactions
- Point fingers or assign blame within the team
- Display a negative, defeatist attitude

Instead, WOW leaders ALWAYS:

- Reinforce positive behaviors and actions publicly

- Consistently acknowledge team and individual successes
- Take time to think, evaluate, and plan their reactions to mistakes
- Conduct constructive, private evaluations to address issues and concerns
- Act with respect, understanding, and integrity
- Admit their own missteps and demonstrate an acceptance of imperfections

Leaders don't have the luxury of following the age-old advice of "saying nothing" when they can't say anything positive. Part of being in charge means evaluating performance and steering those you lead in the right direction, and that means you have to discuss when things aren't working. It's how you go about it that makes all the difference. By criticizing privately and praising publicly, you'll bring out the best in your team and demonstrate your ability to be an effective communicator and to lead like a WOW.

Platform Skills

Presentation skills, public speaking, executive presence, or platform skills: No matter what you call it, a WOW leader needs to be good in front of people. In order to inspire others to rise up and go the extra mile, the clarity, passion, and sincerity of your words must be properly communicated. If you deliver a lackluster, insincere, or rambling message to your team or audience, what they'll hear will be little more than what Charlie Brown and his friends hear when the grownups speak: "Wah, wah, wah."

If you're trying to instill motivation, deliver a call to action, or drive home a point, you *must* keep your platform skills sharp by preparing in advance. You can't wing it, phone it in, or put the responsibility on the listeners to decode a cryptic, disorganized message. In addition, you can't behave like a DUD and rely on your title or reputation to do the speaking for you. People aren't going to be impressed by your name or your position—they will only respond to what you say and what you do. WOWs aren't handed respect; they earn it and work hard to keep it.

To develop and maintain exemplary platform communication skills, you must work at it. You must resolve to WOW by identifying what may be tripping you up at the podium or in the boardroom.

Here are some questions to ask yourself:

- Are you shy, nervous, or afraid to speak in front of others?

- Is your presentation disorganized or lacking in focus?

- Is your vocal delivery flat, hesitant, or unclear?

- Do you have any nervous habits or idiosyncrasies that may be distracting or annoying?

- Are you disengaged or uninterested in who the audience members are and what they need to hear?

- Are you being truthful and humble, or just trying to build yourself up with some hidden agenda?

- Have you adequately prepared what you need to communicate?

WOW in Action

Sharpen Your Platform Skills

To overcome some of the obstacles to WOW platform skills, try some of these techniques:

1. Prepare. Make a checklist before a meeting, presentation, or speaking engagement. What is your objective? What is your point? What are the key messages you want people to walk away with? Also keep in mind factors like the setting, how much time you have, and audience expectations. Write out a rough draft or agenda that includes your main points and several examples. Also allow time for questions, if appropriate, to reinforce that your message was clearly conveyed. The point is to do your homework before you begin speaking.

2. Read your audience. You'll need to adjust your tone, pace, style, and even the message depending on the venue and the audience. If you're speaking to an intimate group of close, familiar coworkers, you can be more informal and direct, but if you're presenting to a large, mixed group of colleagues, you may need to be more formal and careful with your words. If you're giving the same speech to several different audiences, ask yourself how they are different, and then adjust as needed. Will a more logical or emotional approach resonate with a particular group? How much entertainment is expected with the presentation? What is the audience's level of sophistication or understanding of the topic? Is it a friendly or unfriendly environment? Make sure you adjust your platform skills based on the perspective of the audience.

3. *Rehearse.* Go over what you're going to say before you say it. Get in front of a mirror or enlist your trusted advisers or inner circle to listen to a run-through. Better yet, make a "selfie" video of your presentation, then play it back to see how you did. Practice doesn't necessarily make perfect, but it will help you stay organized, tighten up any weak spots, and in general, strengthen your confidence and overall performance.

4. *Seek feedback.* It's not always easy to recognize your own strengths and weaknesses. To get the best picture of your true platform skills, seek feedback from someone who will tell you the truth and provide you with honest input. Enlist a platform skill coach or someone you admire as a speaker and WOW professional. Chances are, people at the top of their game in terms of executive presence did not start out at the top; they had to work at it and build up to it. By seeking feedback, you may learn some "tricks of the trade" or discover some mechanisms used by those who have already solidified their platform skills.

To be a WOW leader, you must have an acceptable level of platform skills. Your job is to inspire, motivate, and communicate effectively in order to lead effectively. Those to whom you present your ideas, directives, and visions are the same people you depend on to step up and push through barriers and challenges. To get the results you seek, you must deliver a WOW message in a WOW way. Investing in improving your presentation skills is investing in yourself, your people, and the common goals and successes you all endeavor to achieve.

———∿∿———

Effective communication is not always a given—it's a skill set that can be learned, enhanced, and shared with those you lead. Transparent, fair, and reciprocal communication is vital to the success of any team. As the WOW leader, set the example by being a positive, clear communicator who encourages the same from others.

Chapter 7

WOW Leaders Are Invested in Others

*"You can get everything in life you want if you will just
help enough other people get what they want."*
—Zig Ziglar

WOW leaders aren't simply out for number one. Instead, they become number one because they're out for the greater good of those they lead. Furthermore, great leaders don't just invest their time and energy in developing the top-tier talent; they lead and inspire each employee on the team.

As a whole, people are driven to grow and develop, especially within the scope of their career pursuits. But many people do not have the skills, tools, or means to progress on their own. They simply don't know how to grow, even though they desire it. WOW leaders capitalize on the strengths of every team member by investing in the development of all employees, regardless of their title or position.

One of my favorite TV WOW leaders, *NCIS*'s Leroy Jethro Gibbs, has a knack for bringing out the best in his team. As the boss, he doesn't soak up the glory of team wins; he deflects any praise directed at him back onto his people. In fact, his track record has earned him countless awards over the years, but instead of basking in the limelight, he ducks it, typically asking another team member to accept the prize on his behalf. Gibbs demonstrates a true team spirit, focusing on investing in the growth of his entire team, from agents to forensic scientists. For this masterful WOW, the goal isn't one-upmanship; it's lifting others up.

Obviously, the boss will have the most interaction with higher-positioned people in the company. Naturally, more time will be spent developing the talents of those at the top. But WOW leaders don't forget about those coming up in the ranks. Every employee has growth potential, and that growth should be encouraged and harnessed through great leadership and guidance. Exceptional leaders do not just expect their team to succeed; they lay the groundwork for success by drawing out the potential within others.

Furthermore, WOW leaders do not just lead those who are already following closely at their heels; they devote their energies and impart their wisdom to people at all performance levels. Since a pyramid is only as strong as its base, WOWs aim to build up and strengthen the resolve and dedication of the people at the lowest tier. They also realize that those at the bottom have the potential to move up the pyramid and become the next top-tier performers. Everyone gets equal respect, because everyone matters in the overall success of the team.

All About Us

When you think about climbing up the corporate ladder, you might picture eager business types starting from entry-level team members at the bottom rung and moving to high-level executives perched in the crow's nest at the top. The journey up this metaphorical ladder is a solo trip: the individual pursuit of a better position, a better paycheck, and a better way of life.

Sounds like the American dream, right? So what's wrong with that?

Nothing . . . as long as you remember to look down, up, and beside you as you scramble up your own part of the ladder. If you pursue the top with the tunnel vision of a "me and only me" leader, you'll soon have nobody holding your ladder in place beneath you.

Unfortunately, the all-about-me attitude is an all too common interpretation of the capitalistic mentality. The thinking is that if you focus on taking care of number one, everything should, in theory, work out just fine. This kind of egotism results in believing that everything will fall into a survival-of-the-fittest type of alignment, with the alpha males/females overpowering the weaker performers.

But all-about-me leadership is an oxymoron. After all, leading is not a solo proposition. By definition, it's about guiding others. DUDs who think only about themselves and not what's best for their company or their people are destined to bring about failure. An all-about-me attitude is bad for business. It's a win/lose equation where the business suffers because the DUD focuses primarily on personal gain.

All-about-me leaders:

- **Are not respected:** How can you respect selfish leaders who put themselves first in every situation?
- **Make bad decisions:** DUD leaders make choices that ensure they come out ahead. Their goal is to win at all costs—which means everyone else loses.
- **Cultivate a negative culture:** Leaders who are all about me have very little capacity for caring about others or helping others achieve their goals. Therefore, they drive a culture with a mentality to "survive," not "thrive."

Who could forget the iconic Aaron Spelling show *Fantasy Island*, with its memorable host, Mr. Roarke, and his enthusiastic assistant, Tattoo? The cool, collected, and mysterious Mr. Roarke made a living helping others—the hopeful and sometimes desperate guests who visited the island. As the fantasy facilitator, Mr. Roarke operated as a behind-the-scenes, hands-off enigma. His methods were never quite clear, but his ambiguous powers were often characterized as otherworldly or godlike. Although the exclusivity of the Fantasy Island experience implied it was an expensive endeavor for guests, the enigmatic proprietor's motivation never appeared to be driven by financial gain. His purpose, it seemed, was not to indulge selfish wishes, but rather to teach the vacationers a valuable life lesson or help them change their often-misguided mindsets. While viewers never quite knew the real Mr.

Roarke, we knew that once Tattoo started ringing that bell, shouting, "The plane! The plane!" it wouldn't be all about Mr. Roarke, it would be all about the guests.

Like the white-suited WOW on Fantasy Island, real-life WOW leaders are devoted to helping others succeed. They make decisions based on what's best for the business, not just for them. A winning attitude comes from implementing leadership strategies to elicit the best outcomes from everyone and for everyone. It's not all about me . . . it's all about us.

Ensemble Casts

A great TV show can't depend solely on its stars to make or break it. The lesser characters are just as important, and sometimes even more important, to the show's success. WOW shows excel in part because the team is stronger than any one player. It's the strength of the ensemble cast that pulls everything together and keeps it clicking with fans. The runaway-hit HBO fantasy series *Game of Thrones* features one of the largest ensemble casts ever, with more than thirty main characters and an expansive list of regular or recurring guests that goes well into the hundreds. With a complex story line interwoven between several warring families, no single character's story stands alone. It's a true group effort that "takes a village" to succeed.

So many great shows featured the best ensemble casts of all time: *Friends*, *Seinfeld*, *Lost*, and *Cheers* to name a few. Would *Cheers* have been a hit without Norm, Cliff, Carla, Woody, or Frasier? Maybe. But it probably wouldn't have survived if it had only been about Sam and Diane and a revolving door of anonymous bar patrons. Like a company, a TV show has power and depth because all of its players interact well together and comprise the whole. WOW leaders—or star cast members—are only as strong as the ensemble supporting them.

Share the WOW

Everyone knows the saying "In order to have friends, you must first be one." Like friendship, leadership is a skill that has to be reciprocated to be fully appreciated. By its nature, leadership is a shared endeavor, with guidance, decisions, and strategies being passed down from the leader to the followers. But WOW leadership needs to go beyond that dynamic to include mentoring, where the skills and life lessons of experienced leaders can be imparted to the next generation of WOWs. The reciprocal value of mentoring is one of its greatest attributes. Mentoring is not only an endeavor to help the up-and-coming leader; it's also a teaching and learning tool for the mentors.

Busy leaders, especially those in positions of power who are tasked with wide-reaching responsibilities, may feel they have no time in their schedule to be a mentor. They may also question the relevance of mentoring, wondering, "What's in it for me?" Although that may not be a WOW attitude, it's a realistic one. In the business world, the day-to-day realities often trump the idealistic larger picture. But people who are quick to brush aside the opportunity to mentor are missing a huge opportunity to grow, improve, and become better leaders.

The political drama *The West Wing* fictionalized the inner working of the U.S. presidency. Among its top players was C. J. Cregg, the trusted, stalwart female press secretary who eventually rose to the position of White House chief of staff. Working beneath her was Carol Fitzpatrick, who served as assistant to the press secretary. In the episode "Access," Carol tells a documentary crew, "She's the best boss. I really look at C. J. as my mentor. They say that a mentor's a wise and trusted guide or friend. I would say that C. J. is all of those things." Under C. J.'s leadership, Carol was loyal and hardworking, always seeking to improve her performance and maintain the respect of her boss.

Mentoring provides numerous tangible and intangible benefits, including:

Self-reflection. Guiding others presents a tremendous organic opportunity to reflect on your own leadership strengths, weaknesses, and current or future goals. In addition, it's a way to hold yourself accountable for your actions.

Connectivity. Via mentoring, you'll be able to stay better connected to up-and-coming generations. For example, a baby boomer's perspective on world issues, broad-based business topics, and life in general is vastly different from a generation Xer's or a millennial's viewpoint. Keeping current will help you rein in the "Back in the day, we didn't have smartphones, laptops, or iPods" comments. Younger generations frankly don't care! If you aspire to large-scale leadership, you will be leading many different generations, so you need to understand their perspectives.

Symbiotic learning. Besides gaining new insights into the psyche of future generations, mentoring provides opportunities for symbiotic learning. Who better to learn new technology-based skills like Twitter and other social media from than the "digital natives" who live and breathe it? What may seem daunting and unfamiliar to those in the baby boomer generation is second nature to the members of the younger crowd who enjoy sharing their wisdom and providing pointers about their tech savvy.

Leadership renaissance. Once we become ingrained in a task, a position, or a way of life, we can end up operating on a kind of autopilot, having supposedly perfected our techniques and adapted to the demands of the day-to-day. Mentoring can provide a reawakening or rebirth that ignites and excites the fresh and idealistic attitudes we had when we were just starting out.

The benefits of mentorship are endless and will depend on how much you put into the process. The bottom line, however, is that you will learn as much from your protégés as they will learn from you. Mentoring can be invigorating, inspirational, and uplifting. It will help keep you grounded as a leader and fulfilled as a person, knowing you're part of a cycle of cooperation and kinship that embodies the spirit of WOW.

Successful Mentorship

Making the decision to become a mentor is a bold, positive step toward leadership training and reciprocal learning. Mentorship is a vital tool in the world of business. It's a win-win situation for any organization, strengthening the skills of its leaders while simultaneously improving the team dynamic and ultimately eliciting better performance results.

Mentors make a profound impression and guide us to become better at what we do and more in touch with who we are. Such is the case in the TV series *Boy Meets World*, where no one exemplified the mentoring role better than principal and teacher George Feeny. The inspirational Mr. Feeny went beyond the typical role of teacher to become a lifelong mentor to several of his students, including Cory Matthews, Cory's best friend, Shawn Hunter, and Cory's main love interest, the enigmatic Topanga Lawrence. Mr. Feeny was a constant, ever-present voice of reason as the kids grew from naive, challenging middle schoolers into floundering, teenage college students.

Although Mr. Feeny was in an authoritative role, his mentoring style was informal, familiar, and personal. He didn't dictate and demand; he encouraged, helped, and guided the younger generation as they faced typical coming-of-age trials and tribulations. Over the course of seven seasons, the TV mentor was a trusted, reliable confidant who helped keep Cory, Shawn, and Topanga on track for success later in life.

Here's how to succeed as a valued mentor and, like Mr. Feeny, help make a difference to those up-and-comers:

Take the "me" out of mentor. Determine why you want to be a mentor. What are your goals and expectations for the relationship? While you will benefit from a mentoring role, those personal bonuses must be secondary to your role as teacher and guide. If you have selfish aspirations, walk away.

Be passionate. Attitude is everything in leadership. If you portray a lackluster, indifferent attitude toward your mentoring role, that's exactly what you're teaching. Be passionate about demonstrating, sharing, and expressing your WOW leadership abilities.

Devote the time. Go all in and stay in. Mentoring is a partnership that requires investing a certain amount of time to keep the commitment viable. Once you make the connection, you need to consistently be present, available, and willing to give of yourself and your time.

Preach practicality. While one of the primary roles of a mentor is to guide and inspire the protégé, it's not always about injecting idealistic, over-the-top, reach-for-the-stars advice or guidance. Instead, it's about helping those up-and-coming leaders navigate the business world successfully by teaching them what they need to do and how to go about doing it. Preach practicality as a way to achieve the WOW dreams.

Be objective. Remember that being a mentor isn't the same as being a motivational speaker. It doesn't mean preparing a speech that you deliver and that your "student" draws lessons from. Mentoring is a communication partnership. Be an objective listener and base your opinions and advice on current facts as well as past experiences. Don't always focus on what you would do; steer your mentees in the direction of their own decisions, teaching them to take ownership of what they choose and to accept the success or consequences of their actions.

Teach transparently. A successful mentor is willing to be an open book about past experiences, including missed opportunities, poor decisions, or outright failures. To teach transparently, you have to possess a level of self-awareness and humility that enables you to be vulnerable at times. Students do not always learn the most from examples of perfection, rather they may gain significant insight and motivation from an admission and honest portrayal of overcoming obstacles, setbacks, and doubts to move continuously in the WOW direction.

By dedicating yourself to mentorship, you'll be setting a WOW example and helping to empower the next wave of WOW leaders.

Melodic Mentors

The runaway hit show *The Voice* took the *American Idol* singing competition format to a whole new level. Not only do the show's four celebrity judges initially select contestants from a blind audition process where they can only hear, not see, the hopefuls, but they eventually become their coaches and mentors. Once the talent pool is narrowed into teams, the celebrity musicians take the start-ups under their wing, offering advice, strategies, singing tips, support, and encouragement. The show is as much about the singers' learning and growth experiences as it is about their actual ability to croon. Even those who don't ultimately triumph clearly benefit from the attention and mentorship of the more-experienced entertainers. As a result of the one-on-one, personal relationships forged between the show's stars and the stars-in-the-making, the "judging" tends to focus on positive encouragement and constructive criticism. *The Voice* may derive its name from its initial impersonal selection process, but it's the relationships, bonding, and teaching between the singers and their mentors that truly make it a winning format.

Helping Others Find Balance

If you're wholeheartedly invested in others, you need to help your team members set and maintain their life/work balance combination. WOW companies and WOW leaders understand the value of their talent pool and care about keeping those assets happy. They want to help their employees successfully manage their life/work combination, recognizing that this fosters enhanced productivity, a more positive attitude, and an appreciation that translates into company loyalty.

Alternatively, companies that ignore the needs of their staff to create a balance between work and personal life are often inflexible, demanding, and uncaring. They drive a wedge between the company and the employee, which breeds hostility, decreased work performance, and stress. Eventually, the top talent leaves for greener pastures.

The popular series *Roseanne* followed the lives of blue-collar working-class family the Conners. Roseanne Conner may have been brash, direct, and inappropriate at times, but she did her best to make ends meet and balance her dual roles as mom and working woman. In the 1990 episode "Chicken Hearts," Roseanne invites her young, silver-spoon-raised boss to dinner at the Conner home in an effort to help him understand the need for a life/work balance.

"I wanted you to see how important my family is and how important it is we're together, cuz weekends are the only time we have together," Roseanne explained to the arrogant manager. He seems to get it at first, saying, "I understand that you need to be with your family and you can't work weekends. That's what you're saying, right?" But when Roseanne agrees that although she wants to be a team player, her family matters too, he won't compromise. "Well, there it is," he concludes. "You can pick up your last check on Monday. You're fired."

Since it's in the best interest of the employee as well as the company to achieve a comfortable life/work balance, here are some ways businesses and leaders can help make it happen:

Harness human resources. When it comes to satisfying the needs of the workforce, WOW leaders and companies should enlist the help of the HR department. HR often has innovative ideas and solutions that help the business be more productive and successful while simultaneously addressing the needs of its employees. Many studies have proven that a happy workforce is a more productive workforce.

Create job share opportunities. To provide the flexibility workers crave, WOW companies should listen to their workforce and create opportunities like job shares. If your company doesn't have a job share program, why not start one?

Adjust PTO. The paid time off (PTO) policies of WOW companies are creative, flexible, and provide the worker with a variety of options. Many companies allow for purchase and buyback of PTO time. This puts more control of the life/work combination in the hands of the employee.

Provide life services. WOW leaders and companies don't just focus on the work part of the life/work combination; they help their workers create balance on the home front as well. Forward-thinking businesses provide child-care services for working parents and even offer solutions for those with elder-care responsibilities. Additional on-site amenities are sometimes offered at large, progressive corporations, including health clubs, eateries, and even laundry, spa, and medical services, all aimed at helping the workforce balance work and life more productively.

When you think about the pinnacle of excellent life/work balance incentives, Google stands out among the crowd. Google and many of its tech-based counterparts (think Netflix, Facebook, and the like) are companies born from a new generation of thinkers and achievers. They don't operate with a regimented, traditional corporate culture—in fact, it's just the opposite. Google reportedly provides its employees with free meals and snacks, offers four on-site gyms, has laundry services available, employs an on-site doctor, and even allows workers to bring their dogs to the office. All that in addition to numerous perks for new parents and an overall attitude of fun, empowerment, and positivity.

WOW companies like Google are mindful and supportive of their workers' life/work combination and as a result can recruit and retain the highest top-tier talent. Sure, it might be unrealistic for your company or you to offer Google-caliber incentives, but try thinking outside the box when it comes to your business . . . think of your employees' lives outside of your business!

Psychological Paycheck

WOW leaders who are invested in their employees make regular deposits toward "psychological paychecks." Workers crave acceptance on the job and look to their leaders for more than just a weekly payout. They also need positive reinforcement, encouragement, respect, and empowerment in the workplace.

In many ways, a psychological paycheck is even more meaningful than the actual salary earned, because it demonstrates an employer's faith in the worker's abilities and potential. The psychological paycheck bolsters people in the work they're doing on a daily basis, giving them meaning, purpose, and motivation to improve and grow, even when raises and monetary incentives are lacking or nonexistent.

With the economy still struggling, many employers have their hands tied when it comes to upping salaries; the money simply isn't available to give. So, without a quantifiable wage increase to boost their wallets and their morale, employees begin to lack the motivation and desire to perform their best. Sometimes they begin to look elsewhere; other times they stay but "check out" in terms of productivity and loyalty to the employer. When money is not reinforcing an employee's value, the psychological paycheck must pick up the slack.

Even people who are financially content or have been given a recent income boost still need the reassurance of a solid, meaningful psychological paycheck. Money itself is not always enough to bring out a person's best, because the positivity of a pay raise only lasts so long. More dollars are always welcome—though hands-off and impersonal—but pay can't stand alone as the sole motivator for doing a good job. When you're in the thick of the work trying to make things happen and wondering if you're on the right track, pulling out your paycheck and counting the zeroes isn't going to provide any answers, encouragement, or feedback. You need to be rewarded not just financially, but psychologically through consistent, repetitive, and real-time interaction and responsiveness.

Here's how leaders can invest in their employee's psychological paycheck:

Listen. Be an active listener; pay attention to what your people are saying. Really hearing and responding to what is being said illustrates your commitment to a reciprocal, communicative relationship.

Show empathy. Put yourself in your employees' place and be empathetic about their issues, problems, and concerns. Verbalizing that you care, understand, and want to help demonstrates that you value them as part of the team.

Be honest/authentic. Lead by example with honesty and integrity, showing your authentic self at all times. People need to feel they are working for someone who's morally sound, trustworthy, and truthful. By being a leader worth following, you're making deposits into the psychological paychecks of your workers.

Praise publicly. When a job is done well, don't pass up the opportunity to praise in public. Call out great performance, extra effort, or exceeded quotas at staff meetings or in widely circulated emails or texts. In addition to boosting the individual employee's psychological paycheck, it will boost morale company-wide and provide an incentive for others to perform well.

Reinforce regularly. Small, regular gestures of positive reinforcement, such as "Good job," "Keep it up," or "Nicely done," take very little effort but reap huge rewards in terms of the psychological paycheck. From the employee's perspective, being acknowledged and encouraged while in the midst of a task gives that extra push to keep moving forward and improving. An email, text, or personal note of thanks after the fact reinforces team members' efforts and demonstrates that you're willing to go out of your way to recognize their contributions.

Encourage growth. Provide opportunities for growth by entrusting competent employees with new tasks and greater responsibilities. Encouraging growth and skill-set expansion instills a sense of pride and accomplishment that strengthens the psychological paycheck.

Employees need to feel connected to their jobs and valued for what they do in order to excel and be inspired to improve. They need to be led by those who are willing to provide intangible rewards as appreciation for hard work, dedication, and workplace achievements. A great boss will not only invest in the team financially but will also invest in its growth, self-confidence, and skill building by consistently funding members' psychological paychecks.

One boss who never had his employees' best interest at heart was the greasy Louie DePalma, overseer of the cabbies on *Taxi*. With the exception of Alex Rieger (Judd Hirsch), most of the drivers had dreams and career ambitions outside of the Sunshine Cab Company. But Louie constantly put down their efforts, bullied and harassed them, and made their jobs as miserable as he possibly could. In the episode "Bobby's Big Break," aspiring actor Bobby Wheeler lands a part on a soap opera, quits his day job, and tears up his cab driver's license. Louie is enraged and unsupportive, saying, "He'll be back . . . they all come back! The only one who never came back was James Caan . . . and I'm still waitin'!" Later, when Bobby loses the acting gig and wants to return, Louie runs around chanting, "Bobby's a loser . . . a loser . . . a loser."

What the fictional DUD dispatcher lacks, besides the basics of integrity, respect, and strength of character, is the ability to foster motivation and self-confidence in his employees. Don't be a Louie; invest in your team's psychological paycheck and help bring out their WOW potential.

Re-recruit Talent

A WOW leader consistently and continually invests in the progress, development, and happiness of the team, especially its top performers. But once the courtship stage is over, why is it necessary to re-recruit your talent? Like a marriage or other committed relationship, you can't take one another for granted once the partnership is in place. Reaffirming your dedication to and concern for your significant other—in life and in business—is vital for maintaining a healthy, happy, and prosperous relationship.

It has been said that people don't leave companies, they leave leaders.

People who are dissatisfied with the level, style, actions, or inactions of leadership will begin to look elsewhere, especially when they have the talents, skill sets, and impressive résumé to easily find other positions. When top talent is recruited, the wooing phase is often laden not only with lucrative offers and promises for future development but also with a great deal of ego stroking, positive reinforcement, and dedication to the prospective employee. However, once hiring is complete, the reality and stresses of the day-to-day tend to overshadow the glory of the initial offering.

While most WOW individuals understand and accept that the recruitment phase can't be sustained past their hire date, they do expect to continue to be valued, invested in, and nurtured in some respect. If their psychological paycheck isn't tended to, they can and often will be wooed away and recruited elsewhere.

Here are some key ways to re-recruit your top talent:

Show support. Catch them in the act of performing well and praise them for it. Use positive reinforcement regularly so they know the work they're doing is acknowledged and valued. Continue to show your support by consistently acknowledging their outstanding achievements.

Keep in touch. Sounds too simple, but keeping in touch with your top talent through meaningful, reciprocal communication is often overlooked. Express your dedication to the relationship by staying engaged and in tune with their needs, concerns, questions, ideas, and contributions. Be an active listener who not only hears what is being said but also responds to it by taking action, getting involved, and making adjustments where needed.

Develop their talent. Back up your initial commitment to your best workers by helping them grow and expand their talents. Give them increasingly meaningful, challenging, and important tasks that keep them motivated and help them feel fulfilled rather than static. Show you trust them, believe in them, and are committed to investing in them and their future achievements.

Be authentic. Don't offer more than you can give or misrepresent your intentions. Be truthful about your expectations and honest about your limitations. Be careful not to offer the world and then yank out the rug from underneath them. Stay authentic, up front, and realistic about the parameters and potential of the relationship, and then continuously maintain that same level of honesty.

Leaders are only as good as their people. So, be good to your people! Be sure you consistently and regularly re-recruit your best workers. If you don't invest in them, someone else probably will.

Investing in TV Talent

In the world of TV, investing in top talent is often a necessity to keep a hit show on the air. Of course, when contracts are being negotiated in the world of TV, it's about dollars and cents, not about pats on the back or psychological boosts. Once ratings begin to soar, the actors and actresses pivotal to the series often start demanding pay raises. And in most cases, the fattened checks are cut.

Two of the most famous salary negotiations in history involved the casts of *Friends* and *Seinfeld*, who negotiated as teams to earn their colossal paychecks. Recently, the top three stars of The Big Bang Theory tripled their already substantial salaries to $1 million per episode each. Johnny Galecki, Jim Parsons, and Kaley Cuoco also upped their ownership stake in the series, negotiating their way into lifetime earnings that could figure close to $100 million for each actor. With the network poised to profit in the billion-dollar region, choosing to meet the cash demands of the show's top performers seems well worth the investment.

However, it's not always money alone that keeps stars content on the set. Sometimes investing in top TV talent means bending to any number of odd, unpredictable, or even unreasonable requests. For example, Shelley Long, who played the persnickety Diane on *Cheers*, was said to be a bit of a diva herself. Ms. Long reportedly once demanded that a flooded parking lot used to mimic the Boston River be drained and refilled with warmer water. Since she wouldn't proceed if the water was too cold, production was delayed and the scene was reset.

In the world of business outside of TV, those kinds of employee demands would be unheard of. However, WOW leaders who believe in their top talent will do what it takes to invest in their growth, happiness, and security on the job.

Be Giving, Not Greedy

WOW leaders do more than pad their own résumés and further their own careers; they inspire, encourage, and give back to others. Giving back to those who need assistance, guidance, or support helps keep you grounded, humble, and positive, and it's simply the right thing to do. There are so many ways to open your heart, lend a hand, and extend goodwill—you just have to be willing to give back.

In an age where we're constantly bombarded with bad news and financial challenges, tensions and stress levels often run high. Average Americans feel as if they're perpetually taking one step forward and two steps back. For many people, it's difficult enough making ends meet at home without feeling that they have to do more. With everyone so distracted by his or her own struggles, who has the time, energy, or means to give back to anyone else? The simple fact is, we all have the means to give back. WOW leaders are giving, not greedy.

Giving back can certainly be a large-scale, grand effort like setting up a foundation, organizing a fundraiser, or donating substantial funds to support worthy causes. But it doesn't have to be that extensive to be impactful and effective. There are countless small but meaningful ways to give back. Small, $5 donations add up when enough people chip in; an hour of time volunteering at a local food pantry or shelter touches the lives of many needy families.

You probably equate the show *Baywatch* with bikini-clad lifeguards running in slow motion up and down the beach. And yes, that's much of what it was. But like the pages of that infamous men's magazine that also "has great articles," there was often more to *Baywatch* than just the red-suited eye candy. Several episodes featured one or more of the lifeguards participating in charitable events.

In "Money, Honey," Shauni embarks on a campaign to raise money for an animal rescue group. In "The Child Inside," the gang hosts the Special Olympics. Mitch and Hobie take in a lost boy during Christmas in the episode "Silent Night, Baywatch Night."

In yet another episode focused on giving back, "Desperate Encounter," the lifeguards team up with country star Jesse Lee Harris to raise funds to save a horse-rescue ranch. The gang, along with Hulk Hogan, hosts a charity wrestling match to benefit a youth recreation center in "Bash at the Beach." C. J. and Cody show their charitable side in the episode "Lost and Found" by helping a physically challenged man achieve his dream of swimming in the ocean.

In addition to their career-based lifesaving acts, the lifeguards of *Baywatch* frequently went above and beyond for each other and those in need. Through their charitable and giving acts, they proved they weren't just WOWs on the outside, but WOWs on the inside as well.

Positive Impact

WOW leaders don't just rack up personal successes; they positively impact others. In terms of business and personal goals, quotas, and strategies, most leaders in key positions have learned how to deliver. But WOW leaders take it a step further, making up their minds to go beyond the bottom line of business by also helping to make a difference in their corner of the world. While WOWs are motivated and determined, they are also realistic. They know that they can't accomplish absolutely *everything* that is asked of them or impact every single individual they encounter, but they're driven to do what they can to the best of their abilities.

Early in my leadership career, I helped a direct report who was facing a difficult situation. While I didn't think I was necessarily offering anything unique in the way of advice, my encouraging words apparently hit home. Later, I was touched and surprised when I received a heartfelt thank-you card and a box of chocolates with "The Starfish Story" printed inside the lid. The box and note remained on my desk for some time, serving as a reminder that even seemingly small gestures can have an impact.

Here's the story, adapted from the essay "The Star Thrower," written by Loren Eiseley and first published in *The Unexpected Universe* (New York: Harcourt Brace and World, 1969):

> Once upon a time, there was an old man who used to go to
> the ocean to do his writing. He had a habit of walking on
> the beach every morning before he began his work. Early one

morning, he was walking along the shore after a big storm had passed and he found the vast beach littered with starfish as far as the eye could see, stretching in both directions.

Off in the distance, the old man noticed a small boy approaching. As the boy walked, he paused every so often and as he grew closer, the man could see that he was occasionally bending down to pick up an object and throw it into the sea. The boy came closer still and the man called out, "Good morning! May I ask what it is that you are doing?"

The young boy paused, looked up, and replied, "Throwing starfish into the ocean. The tide has washed them up onto the beach and they can't return to the sea by themselves. When the sun gets high, they will die unless I throw them back into the water."

The old man replied, "But there must be tens of thousands of starfish on this beach. I'm afraid you won't really be able to make much of a difference."

The boy bent down, picked up yet another starfish and threw it as far as he could into the ocean. Then he turned, smiled, and said, "It made a difference to that one!"

As leaders, we don't always know when we make a difference. We don't always receive notes or thanks from the people we lead. But that's not the point, is it? We're driven to impact others because in the end, making a difference for one is making a difference for all—including ourselves. When we give, we also receive. The boy in the story won't ever know the eventual fate of the starfish he saves, nor will he be shown any gratitude from the oblivious sea creatures. But he's committed to the task nonetheless. He knows it's the right thing to do, and he's determined to make a difference.

Leaders who share their good fortune and look for opportunities to give back to the community demonstrate that they see a larger picture beyond their own office doors. They impress by not just focusing on themselves but also by connecting with those around them, on and off the job. Even thoughtful, friendly gestures like waving a car through in traffic, giving up your seat on the train, or holding the door for a stranger are ways to pay some positivity forward. You never know how much your small act of kindness may mean to those who are down on their luck, feeling lost, or struggling in some way. WOWs don't just look for ways to succeed; they find ways to inject positive energy into the world and help others be successful as well.

Chapter 8

WOW Leaders Are Inspirational Motivators

"Leaders must be close enough to relate to others,
but far enough ahead to motivate them."
—*John C. Maxwell*

WOW leaders are passionate inspirational motivators. If they're gifted leaders, they are motivated to empower and inspire others to share in and work toward a common goal. WOW leaders set an example that encourages team members to be engaged and passionate about their own abilities and their own success on the job.

Part of being a great leader is recognizing and advocating the achievements of others. Superior leaders aren't simply focused on their own successes; they are dedicated to seeking out team members' strengths and encouraging their staff to achieve its full potential. WOW leaders never suppress the talents of the people they lead; they help build up those talents through guidance, praise, and support.

In sports, motivational leadership can be the cornerstone of enhanced team performance. Locker-room pep talks or on-the-field encouragement can help players muster their inner strength, focus on the positive, and push themselves to greatness. It's the same in business. The fictional Coach Eric Taylor on the TV show *Friday Night Lights* was that voice

of encouragement for his football team, often espousing words of wisdom that inspired and motivated his players to give their all—in life as
well as in the game.

In the episode "East of Dillon," the coach pumps up the team:

> There's a joy to this game, is there not? There's a passion;
> there's a reason why we're all out here. Other than the pride
> that it gives us and the respect that it demands, we love to play
> the game . . . so let's go out there and have fun tonight. Do
> you understand? Because tomorrow, if you give 100 percent
> of yourself tonight, people are going to look at you differently.
> People are going to think of you differently. And I promise
> you you're going to look and think differently about yourself.
> Clear eyes. Full hearts.

With his heartfelt expression and motivational call to action, the
coach instills a mood, elicits a feeling, and injects an attitude to grab
hold of. He doesn't demand an outcome; he lays the groundwork for
success by inspiring the desire for success in his team.

Like the fictional Coach Taylor, leaders set the tone in their group.
When leaders are negative, those following tend to be negative, which
in turn means productivity is negative. When leaders inspire, they lift
up morale and create a positive work environment ripe for success.
A little encouragement and empathy from the boss goes a long way
toward boosting the output and attitude of those working hard to succeed at their jobs. When things go wrong, as they sometimes do, WOW
leaders support their team members and back them up rather than feeding them to the sharks.

As mentors and role models, WOW leaders have the ability to steer
their teams back on course when challenges or bumps in the road arise.
Rather than condemning or berating people when problems occur,
exceptional leaders will lead the charge to pick up the pieces and move
on. They will encourage action and drive their people forward with the
understanding that while the goals and objectives that need to be achieved
are not easy, they are possible. By demonstrating and voicing their faith
in the team's success, WOW leaders foster and enable that success.

People want to put their hearts and minds into their work, but sometimes they need an inspirational leader to help them get to that place. Challenges and obstacles can be like a brick wall standing in the way of moving forward. In order to succeed, the team needs to power through that brick wall. Motivational, inspirational leaders facilitate the courage and the drive needed to break through any barrier.

Being passionately driven is imperative for WOW leaders. When those in charge are enthusiastically in pursuit of success, those following will inevitably feel the same. Passion and conviction can be contagious, but so can apathy and inaction. WOW leaders inject their employees with their own positive energy and spirit, giving them the motivation they need to do every job with an equal passion.

Motivational Medium

TV is one of the most powerful mass-communication tools ever invented. Through television, we've certainly been entertained, but we've also been moved and inspired as history unfolded before our eyes. As a society, we watched the first-ever moon landing on our TVs, we witnessed 9/11 as it was happening, and we saw the bombs dropping on Baghdad as the Gulf War began. Through news reporting and TV coverage, we've been transported to the Olympics, invited to political debates, and exposed to horrific and moving stories from around the world. We've been collectively awestruck as real-time, inspirational images were broadcast in our living rooms. And at times, we've even been motivated and inspired to do more than just watch—we've been driven to take action and make a difference.

In 2004, the Indonesian tsunami made headlines everywhere with its unfathomable destruction. Television coverage of the natural disaster's aftermath sent shockwaves of horror and empathy to a world held in suspended disbelief. The TV exposure inspired countless fundraising efforts, telethons, and an outpouring of viewer support for the victims of the tragedy—resulting in billions of dollars of relief donations. Television's swift, comprehensive, and visually motivational reporting of the tsunami demonstrates that the medium is more than just an idiot-box; it's an information box as well—one that can move, motivate, and inspire the masses.

Motivate Through Caring

In much the same way TV, movies, books, and music drive popular culture and influence the masses, leaders have the power to drive performance within their companies, teams, or groups. The corporate or business culture they create shapes the way their teams perform and ultimately impacts the likelihood for sustained success.

In business, there are people who lead through fear and aggression and expect top performance as a result. They believe in the mantra "The floggings will continue until morale improves" and purposely keep their team off-balance and struggling to survive in an effort to maintain control.

But does this kind of corporate aggression positively drive performance? Or is an atmosphere of caring and cooperation a more effective approach to garnering motivation and peak performance?

Sadly, the aggressive attitude found driving the culture of many corporations these days has only been made worse by an uncertain economy. When the going gets tough, sometimes the tough get even tougher—and often not in a positive way.

Financial pressures, tight bottom-line earnings expectations, and fierce competition in sometimes-struggling markets often cause the corporate fangs to come out, creating a hostile, bloodthirsty environment where everyone fears being bitten. But in times of stress, uphill challenges, and increasing pressures, a leader's real character emerges. Likewise, the true culture of a corporation reveals itself. Those who drive a culture of fear and aggression in the workplace expect subservience, allegiance, and productivity as a result of their harsh demands. In most cases, the people respond. They perform because they must in order to survive. In a kill-or-be-killed culture, the strongest prevail; their survival instincts kick in and they push themselves to achieve more and stay ahead of the pack. In that respect, performance is, in fact, driven by aggressive tactics.

The cutthroat culture on the reality show *Survivor* is like a microcosm of real-life leadership styles—running the gamut from good to great and bad to worse. The "characters" aren't billed as actors, but rather as everyday people from all walks of life competing to survive in remote locations under dire and extreme circumstances. At first, alliances form and the survivors lean on each other to win challenges and move forward in the competition. But it is, after all, a game with a $1 million prize—for one winner. The castaways' true colors eventually emerge, and in the end, it's winner take all. Established teams and trusts frequently break down as tensions rise, difficulties emerge, and the self-serving goal comes closer into view. When all is said and done, the victor gets the money and the title, but often at the expense of friendships, personal integrity, and even self-respect.

In business, as in the world of *Survivor*, do the pressures and demands of corporate aggression eventually take their toll, causing the system to ultimately break down? Certainly! After all, people can only withstand the flogging for so long. Over time, they either crack from the pressure or they find the strength to rise above the hostility and ignore the whip.

Naturally, there are all types of personalities and leadership styles. Some people thrive in a pressure-cooker environment. They are constantly motivated to do more, work harder, and improve outcomes. But does the cattle-prod approach last over time? Do the cattle keep moving constantly forward, or do they eventually lie down and die?

Perhaps a more familial, easygoing, caring style of leadership can elicit more greatness than the corporate overlord methodology. Employees, and people in general, want to be led by a leader who cares. Leadership can be simplified into three C's: communication, consistency, and caring. Great leaders must possess all three. They must lead with courage and passion, but above all, they must exhibit respect and caring for the people who follow them.

Whether or not you'll admit to being a fan of the series, I'll bet you can whistle the tune to the opening sequence of *The Andy Griffith Show*. Sheriff Andy Taylor was far from the gun-toting, tough-guy cop persona of today's cutting-edge police dramas. As the levelheaded, patient, and compassionate public servant of the small town of Mayberry, North Carolina, Andy proved you don't have to be a tyrant to be an influential leader.

In the episode "Andy on Trial," Andy's character is called into question when a big shot from the city is caught speeding in Mayberry. Rather than admit to his mistake, the out-of-towner attempts to put the blame on Andy. In his defense, dim-witted but loyal Deputy Barney Fife stands up for his boss:

> As far as Andy knowing his job . . . I'd just like for you to take a look in the record book, Mr. Jackson. You know there ain't been a major crime committed in this town thanks to Sheriff Taylor? The only ruckus you'd ever have in Mayberry is if you tried to remove him from office. Then you'd have a riot. You asked me if Andy runs a taut ship, Mr. Milton. Well, no, he don't. But that's because of something that he's been trying to teach me ever since I started working for him. And that is, when you're a lawman and you're dealing with people, you do a whole lot better if you go not so much by the book, but by the heart.

People who are working hard to succeed want to be enthusiastic about their part in the organization. They want to feel free to contribute their best efforts and, as a result, be engaged and passionate about the possibility of growth and improvement. Most people do not want to live with their guard up, constantly in fear of making the wrong move. No one wants to be so terrified by the repercussions of failure that they lose their motivation to succeed.

Leaders who drive the hard line might maintain that a more familial corporate environment, in which employees are rewarded and trusted, will not yield high-performance results. They may argue that loosening the reins would create a soft, flimsy atmosphere where workers get lax because, without threat of punishment, there is no motivation to succeed.

However, WOW leaders typically believe in creating a performance-driven culture that celebrates success, stresses continuous improvement, and encourages passion and engagement in the process. They know that the team needs to communicate often in order to share personal strategies and best practices. There should be no fear of failure as long as calculated risks are taken. A successful corporate culture should encourage innovation, change, and adaptation with purpose, rather than trying to keep people in line with an iron fist.

When it comes to corporate culture, "The fish moves from the head," or the organization will move in the direction of the leader. Leaders, owners, and CEOs dictate the culture of their business. They set the tone and everything else trickles down from there.

With a fear-based mentality, employees perform based on terror and aggression, which consequently encourages the leader to operate with more and more aggression. The floggings continue despite improving performance. The culture is set.

But when leaders guide and motivate with compassion, there are no floggings. People are driven to perform at their best level because they respect their leader, they believe in the mission, they are a part of the plan for success.

What drives performance, then? Is it the culture of fear or the culture of caring? Generally speaking, it's both. But not all success stories are created equal. How does a fear-based approach to performance help sustain the best productivity and best practices from those people who are subjected to it? Does it change those who must compete for every win in that culture? Does it elicit a cooperative team environment, or pit one worker against the other?

At the end of the day, all you have is your character, your integrity, your credibility, and the respect of those around you. Strive to lead with a culture that helps others develop their character in a positive way. Protect your own ideals, and don't sacrifice your motivation, drive, and passion because the field you play in sometimes seems to be pushing you back. Be the voice of caring, understanding, and encouraging motivation that your team needs, rather than the voice of doom that crushes everyone's morale. Strive to succeed without having to succumb to the pressures of an aggressive, unsupportive business culture.

Encourage Employee Engagement

WOW leaders aren't out solely for themselves; they oversee the team and therefore must be an advocate and inspirational voice for the team. The business management concept of employee engagement holds that a positive, emotionally connected employee will further the organization's success, while the opposite, a zombie employee, is ultimately a detriment to the company by being disengaged, unmotivated, and negative. But what drives employee engagement? The employer!

As a leader, regardless of your title or rank within a company, if you're a decision maker and overseer, you're representing the "employer." However, for those people who are leaders in the middle, you're also the "employee." You're being led by those above you while simultaneously leading those below you. You need to be engaged as both the employer and the employee.

Without employer engagement, there's no motivation for employees to be held accountable, to excel, or even to care about the job they're doing. While some individuals have a more innately positive attitude and conduct themselves with a work ethic and pride in their performance that goes beyond, that isn't always enough to sustain or grow employee engagement. Even the best-intentioned employees have to know they're working for something of value and that they are, in fact, valued in return.

It's easy to assume that the leadership of the fictional "Total Bastard Airlines," a featured sketch on Saturday Night Live, does not encourage (or expect) employee engagement. The disgruntled flight attendants of the airline, portrayed by David Spade and host Helen Hunt, are rude, condescending, and dismissive of their passengers, answering nearly every request with a mocking "buh-bye." In one skit, the "welcome greeting" comes over the intercom. "This concludes the safest part of our journey. Thank you for flying Total Bastard Airlines. As we indicated at the start of the flight, we at Total Bastard Airlines are bitter about the career paths we have taken, and we do then take that out on our passengers." It's not difficult to see that this type of "encouragement" would only make employees and customers tune out.

To elicit employee engagement and motivation, a company and the leaders who represent it must do their part as well. Optimal employee performance, unwavering loyalty, and a positive, enthusiastic attitude isn't a given or a guarantee, even if it's "demanded" or "expected." It's the result of working in a supportive, communicative, and motivational culture that doesn't just require respect but also gives it.

Here's what an employer should do to be engaged and, therefore, facilitate employee engagement:

Be an active listener. The leaders who drive the organization's culture need to be engaged, active listeners. Rather than issuing directives without hearing the voices of their workers, engaged employers should be open and responsive to what their employees are saying.

Care about the customer. If the customer is not happy, the boss isn't going to be, either. For a company to succeed, it must be in tune with the needs of its customers. But those at the top are not typically the ones dealing directly with the customer—the employees are. So it's vital that the employer respect the "middleman" as a valuable, knowledgeable connection to the customer. The engaged employer must be open to suggestions, opinions, and employee feedback if customer relations are to move in a positive direction.

Take action. Engaged leaders must not only be active listeners: they must also demonstrate that they value their employees' opinions by doing something about it. They must make decisions and take actions in response to discussions with their staff. Listening without following through is no better than not listening at all. If there's a reason for not moving forward, an engaged employer needs to communicate the why behind it and involve the employees in the process of seeking compromises or alternatives.

Be sincere. You can't stonewall your employees and then expect them to stay motivated to deliver peak performance. Engaged employers must hear the message coming up, react to it appropriately, and be honest and sincere about what is or is not being done about it. Employers must be consistent about doing what they say, and not just saying what they're going to do. Employees need to trust that their leaders will follow through and that they aren't going to make promises they can't—or won't—keep. Engaged employees are those who know they can count on their leaders and their company to be sincerely invested in them, and not just the other way around.

By demonstrating a reciprocal, communicative, give-and-not-just-take relationship with your staff, you'll help facilitate engaged employees. And since engaged employees help drive a successful company, everyone wins—and WOWs.

Empowering Employees

WOW leaders realize that the best performance results are achieved not when employees are told to perform well, but when the employees care enough to *want* to perform well. Empowering employees helps them to grow, improve, and succeed on the job, and it also facilitates a culture of cooperation and mutual respect that benefits the organization as a whole. WOW leaders have a vested interest in empowering their employees, rather than just seeking power for themselves. They know that to bring out the best in their followers, they must provide them with a sense of worth, value, and pride in their accomplishments.

In the *Friends* episode "The One Where They're Going to a Party," Rachel Green is employed at Bloomingdale's as a buyer's assistant. Her boss, Joanna, thinks very highly of Rachel's work performance, entrusting her with numerous responsibilities and projects. Overall, Rachel is empowered and engaged in her career, which in turn, brings out the best in her abilities. However, for Joanna, that becomes problematic. Rachel becomes so good at what she does that she becomes a candidate for a promotion outside of Joanna's department. In an effort to keep Rachel at her side, Joanna sabotages her assistant's chances at the job. Empowering employees is not about finding ways to improve the bottom line for the leader, but it is a reflection of the leader's effectiveness. WOWs don't try to stifle their employees' growth; they empower their workers and encourage their potential for success.

Here are several key elements essential to empowering employees:

Clear communication. Providing employees with clear, specific information is vital to helping them succeed. They need to know what's expected of them, what the company's goals are, and why certain policies and procedures are important. Employees must also feel free to ask questions, make suggestions, and voice concerns. Listening to the people who are carrying out your directives is crucial to creating a reciprocal, team dynamic. If your employees don't feel they're being heard, they'll also feel they have no voice, no power, and no motivation to succeed.

Accountability. When employees are held accountable for their actions, they know that what they do really matters. They realize that, as part of a team, others are counting on them and relying on them to do their share. And at the same time, the rest of the team is being consistently held to the same standards. Nothing shatters morale and performance quicker than watching others sabotage team efforts and not be held accountable. When standards, rules, and expectations are laid out, they need to be adhered to and respected in order to be effective. Only through consistent accountability are employees empowered to do their best.

Reinforcing the good. Part of accountability is ensuring that the wrong things aren't being done, but the most effective way to empower employees is by rewarding them for doing things right. When you catch employees in the act of exceeding expectations, going the extra mile, or putting forth their best efforts, tell them it's appreciated. Point out the positive rather than only acknowledging mistakes or shortcomings.

Trusting their decisions. Don't micromanage your employees; trust them to accomplish tasks on their own. Providing employees with decision rights enables them to be more connected to the importance of their role and demonstrates that you have faith in their judgment and belief in their value. When you give employees the authority to use their own mind, skills, and voice to get things done, you give them the confidence and drive to continuously improve and grow.

Consistency. Be consistent with everything you do as a leader. Your employees must be able to trust the leadership guiding them if they are to believe in it. If your employees can't count on you to be clear, reliable, fair, and authentic, there's no anchor to grab hold of to keep them grounded. By creating and maintaining a culture of empowerment, your employees will rise to the challenge and prove how powerful they can be.

Empowering employees benefits everyone. After all, when the employee is happy, the customer is happy; and when the customer is happy, business is good, so the leader is happy. And that's the power of WOW!

Meet and Motivate

Employees are motivated and inspired through positivity, caring, and empowerment, but you must also provide them with specific opportunities to reinforce and increase that drive. Business as usual can be a good thing, but it can also mean a stale, stagnant workplace in need of some serious motivation and inspiration. To rejuvenate morale and inject a little bit of energy into your meetings, try employing one—or all—of these creative strategies.

Meetings That Matter

1. Mix up the meeting. Steering away from the usual routine, even in simple ways, can take the monotony out of staff gatherings. Eliminate ineffective or unnecessary tactics and replace them with something new. Do you always begin meetings with the same overview of weekly numbers? Do you repeat the same mantra to improve ABC or the same reminder to stop doing XYZ? Time to mix things up and move your team from checked out to engaged.

2. Bring the outside in. Invite a guest presenter or motivational speaker to deliver a fresh perspective and introduce new ideas to the group.

3. Get your game on. Try a few mind-stimulating games or exercises like word association or prompting with props, where you try to come up with as many uses for an ordinary object as possible. Coaxing the brain into thinking in new ways should help breathe new life into anyone who's feeling uninspired.

4. Create a contest. Nothing shakes things up quite like a friendly contest among coworkers. Introduce a challenge or goal that aligns with your business strategy and will help everyone improve the bottom line. Offer a reward of some kind—event tickets, an incentive trip, a plastic trophy, or simply bragging rights—whatever makes sense for your team. You make the rules. There could be a solo winner or it could be a team prize. Either way, the point is to provide motivation through reward.

5. Throw a "positivity party." Ban negativity from the meeting, then take it a step further and require positivity. Have each person compliment or praise the person to their right, going around the room until everyone has said something positive and has received some form of positive feedback. Patting each other on the back will help boost morale, confidence, and camaraderie.

Mockumentary TV show *The Office* is hardly a realistic portrayal of the typical corporation, but its comedic take on interpersonal business relationships provides some interesting and humorous examples from which to draw. In the season eight episode "The Incentive," office manager Andy Bernard (no, not Michael Scott this time) tries to impress corporate with the goal of doubling paper sales. To motivate his lackluster team, he improvises by offering a points system that could earn them big prizes: his wearing a dress to work, running naked through the parking lot, or even being branded on the buttocks with a workers' choice tattoo. Humiliating the boss proves to be the ultimate motivation for the Dunder Mifflin staff, and sales are doubled within the day, much to Andy's delight and simultaneous horror. In the end, he reluctantly follows through with his promise and faces the needle, prepared to be forever scarred with the horribly offensive artwork his workers have decided on. At the last minute, however, the team surprises him with a more personalized tattoo, which he actually seems to like, and everyone shares in a celebratory cheer.

Now, I'm certainly not suggesting that you get inked in the name of motivation . . . but spicing up your meetings a bit every now and then will help keep the ideas fresh, the attitudes upbeat, and the inspiration piqued, which in turn will keep the momentum flowing and bring out the WOW within the team.

Leadership, by definition, is about guiding and directing others—not about embarking on a solo endeavor to success. To elicit greatness from your followers, you must empower and engage them, motivate and inspire them, and set the example by being a caring, passionate, WOW leader.

Part III

On the Air—
Keeping It WOW

Chapter 9

WOW Leaders Are Agents of Change

"He who rejects change is the architect of decay. The only human institution which rejects progress is the cemetery."
—*Harold Wilson*

The marketplace and economy as a whole are wrought with the ups and downs of change. Corporations and individuals working for those companies are challenged with navigating an often complex and confusing path to survival and success. Today, more than ever, we need WOW leaders who are able to face these changes head-on, without fear or hesitation.

Great leaders are not impervious to change, but rather are impervious to the fear of change. As has once been said, "A real leader faces the music, even when she doesn't like the tune." WOW leaders have the ability, confidence, and gumption to lead from the front, helping their team deal with and thrive in a changing environment. People who resist changes that are inevitable or who lead through inaction end up facilitating the breakdown of a department or even an entire organization. When fear of change takes hold and when leaders are not agents of that change, productivity wanes and a general workplace paralysis sets in.

WOW leaders have the skill and talent to implement solutions and new approaches when challenges arise. They mobilize their team by setting forth clear strategies to work with, rather than against, the impending changes. Through the strength and motivation of a WOW leader, a successful team will thrive and grow, even in these uncertain and ever-changing times.

Most people only like change when they are driving it, not when change is forced on them. Change can be invigorating, refreshing, and exciting when the perceived outcomes are positive and desirable. But when it's forced and the outcome of that change is uncertain or unpredictable, it can be stressful and scary. As a result, change is often feared, avoided, and resisted. Companies or individuals in a company who refuse or are unable to move along with the transformations happening around them will become stagnant and unsuccessful. They'll eventually fade and become part of the backdrop of everything that existed before the changes occurred. They'll be obsolete.

To survive and thrive in an unpredictable, uncertain culture of change, business leaders must not only guide their staff through the changing times but also must be agents of change within their organization. They must drive change in the right way, injecting a positive outlook and assuaging the fear of uncertainty.

TV programming often reflects current culture and changing times. It can also be a catalyst of change. In the 1990s sitcom *Ellen*, Ellen DeGeneres starred as Ellen Morgan, a neurotic bookstore owner dealing with the ups and downs of life. Up until the fourth season, Ellen's on-show dates were traditional: She dated men. However, as is widely known now, the actress herself was a lesbian and wanted her character to reflect that status as well.

The decision was made to "out" both the actress and her character simultaneously in "The Puppy Episode." This bold, controversial move was widely regarded as a defining, pivotal moment for the LGBT community and for TV itself. It paved the way for other series that did more than marginalize or mock gay characters, bringing a realistic gay lifestyle to the forefront. Shows like *Will & Grace*, *Queer as Folk*, *The L Word*, and *The New Normal* followed, along with a perceived gradual but marked change in the way the American viewing public accepted the portrayal of alternative lifestyles in their favorite TV programs.

Ellen was an agent of change, proclaiming her own ideals and point of view despite the initial backlash, outrage, and negativity surrounding the "coming out" episode.

The best WOWs embody change leadership, which means they don't just move with the change, they lead the change. They set the course that steers the train out of the loop and onto the track bound for new, uncharted territory. Change leaders are innovative and inspirational in a way that moves people into action and empowers them to drive the change. They set the vision, strategy, and implementation plan, establishing a new direction for the team and providing leadership guidance, but not management interference. As visionaries, they set the path and light the way but aren't necessarily involved in the day-to-day execution of the change.

Communication is key for any team structure, but it is especially vital when changes are being made. As previously noted, WOW leaders are effective communicators, which also plays into their superior skills in driving change. Providing truly open and transparent communication, and not just regurgitating a one-way podcast produced by the PR department, demonstrates a connection to the team and to the changes being made.

Change leaders do more than just tell; they listen. They pay attention to what the influential leaders (even those without titles) are saying about the change, and they are cognizant of the uncontrollable ricochets occurring as reactions to newly implemented plans. Based on the two-way communication feedback, they make adjustments, if needed, to move the company in the right direction.

WOW leaders also explain and clearly outline the "why" behind the changes taking place. They don't just back into it, making the reasons fit the actions after the fact. Instead, they are forthcoming and up front about the worthiness of the change, giving the people who are affected the time to realize they are better off with it than without it.

When changes are imminent, there's nothing worse than being dictated to by an enigmatic taskmaster who anonymously doles out orders from above. Effective leaders of change are people who realize that new methods, strategies, and situations are not just affecting things on paper, but also have a direct and profound effect on the people within the company.

Leaders must care about their people and demonstrate that care if they want the team to perform at its best, especially during the uncertain times of change. Most employees want to love where they work; they want to love their organization. But people don't want to love what doesn't love them back; it hurts too much. Great WOW leaders are the facilitators who show people that the organization loves them back.

WOWs often emerge in times of change. When the situation is dire and action must be taken to avoid certain doom, leaders with the potential to WOW will climb out of their cocoons of mediocrity and begin to fly. Those who do nothing or who freeze out of fear or doubt may end up missing their WOW moment.

Enduring Change

The WOW series *Nightline* began when Roone Arledge, then-president of ABC News, seized a moment and created a new TV concept. In 1979, when the Iran Hostage Crisis began, Arledge decided the best way to keep the public updated was with a regular nightly special report, titled "The Iran Crisis: America Held Hostage." While Frank Reynolds originally hosted the series, Ted Koppel soon took over, becoming as popular in his own right as the show itself. Once the crisis ended, the series took on a new name but maintained its hard-hitting, investigative news format.

What began as an opportunity to change gave way to an enduring legacy that continues to this day, more than thirty years later. Had ABC's Arledge been gun-shy about changing the traditional format by which news had been previously reported, the WOW that has become *Nightline* and the WOW that became Koppel's career would have never happened.

Be Fearless

Leading change requires fearlessness. All too often, fear causes leaders to fall. And when the leaders fall, the rest of the team inevitably tumbles down like dominos, unable to stand against the momentum of fear sweeping through the corporate ranks. As a WOW leader, you must learn how to be fearless in the face of what scares you the most.

Jobs are precious commodities in today's economy. No one is immune to the fickle and unpredictable nature of the current market. Downsizing, company closings, and jobs being lost to a cheaper, overseas labor pool are a harsh reality for businesses of all kinds. With new graduates scrambling for sought-after positions and seasoned veterans being pushed out before their time, the workplace has become a hotbed of fear and anxiety for people on all levels of the corporate ladder.

Often, those trying to outmaneuver the wild, erratic swinging of the corporate axe end up ducking into a corner, trying to avoid the fatal blow. But cowering in fear makes you weak, and weakness only makes you even more vulnerable to attack. After all, it's much easier to strike a frightened, paralyzed target than one that is up and moving, fearless, and strong with a conviction to survive.

If you're operating in an atmosphere of paranoia and suspicion, you're likely caught in a downward spiral that is all but crippling your productivity in the workplace. And if you're in a leadership position, the fear that you project will infect those around you like a virus, in essence destroying your authority as well as jeopardizing the careers of your employees. To end this debilitating cycle, you must empower yourself to accept your fears, face them head-on, and then take action to be fearless against them.

In the words of Frank Reagan, the steadfast, morally secure police commissioner on the TV police series *Blue Bloods*, "It takes guts to stand by your principles, not just when it's easy, but when it can cost you something."

Here are some principles that can help WOW leaders deal with fear:

Face your fears. Being fearless in the face of adversity does not mean you're completely unafraid. In fact, you need to acknowledge and understand that you do have fears in order to combat them. No matter what your job description, title, or seniority level may be, there will be issues to face, rumors to deal with, and obstacles to overcome at work. It's perfectly natural to experience some fear surrounding your unique workplace situation. The trick is to face those worries head-on and move forward with real solutions, rather than becoming frozen with indecision and inaction. Overcoming fear means being courageous enough to move forward despite the possibility of failure. If you make decisions with confidence and conviction, you will ultimately demonstrate your power, authority, and overall worth as an employee and leader.

Be fearless, not reckless. Confidence and self-assuredness in your actions is not the same as throwing all caution to the wind and making career choices that are reckless or haphazard. Fearlessness does not mean acting without a carefully considered strategy or plan. More than ever, you'll need to make calculated business decisions in order to stay afloat or get ahead. Remember: Proceeding with caution and care is not the same as acting out of fear. After all, you wouldn't demonstrate your courage by skydiving without a parachute, would you? Instead, you would show your fearlessness by taking the plunge in a responsible, well-planned way, with the foresight and consideration to land safely on your feet. Similarly, proving your fearlessness in business does not mean making careless, rash moves. It means proceeding with both caution and confidence: with the bold conviction that you are moving toward an achievable goal.

Be focused, not fearful. Confidence is key in the battle against fear. Taking a firm, focused stance in all your business dealings will secure and strengthen that confidence. Although it sounds simple and perhaps a bit cliché, if you believe in yourself and if you trust your instincts and abilities, you will succeed. If you fear failure so much that you question your every action and decision, you will immobilize yourself, and you will never succeed. Fearless individuals are focused on the process and the methods required to achieve winning results. They play to win by employing winnable strategies and, quite frankly, having a winning attitude. They do not let fear creep in and erode their resolve to succeed. Being fearless means being tenacious and self-assured, conducting yourself with aggressive, forward-moving actions in all matters. Fearlessness is having the fortitude to get the job done regardless of any underlying fears or perceived threats. It means demonstrating the strength, determination, and courage to follow through with your ideas and to pursue new or bold courses of action. Only then can you move forward and achieve true success, improving your job security by enhancing your value as an employee of substance.

End the vortex of fear. Fear begets fear. It feeds on itself and will only grow larger and more powerful if left unchecked. And it will spread through the ranks of your office or team, destroying the trust and communication needed to continue working effectively and productively. For WOW leaders, it's especially damaging to act in a fearful and immobile manner. People who follow your lead will not only begin to doubt your capabilities, but also their own performance will surely flounder without the guidance and support of a strong, fearless mentor. And at the same time, those above you in rank will smell the blood in the water, and the sharks will begin circling. Treading water in a swirling vortex of fear will make you easy prey. Inaction because of fear will ultimately spell your demise. It is only through fearless action that you will have the confidence and strength to survive—to stop treading water and start swimming.

Whatever your workplace fears may be—fear of losing your job, fear of making mistakes, fear of not succeeding, fear of being judged by your peers, fear of change—you must be confident and strong enough to soldier on despite your doubts. You must believe in your own actions and recognize that it is not what you do, but rather what you don't do because of fear that could ultimately cause you harm. Be fearless, and you will prevail as a WOW leader.

A Fearless Medium

Launching a TV show requires a great deal of fearlessness, as does any entertainment venture. The writers, creators, producers, and even performers must face their fears of rejection or low ratings. They must boldly stand behind their concepts and ideas and present them to a fickle, critical audience. If the fear of failing were stronger than the will to succeed, there would be absolutely nothing to watch on TV!

Besides the general risk involved in creating a television program, many shows have taken monumental chances by portraying controversial characters, sensitive subject matter, or untested new concepts.

The pioneers of TV have been and continue to be courageous and
confident enough to be authentic to the message they want to convey.
Many have failed or fallen short in their objectives, but through their
fearless actions, they have paved the way for future success and continued progress in the art of television programming.

Crisis Management

Change often occurs in times of crisis. When people are asked to name
the biggest crisis our nation has faced, 99 percent of us would say 9/11.
But other crises would inevitably come to mind: natural disasters like
those in Oklahoma or New Orleans, violent acts such as the Newtown
or Boston Marathon tragedies, or national woes like unemployment or
the housing bust.

If you get more personal, each of us has faced individual life crises of
varying degrees. How we deal with those disasters makes all the difference. Do we lie down and give up, or do we soldier on and find a way
to overcome the situation?

In business, the same holds true. When faced with a career or company crisis, the actions we take in response can make or break us.
Whether you're a bigwig at a large company or the leader of a small
team, you'll eventually need to manage a crisis. Crisis management is
paramount when situations arise that may risk your (or the company's)
reputation, jeopardize revenue, or significantly detract from opera-
tional productivity. When the stakes are high, time is of the essence,
and careers are on the line, you're in crisis mode—and it's time for a
WOW leader to step up and manage.

Typically, as with any national or personal crisis, a business crisis
comes about quite suddenly and will more often than not catch you off
guard. As swiftly as the crisis swoops in, decisions need to be made to
offset the fallout and deal with the repercussions. The faster a leader
responds to an unforeseen crisis, the more secure the team members
will be and the more likely they will be able to recover and rebound
from the situation.

The reality cooking show *The Great Food Truck Race* is a

competition-based TV series that challenges eight food truck businesses to outdo each other in a series of tasks. At the end of each episode and corresponding challenge, the truck team earning the lowest total sales is eliminated. Crisis management comes into play as the inevitable twists in the challenges are revealed: usually something akin to cooking with a strange ingredient, cooking without a vital ingredient or tool, or having to acquire hard-to-find ingredients before preparing dishes. Coming up with quick, effective solutions on the fly is vital to the survival of each truck as every new challenge brings about its own mini-crisis. Those who manage the unforeseen complications the best typically end up bringing home the win. However, those who fall short in handling the "speed bumps" must ultimately close the window on their food truck's competitive journey.

Since it's impossible to gauge the effect a crisis will have on a business, skilled crisis management becomes vital. If a crisis is managed incorrectly or not at all, it could have a deleterious effect on morale, performance, and the business as a whole. And while it seems obvious that leadership needs to take the reins in times of trouble, some companies are rendered helpless when a crisis hits. Some can't—or don't—handle the rough waters in a WOW manner. But why?

The classic, textbook crisis management case cited by all business schools is Johnson & Johnson's handling of the Tylenol scare in Chicago. If you recall, seven people died in 1982 after ingesting cyanide-laced Tylenol capsules. While the act was criminal and not the doing of the manufacturer, it was certainly a corporate crisis for the makers of the drug. The way in which the situation was handled directly impacted the future success of the brand. Since Tylenol still lines drugstore shelves, we can safely assume that the company's crisis management saved the day.

However, not all companies have taken a page from the Johnson & Johnson book on crisis management. Here are a few reasons why companies fail at crisis management:

Attitude. A positive attitude is one thing, but ignoring the possibility for disaster is negligent. The overconfident attitude that a crisis would never affect your team, company, or product marks an obvious shortcoming in the ability to manage one when it happens.

Lack of planning. In school, fire drills and lockdowns are practiced so everyone is prepared in the event disaster strikes. A plan is formulated and simulated in advance so everyone knows his or her role. Crisis management procedures need to be considered, planned, and made a priority well before a crisis presents itself, or the ball will certainly be dropped.

Ignoring the risks. All business includes a level of risk. If you don't recognize and identify those risks in advance, you won't be ready to handle the fallout when the worst happens.

Blindness. Turning a blind eye to an obvious crisis and hoping it goes away on its own is a mistake made by weak, ineffective leaders. Remember the maxim "Hope is not a plan." Crisis blindness leaves people floundering and trying to find their footing, with no one to lead them through the darkness.

Indecision. Taking too much time to act on a crisis can compound the situation. When leadership is halted with indecision and no response or direction is dictated, things start to unravel quickly.

Communication. The details of a crisis need to be openly and clearly communicated internally as well as externally (when applicable). Communication needs to be transparent from the top down, or rumors and false information will exacerbate the problem.

Succeeding at crisis management is often synonymous with succeeding as a business or a team. People who fail to lead effectively during a crisis or times of change may be sealing their own fate as well as that of those they lead. The 2004 TV series *Battlestar Galactica*, a reimagined version of the 1978 sci-fi TV show of the same name, revolves around a crisis of epic proportions. After the population of humans living on a group of planets in a distant solar system is attacked by a race of robotic enemies, only one military space ship, the *Galactica*, has managed to flee and survive. A complement of civilian ships have also escaped and are now being led by the *Galactica* and its crew to seek refuge on a fabled planet called Earth.

Commander William Adama, the ranking military officer, along with civilian president Laura Roslin, must lead and manage a group of 50,000 human survivors in the wake of an apocalyptic crisis. While Adama's initial plan is to fight the Cylon enemy, a more realistic Roslin convinces him to rethink his strategy and flee to safety. Although he craves revenge for the billions of lives lost, he realizes that their efforts would likely be futile against such superior enemy numbers. Adama manages the crisis with a responsible, clear, and steady mindset, keeping those in his charge at the forefront of his decision-making process.

Always assume you'll need crisis management at some point, and plan accordingly. If a disaster strikes, make quick, thoughtful decisions and react with open, transparent communication on all fronts. Never ignore a crisis or try to sweep it under the rug. Deal with disasters honestly, openly, and with a caring, responsible approach, and you'll lead your team through the storm without sinking the ship.

Don't Knock Opportunity

More often than not, people regret what they didn't try more than what they did try—even if they failed at the attempt. As Wayne Gretzky famously said, "You always miss 100 percent of the shots you don't take."

In business, missed opportunities due to fear or resistance to change can be the kiss of death. Look at Kodak, for example. They invented the digital camera but resisted the chance to spearhead the market, fearing they would suffocate their film developing business in the process. But as someone once said, "Opportunities are never lost; someone will take the one you missed." Others entered the digital camera arena first, and as a result, Kodak fell far behind in the industry, eventually filed for Chapter 11 bankruptcy protection, and remains struggling to this day.

In life, we miss small opportunities on a daily basis: the chance to pay someone a compliment, try a new food, join in an activity, change a habit, or even check something off our to-do list. We tell ourselves we'll take things on later . . . tomorrow . . . next week . . . eventually. But by continually procrastinating, we're really just choosing not to try. And by doing that, we'll eventually find ourselves wishing we'd only had the courage and initiative to do so in the first place.

But does that mean you have to accept every challenge that comes your way? To try simply for the sake of trying? Never pass up an opportunity? Certainly not. You've got to take calculated risks, not jump headfirst over a cliff just because it's there. The point is to try what you know you should without letting fear, doubt, or lack of motivation prevent you from taking action.

As a WOW leader, you must guide and encourage your team members to try innovative approaches, accept new challenges, move in different directions, develop new ideas, work toward their goals, and never back down from an opportunity to succeed. And most important, you must also do the same! When opportunity knocks, don't knock it . . . fling the door open and try!

Rethinking Failure

People often resist change because they fear failure. In fact, "fail" is often regarded as the other F-word. And although everyone dreads the thought of failing, failure can ultimately be a springboard to success. Those who eventually become successful know that failure is just a stepping-stone along the way.

Criticism, rejection, mistakes, and even total flops are all part of the hidden résumé of any top achiever. The more successful the person, the more failures they've experienced throughout their career. As a WOW leader, you should keep in mind that failing is not a destination unto itself; it's a journey toward discovery—a learning experience through which continued growth is assured, as long you pick yourself up and continue to move toward your goals of achievement.

The next time you slip up, try these techniques, and soon you'll be picking yourself up, dusting yourself off, and leaving your failures behind you.

Recovering from Your Mistakes

1. Keep a positive attitude. Success is 90 percent attitude. People who are able to put a positive spin on a negative outcome are more apt to turn things around and steer in the direction of success. Keeping an optimistic, determined frame of mind, rather than giving in to a defeatist negativity, will help you turn your missteps into opportunities rather than endings.

2. Reflect on your failure. Don't wallow in self-pity when things go wrong. Ask yourself why you failed. Think about the variables that contributed to the unfavorable results. Take the time to do an honest self-evaluation and reflect on what you could have done differently and how you could have prevented the failure.

3. Own up to your actions. Don't try to justify your failures by blaming someone else. Own up to your decisions and strategies and realize that you alone are responsible for your successes and failures. Realize that you are not infallible, and forgive yourself for those imperfections. Recognize that you can only improve if you admit there is room for improvement.

4. Follow up the failure. After coming to terms with a failure, strategize your next move. Make a plan that takes into consideration what you learned from your previous course of action. Employ new moves, engage in new activities, try new methods. Do something that keeps you focused on the goal, not the hurdles.

5. Stray the course. No, that's not a misprint! If you've failed on your current course, stray from it! Look for the next opportunity that comes along. Be open to new possibilities and explore uncharted territories. As they say, when one door closes, another one opens. You just have to be courageous enough to stray onto a different path and find a new door to open.

6. Face your fear. Fear of failure will ultimately cause you to do just that: fail (see the beginning of this chapter). The debilitating grip of fear will hold you back from taking the risks necessary to succeed. To move beyond failure, you must face your fear of failure. You must be unafraid to make mistakes. You must trust your actions and accept that the consequences that result—even if they are less than favorable—are simply one part of the larger picture that is your journey.

7. Change your perspective. If you look at it from a different angle, what you view as failure can be seen in a whole new way. Think of your mistakes as change catalysts that will ultimately strengthen your resolve and push you to improve and grow. If you view failing from a perspective of success—if you can see from a distance, where you are standing at the summit of your dreams looking back—you can take failure for what it is and move on.

Great leaders fail. But that doesn't make them failures; it makes them human. What makes them great is the ability to learn and thrive and prevail despite those mistakes and missteps.

One of the most celebrated and award-winning medical dramas of all time, *ER*, followed the lives and careers of emergency room doctors, nurses, and staff of the fictional County General Hospital. In the freshman year of the long-running series, Chief Resident Mark Greene was reliable, confident, and self-assured. He was the voice of authority and reason among the staff, the one we as viewers counted on to save the day. However, in the touching, emotional episode "Love's Labor Lost," the seemingly infallible doctor "fails" when he makes a critical error delivering a baby in the ER. The baby survives, but the mother dies, much to the shock and horror of Dr. Greene, the woman's husband, and the viewing audience.

The mistake Dr. Greene makes is a costly one, not only to the family affected by the tragedy but also to the doctor himself. His guilt in the matter is called into question on a professional level (he has to go before a review board to decide his fate), and he begins to question his own ability to successfully move forward with his career. Eventually, he overcomes his depression and comes to terms with the failure, making peace with the fact that a mistake—even a catastrophic kind—cannot altogether define him or his doctoring abilities.

Remember, careers are not straight ladders to the top. The workforce and business arena is more like a complex lattice, or a maze that must be navigated up, down, and sideways, often making it difficult to determine if you are succeeding or failing in your quest for career advancement. What may seem like a lateral move, or even a step down, can actually be an opportunity to learn new skills, meet new people, or gain new experiences that could parlay into a greater position or new career path.

Never let the idea of failing hold you back from moving, changing, and growing. If you do fail, learn from your errors, tweak your strategies, and fine-tune your attitude. Failing builds character and opens new doors. Be brave, be bold, and above all, don't fret your failures!

Don't Fret Your Failures . . . They Didn't!

Nearly every success story is peppered with failures. Throughout history, there are countless examples of individuals who have failed, sometimes repeatedly, before becoming the success stories we know them now to be. Well-known greats like Abraham Lincoln, Thomas Edison, and Bill Gates weren't always winners in every venture. In fact, they all stumbled at one time or another, but each refused to give up when he got knocked down.

TV is also laden with examples of perceived failures: canceled shows, fired actors, poor production choices, low ratings, and more. But as they say in the entertainment business, "The show must go on." In the following examples, failure wasn't an end, but rather a new beginning that eventually brought about success.

Winfrey Didn't Always Win: Oprah Winfrey

The media queen and billionaire came from humble, some would even say tragic, beginnings. She was born into poverty, lived in an inner-city environment, and endured years of physical and emotional abuse in her youth. Eventually, Oprah began a career in radio and then television, but faced numerous challenges during her rise to the top. Early on, she was even fired from a reporting job, having been told she wasn't suitable for TV. Guess she proved them wrong!

New Developments: Arrested Development

Arrested Development aired for three seasons (2003–2006) on the Fox network before being canceled due to low ratings. However, a strong fan base and critical acclaim remained for the series. Although the show's producers felt the TV format had run its course, interest in a feature film based on the original series led to an almost unprecedented revival of the TV show. A fourth season was filmed in 2012 and picked up by Netflix to run in 2013. Currently, the show is receiving new buzz and new success, despite its original "failure" to captivate and retain a large TV audience.

Found Its Following: Family Guy

The cult phenomenon *Family Guy* had a rough start on TV, to say the least. During its first three seasons (1999–2002), the show was frequently moved into different time slots on the Fox network, aired irregularly, and received consistently low ratings. The show was officially canceled but was brought back into syndication by Cartoon Network, airing during the late-night "Adult Swim" broadcast. *Family Guy* reruns finally found an audience, increasing the show's fan base exponentially. Things only got better when the first two seasons were released on DVD and record sales were achieved. Based on the new-found popularity of the series, Fox decided to pick the show back up in 2005, and it's still going strong to this day.

Didn't Always Have Game: Merv Griffin

Merv Griffin is not a name you might associate with failure in TV. After all, this icon of television history was responsible for the award-winning *Merv Griffin Show*, created and produced game show sensations like *Jeopardy!* and *Wheel of Fortune*, and amassed his own fortune in holdings worth nearly a billion dollars. But not everything Griffin touched turned to gold. He failed as a daytime talk show host in 1962 and then had troubles in a late-night spot opposite Johnny Carson. While he created and hosted numerous successful game shows, many of his ideas tanked, including a wild, stunt-based show called *Rukus* and a TV version of the board game Monopoly. But despite the occasional (and inevitable) misses, Griffin was a WOW in the world of TV . . . because he didn't fret his failures.

In addition to these TV examples, there are millions of examples of ordinary people who have triumphed after facing overwhelming obstacles or outright failures. Sometimes, the successes are small or even private, with personal goals being met after multiple attempts. Sometimes, the successes are life changing and impactful on a large scale. You have probably witnessed many such examples. Maybe you've been a successful "failure" yourself.

Often, when you hear about a success, you don't know about the failures that it was built on. But rest assured, behind every great success is a string of missteps or mistakes. Obviously, being a success does not mean you've never had failures; it means you've survived them. Take a cue from the accomplished successes of TV—rethink what failure really means.

We often avoid change because the outcomes are unknown, while the status quo, even if not ideal, provides a comforting, secure familiarity. But WOW leaders aren't afraid of change; in fact, they drive it, knowing that change is synonymous with growth, innovation, and business sustainability. Because there can be no progress without change, WOW leaders not only accept the curve balls as they come and lead effectively through forced change, they also become agents of change themselves by encouraging their team to try new things, suggest new ideas, and pave new paths to success.

Chapter 10

WOW Leaders Are Bold Decision Makers and Problem Solvers

"Each indecision brings its own delays and days are lost lamenting over lost days . . . what you can do or think you can do, begin it. For boldness has magic, power, and genius in it."
—*Johann Wolfgang von Goethe*

Making decisions based on critical thinking, innovative strategizing, and past experiences sets WOW leaders apart from those with a grandiose title but no backbone to commit to their choices. People look to their superiors for direction, advice, and guidance. They trust their leaders to be responsible and proactive—to be the voice of experience and reason.

Above all, leaders are expected to pave the way by *choosing* the way and then *showing* the way. WOW leaders are not afraid to carve out a path and leave a trail of breadcrumbs for their teams. Leaders who cannot or do not choose a road and a direction will leave their employees lost and wandering through the woods.

Being a decisive problem solver means having the courage as well as the knowledge to make informed but perhaps unpopular judgment calls. WOW leaders make decisions based on facts, foresight, and faith, even in the face of adversity or negativity. Those steering the ship should know the course better than those manning the decks, and they should keep the vessel steady even in rough waters. Those who jump ship or drop anchor at the first sign of trouble will only drown the crew. Great and respected leaders face all challenges with swift and steady action and are able to lead their team to greatness in all aspects of the job.

Captain Frank Furillo, the fearless leader on the genre-leading cop drama *Hill Street Blues*, is a bold and courageous decision maker, never one to compromise his own ideals to please the top brass. In the episode "Trial by Fury," Furillo and defense attorney Joyce Davenport are discussing a case. Joyce disagrees with Frank's methods for obtaining a confession, even though he technically went by the book and didn't break any laws. "I can live with what I did, Joyce. I went by my instincts and they were right. Under these circumstances, I'd do it again." Furillo made choices based on gut feelings, experience, and courage to do what he felt was right, not what was perceived by others to be right.

WOW leaders encourage their team by example, demonstrating how to make decisions and act on them. They show that even when mistakes or missteps occur, problems can be tackled by thinking outside of the box and then moving to remedy the situation. Exceptional leaders are at the top of their game and have a wider view of the landscape. WOW leaders utilize that unique vantage point to aid in their decision-making process, enabling them to confidently advise their team and blaze the trail to success.

Decision Is Key

WOW leaders know the importance of making a decision, even when the outcome isn't guaranteed. In order to succeed, they must accept the bad choices they make as well as the good ones. They have to make decisions. A WOW leader understands that the most important part about making decisions is not whether they are right or wrong, but simply that they are made. In that respect, the only bad choice for WOW leaders is indecision—not making a choice at all.

Naturally, there are some pretty clear and obvious bad choices. If you know for a fact the outcome is likely to be negative before you make a decision, you should steer clear of that path. For example, drinking and driving is a bad choice. Swimming with sharks during a feeding frenzy is a bad choice. Anything illegal is a bad choice.

Walter White, the high school chemistry teacher from TV's *Breaking Bad*, makes a bold decision when diagnosed with terminal lung cancer. To pay for treatment and ultimately provide a secure financial future for his wife, teenage son, and unborn daughter, he enters the illegal drug trade. After stealing equipment from the high school chemistry lab, he begins to supplement his straight-laced, middle-class, honest lifestyle with a covert career cooking and selling crystal meth. The consequences of that choice naturally lead down a path of violence, theft, and destruction, ultimately putting him and his family at risk. Becoming a drug lord? Clearly a bad decision.

But not all outcomes are that apparent. A WOW leader analyzes the information and facts at hand and researches all the options before making a choice. The intention is always to make the most well-informed decision, but there aren't any guarantees. Still, moving forward is the only good choice, no matter what the decision, no matter what the outcome.

Once a choice is made, good leaders set a course of action. But the strategy can always be tweaked or altered along the way to improve the decision or change the details of the choice. WOW leaders make decisions to get the ball rolling and move toward a favorable outcome rather than doing nothing and staying stagnant with indecision.

Making good or right decisions is important to a degree, but all choices, whether thought to be good or bad, have their own set of consequences. A negative outcome can eventually lead down a positive path. A failure in one regard can lead to a new, unplanned opportunity for success. Sometimes our mistakes teach us more than our triumphs. We never know where our decisions will ultimately take us, so we can't really ever judge our choices to be bad. We can only decide to choose.

Intuition Helps Guide Decisions

Hard data and raw facts are indisputable tools used to shape the decisions and strategies of business leaders. But effective leadership involves much more than just gathering and processing the right information set. WOW leaders combine their experience, knowledge, and know-how with their own intuitive reasoning. In other words, great leaders trust their gut feelings.

The detective dramedy *Psych* centers around Shawn Spencer, a police consultant who uses his "gift" of intuition to help solve crimes. The protagonist's father, an overzealous police officer, taught Shawn at an early age to zero in on the most minute details, thus giving birth to his unique abilities. While he feigns a psychic ability, Shawn's skill set doesn't involve any sort of clairvoyance. Rather, he's learned to process information using a combination of detail-oriented observation and gut-feeling guidance to reach the best possible conclusions.

No matter what you call it—gut feeling, intuition, instinct, sixth sense, hunch, premonition, or inner voice—that initial response or feeling you perceive when faced with a decision is based on collective life experiences and observations. Most people have found themselves in situations where a decision needs to be made despite limited information or without having the proper time to study all the options. Likewise, everyone has been faced with choosing directions when faced with an overwhelming, overabundant amount of data, details, facts, and possibilities. In either scenario, the right path cannot be logically concluded based on some sort of fact-based equation. You must follow your gut.

WOW leaders are tasked with being the guiding voice of a team, department, or even an entire corporation. They draw on the expertise and opinions of trusted advisers and respected colleagues and employees. They rely on carefully researched marketing or financial outcomes and probabilities. But at the end of the day, WOWs are the navigation system that points the way; they need to make the call. While mediocre leaders might make shaky decisions based on percentage-point strategies alone, WOW leaders combine what they know with what they feel. The strongest leaders trust their intuitive nature, knowing that the merging of business acumen and judgment is the most logical way to come to the best solutions.

Daring Decision

When Charlie Sheen famously went off the deep end in 2011, he was TV's highest-paid actor as the star of the hit series *Two and a Half Men*. Following a stint in rehab for substance abuse, Sheen had a public meltdown that included derogatory and inflammatory comments aimed at the show's creator. He also demanded a substantial pay raise to return to the set, which had temporarily shut down production while he was in recovery.

With *Two and a Half Men* still going strong at the top of the ratings and a fan base dedicated to the show's star, producers were faced with a tough decision: meet Sheen's demands and hire him back, cancel the popular series, or continue without one of the "two" men. Since Sheen had been a mainstay of the show for eight seasons, making the choice to kill off his character, Charlie Harper, was risky, to say the least. But the executives made the decision to replace Sheen and introduce another character to fill the space.

Ashton Kutcher was hired on, taking the show in a completely new direction. With substantial revenue at stake, the bold decision was a WOW move, regardless of the outcome of the choice. Only through action can results be achieved. In this case, the show remained a hit even without one if its lead characters and continued to be a profitable and popular series.

Emotional Decision Making

Emotional decision making is often a recipe for disaster. Certainly, there's a level of emotion involved in every decision made, whether of a personal or business nature. But your emotions cannot take the lead when you're making the choice, or you may end up regretting it later.

When weighing your options, gut feelings and intuition play a significant and necessary role. Those instinctive reactions are often quite telling and shouldn't be ignored when making decisions. But while gut feelings and intuition are like cousins to emotions, they aren't the same. The root of intuition is based in experience and intelligent past observations. Your brain recalls those previously learned lessons and sparks an instantaneous reaction that goes off like either a warning bell or a positive cheer.

Emotions, however, aren't drawn from collective life experiences but are born from immediate responses of pleasure, fear, or excitement. Emotions often cloud, mask, or shield rational or well-thought-out judgments, which is why emotional decision making can lead you down a path you might not ordinarily traverse.

If you've ever sat in on a timeshare presentation, you know what I mean by emotional decision making. The salespeople play to your emotions and capitalize on your desire to capture and retain the excitement of a vacation experience. Those selling a piece of property at an exotic destination are really selling a feeling, one they want you to buy into before you get a chance to think. A timeshare employee once confided in me that nearly all successful sales are made on the spot. Those who leave the presentation and take the time to mull it over almost never make the investment. Once free of the emotional attachment, they make the rational decision to pass on the offer.

The hapless *Ugly Betty* heroine, Betty Suarez, lets her emotions get the best of her in "The Manhattan Project," as she endeavors to achieve her goal of getting her first apartment. When she attends a showing at a beautiful Manhattan flat, she instantly falls in love with the bright yellow walls and open space. And when a pigeon lands on an open window ledge, she takes it as a sign that she should rent the unit. However, she's a split second too late, with another buyer signing the lease under her nose. In her emotionally charged excitement, she agrees to rent another unit in the building, sight unseen, with the realtor's promise that it had "sexy views" and would be snatched up quickly. Naturally, after sinking her life savings into the deposit, the place turns out to be a dive, complete with moldy tub, leaky roof, and a sexy view of the two elderly nudists across the street. Betty's hasty decision proves disastrous. If she had done her due diligence and actually viewed the apartment in advance, she would have never jumped in headfirst.

In business, emotional decision making that disregards pertinent information, intuitive reactions, and potential consequences can lead to an irreparable DUD situation. It's not the failure of the outcome that makes the decision a DUD but the method by which it's obtained. Even rational, well-thought-out decisions can lead to failure or less-than-stellar results. After all, no outcome is guaranteed. But if you've reached a conclusion carefully and with the right motivations, you'll learn and grow.

When faced with the potential for emotional decision making, here are few ideas to get you on the right track to thinking before reacting:

Step away. Remove yourself from the situation, both physically and emotionally. Move to a different location or partake in an alternative activity. Go for a walk, grab a bite to eat, or head for the gym. Clear your mind and look at the situation from a fresh, neutral perspective.

Release the pressure. Decisions have to be made, no doubt about it. But don't make a decision if you're feeling pressured to choose when you're not adequately prepared. When you're being pressed, persuaded, or prodded in the direction of a choice you're not comfortable with, think twice.

Take the time. There comes a time when a choice must be made and an action must be taken. But when critical decisions are at stake, that time is not instantaneous or immediate; it's only after allowing for intelligent consideration and reflection.

Write it out. Sort out your decision-making process on paper, making a list of pros and cons or potential positive or negative outcomes. This will help you slowly and carefully outline the situation's details rather than emotionally reacting to them.

Be realistic. As the cliché goes, "If it seems too good to be true, it probably is." Consider every angle of the proposal and break it down rationally and realistically before jumping at a "sure thing" or a "can't miss" opportunity. Trust your gut and your intuition, but never let your emotions overpower your ability to reason.

While it's true that the only bad choice is no choice at all, it's pertinent to make your decisions using the right criteria and the best tools in your arsenal. If you jump into a scenario based on emotional decision making, the consequences can be regrettable or even catastrophic. Keep your emotions in check when making a decision, and instead draw upon research, experience, intuition, and strategy to elicit the best results.

Deciding to Say No

As a WOW leader, you're naturally a person who gets things done. You're a go-getter and probably a bit of a perfectionist. You know what it means to work hard, and you don't shy away from a challenge. That's all well and good. But there comes a point when you may be doing too much and spreading yourself too thin, and as a result, areas that really need your attention end up suffering.

That's why it's important, every once in awhile, to just say "no!" Saying no isn't about admitting defeat or suggesting that you can't do the job. It's about setting boundaries that make sense. By delegating responsibilities and tasks of lower priority that can just as easily be accomplished by someone else, you are being more, not less, efficient.

"Freedom," the two-part fourth season finale episode of hospital drama *Grey's Anatomy*, provides a fictional example of an overachiever just saying no. In this case, Dr. Miranda Bailey, who served not only as chief resident at the show's Seattle Grace Mercy West Hospital, but also the founder and director of the hospital's free clinic, decided that it wasn't possible or fair to her family to attempt to "have it all." With her marriage on the line and her son recovering from recent serious injuries, the successful career surgeon had an epiphany of sorts. She decided to say no to herself—to her stubborn drive and workaholic tendencies—by delegating one of her main responsibilities to another doctor. "I've seen the bigger picture. And I can't do everything and still have everything, so I have to let some of the pieces go," she confessed to Dr. Izzie Stevens. Handing over the keys to the clinic and passing the torch to her colleague, she said, "I love running the clinic, but not as much as I love surgery. I don't love it as much as I love being chief resident. I don't love it as much as I love my husband and child."

Just as the fictional doctor decided to prioritize her life and focus on what mattered most, the most successful WOW leaders must also do the same. By occasionally saying no, you'll find room in your schedule to take care of what's most meaningful and important to you or your career. You'll be less stressed throughout the day if you don't overburden yourself by taking on more than you can or more than you really need to. Less stressed translates into more productive, so in a sense, by doing less, you'll really be doing more.

When to Say No

Saying no is vital if you want to operate at peak efficiency for what really matters. But when should you say no? You can't adopt a policy of always saying no when someone asks for a favor, requests your input, or needs your help. But you can't always say yes, either. Obviously, you must strike a realistic balance and understand when it's best to step up and when it's better to turn something down.

When it comes to your family, especially with your children, it's hard to say no. However, everyone will benefit from you not stretching yourself so thin that you ultimately snap. Say no when the request is unreasonable (as it often is with kids), when an alternative exists that is equal to your own involvement, or when it's just not possible without setting yourself up for failure. Occasionally saying no doesn't make you a bad parent or an ungrateful spouse; in fact, it's a smart, honest way to maintain a healthy family relationship.

From a business standpoint, saying no is about setting boundaries and establishing acceptable parameters by which you take on new tasks, roles, and responsibilities. You can't be known as the go-to person for everything. You'll never get any of your own work done if you're constantly saying yes to every request.

Always say no when you're uncomfortable with the request. If it doesn't feel right or if your intuition sends up red flags that you shouldn't do what's being asked, just don't do it. Your gut is usually right. In addition, when you're already swamped and your in-basket is overloaded, you need to put your foot down and say no to more work, especially if can be handled by someone else.

Moreover, don't get "guilted" into picking up extra duties. Loaded phrases like "If you don't do it, no one will," or "I thought I could count on you" are meant to goad you into doing something you don't want to do. Stick to your guns and resist the urge to please at your own expense.

How to Say No

Learning how to say no is an art form but one you can master with the right mindset, a confident approach, and a little practice. The key to refusal is to do so with tact and care but without ambiguity. When you say no, you must mean it. You can't leave it up for debate or imply a "maybe" when you mean "absolutely not."

Here are some ways to say no tactfully, but resolutely:

Answer the request immediately. Don't say, "I'll get back to you on that," or "Let me think about it," unless you truly aren't sure about your answer. If you want to say no, say it right away; stalling will only work to your disadvantage, because it will give the asker more time to talk you into it and less time to find someone else to do the job.

Keep it simple. Don't over-explain yourself. There's no need to come up with a laundry list of reasons why you're saying no. A simple "Sorry, I'm overloaded right now," or "I wish I could, but my schedule just won't allow it" is all the explanation you need. In fact, the more you talk about why you can't, the more likely you are to talk yourself into finding a reason why you can.

Stick to your word. Once you say no, don't backpedal and then do it anyway. Going back on your intent to say no often happens out of guilt or because you're afraid to relinquish control and let someone else do the job. Learn to let go and cut yourself some slack. Remember, no means no.

Stay positive, even when the answer is negative. Although you might be turning someone down, you can still spin it in a positive direction. For starters, don't reply with a hostile, frustrated tone. You can say no and still be cordial, polite, and even encouraging. Try something like "I'm sure you'll find the right person for the job," or "I know you'll figure it out."

Offer an alternative. Suggest an option other than doing it yourself. That way, you're being helpful even if you can't be the one to do the job. But be mindful to offer an alternative without passing the buck. If you know that Johnson is just as swamped as you, don't mention her name. However, if you think Smith might be a good fit and you're pretty sure he has the time for the task, point the asker in his direction.

Choose Your Yes Moments

Although saying no is necessary to keeping your sanity, maintaining a doable schedule, and working to your fullest potential, you don't want to become known for being uncooperative or unhelpful by never saying yes. Like the art of saying no, it's just as important to learn when *not* to say no.

Exercise your right to say no, but don't pass up an opportunity. There may be times when taking on something extra is not only called for, it's beneficial and important to your career. Here are some tips on how to choose your yes moments wisely:

- When the big boss personally requests you for a task, the answer should be yes.
- When the chance for redemption of a past mistake comes along, take it.
- If your first instinct is to say yes because you truly want to do the job, then find a way to make it happen. Your gut reaction usually won't steer you wrong.
- When you're returning a favor, it's a yes moment. If you've reached out for help and it has been given, be sure you give it back when you're called on.
- When you're the only one capable of doing the job, you'll need to step up and do it. For example, if you're the only one who speaks Chinese in the office, you need to be the one to take the call from Beijing, even if it's not technically your responsibility or your client.
- When there's a clear career advantage, an opportunity to learn a new skill set, or the chance to move toward a personal goal, find the room in your schedule to say yes.
- When someone really needs your help and will fail or suffer without your intervention, take the high road and say yes. There's a clear distinction between a genuine need for assistance and a casual request for help. You'll know the difference when it presents itself.

Along the road to success, you'll find yourself wearing many hats—but you can't wear them all simultaneously. From time to time, you have to remove one hat to make room for another, and occasionally, you'll have to leave a hat on the rack and walk away. The key to being a WOW is picking your yes moments but also knowing when, how, and why to say no.

The Art of Delegation

Delegation is perhaps one of the trickiest leadership skills, because it goes against the grain of most overachiever types. Successful, driven WOW leaders don't shy away from hard work. In fact, many aren't content unless they're busy. They take pride in their work, believe in their efforts, and want to accomplish great things—which is why they have a tendency to take on too much and resist the delegation of tasks.

Even leaders who recognize the benefits of delegation often have a hard time following through with it. Part of the apprehension involved in letting go is the "if you want it done right, do it yourself" mentality. WOW leaders are accustomed to stepping up to the plate and making things happen on their own. They have honed their own abilities and skill sets and will push themselves to reach their goals. Trusting others isn't quite as easy as depending on yourself, so delegation gets put on a back burner.

There's also the issue of time. Busy leaders are pulled in several directions on a daily basis. While they're used to the pace and often thrive on it, it can take a great deal of extra effort, time, and patience to delegate tasks to others. Delegation lightens the workload in one respect, but adds the responsibilities of training, overseeing, and following up on what's been delegated.

Time also plays a role on the other end of the equation. Mindful leaders don't want to overwhelm their people, especially if they're operating efficiently and successfully in the current culture. They don't want to rock the boat with the delegation of new tasks that their staff may not have time to tackle. They don't want to push too far by introducing additional stresses, so they hold on to the tasks themselves.

And therein lies the rub. Doing it all holds everyone back from moving forward, because no one is being given the chance to learn new skills and take on new experiences—including the leaders! By teaching others through the delegation of tasks, leaders are deciding to invest in their staff as well as in themselves. Eventually, by relinquishing certain responsibilities, they will free up some of their own time to make room for tasks delegated down to them from higher-ups. In other words, progress and skill advancement requires the delegation of jobs, not the hoarding of them.

To master the art of delegation:

Be selective. Delegation works best when you carefully match the right jobs with the right team members. Don't simply pass along your headaches to someone else or task others with the busywork you don't feel like doing. Be selective about what assignments would be most beneficial to teach another, then carefully decide who's up to the challenge. Make sure the candidate is ready and has the potential to succeed.

Be strategic. Don't begin by delegating the most critical tasks on your plate. When the consequences of failure could be catastrophic or career altering, it's best to keep those jobs close at hand. Start with the delegation of less critical, but nevertheless important tasks. Once those skills have been learned and the team members have proven their capabilities, introduce more and more challenging assignments. Strategically build up the levels of confidence, trust, and performance as you relinquish duties through delegation.

Be supportive. Once you've delegated a task, your involvement isn't immediately over. Often, you'll need to teach the skill or at the very least oversee the process for some time. Be supportive by being encouraging, communicative, and available should questions or issues arise. There's always a transition period when delegation first occurs. Be ready, willing, and able to commit to the interim phase. You can be more hands-off once the skill is more practiced, but as the leader, you'll always need to stay connected in some way.

Be proactive. Don't wait for employees to come to you with problems or skill gaps regarding the newly delegated task. Be proactive about checking in, asking questions, listening, and in general, keeping an eye on things. Don't just throw a new assignment at someone and then walk away, washing your hands of the responsibility. Make a point of being present and on hand so you can identify any barriers that may need to be removed or any hurdles that need to be crossed.

Be realistic. Change takes time. Don't expect perfection or an incident-free transition period when implementing the delegation of tasks. Have realistic, attainable goals for passing along the new responsibilities. Be patient and unafraid, allowing the time for the necessary growth to occur. When failures or missteps occur, help team members learn from them and move forward so they can ultimately be successful.

A friend of mine once said the only way he'd watch the show *Duck Dynasty* was if it were a reenactment of the 1980s show *Dynasty* using ducks as the cast members. Now that would be something to see! Not one to hunt or wear camouflage myself, I could see his point. Still, I had to believe the show had merit; after all, it had become a cult phenomenon of sorts and was watched and loved by millions of viewers on a regular basis. In any case, I watched it. And what I discovered, surprisingly, was that there are brains behind the beards. What I feared might be another *Here Comes Honey Boo-Boo*-type reality series was actually a humorous and thought-provoking look at a family of businessmen and entrepreneurs.

The Robertsons, I learned, founded Duck Commander, a business that produces and sells duck calls for the hunting trade. The show depicts their experiences running the multimillion-dollar enterprise as a family business. On the episode "CEO for a Day," Willie Robertson delegates his entire job to his brother Jase for a single day, aiming to teach him a lesson about respect. In the beginning, it seems the eager new boss is on the right track when left to his own devices. With Willie out of the office, Jase tells the team "there are no rules," then sets out to have a day of fun that includes warehouse box jousting and a duck-call assembly contest. Work seems to be getting done and morale is high, with all the camaraderie and horsing around.

However, near the end of the business day, Jase and the team discover that there was a large shipment that needed to be delivered. Needless to say, they can't make the delivery, and Jase learns it's harder being in charge than he had thought. Willie's none too happy about the mistake but knows his point was made. "He's not the best CEO in the world, but that's why it's a team," Willie says in his Southern drawl. "We have to rely on each other . . . after a while you come to realize that working hard and having fun ain't that much different."

While Willie's approach to delegation was not ideal, it illustrates the point that a leader has to rely on his team. Had Willie not made the lesson an all-or-nothing task by delegating all of his duties and giving nothing in terms of guidance, there would likely have been a more favorable business outcome. If Willie had taught his brother a skill or schooled him in the demands placed on a CEO, Jase would likely have been able to perform up to par. Willie wasn't selective, strategic, supportive, proactive, or realistic about delegating his job to his brother. Truth be told, he just wanted to see him squirm! Remember, delegation isn't simply giving up your job to someone else; it's a teaching tool that helps others grow.

The art of delegation, like any other skill set, takes time, effort, commitment, and practice to master. Only by loosening your grip on some of the tasks on your own to-do list and delegating them to others can you facilitate their growth and advancement. Being a WOW leader doesn't mean doing everything yourself; it means knowing how to elicit the best from the people in your charge. When you master the art of delegation, you're making a bold decision to trust and empower those you lead, helping them become WOWs in the process.

Be Bold

Being a WOW leader often means making choices that may not be popular but are right for the company or the team. It also means possessing a self-awareness and confidence that guides your informed decisions and enables you to continuously move forward.

Whatever your position in the career cycle, take a stand by being bold, courageous, and authentic. Never compromise or alter your choices due to fear, insecurity, or peer persuasion. WOW leadership is an attitude backed by action.

Here are some ways to be bold:

- **Make a change.** Sounds simple, right? But change is often feared. Leading confidently in a new direction is a bold, positive move.

- **Speak the truth.** Honesty may be the best policy, but it's not always easy. Have the courage to be truthful, even in the face of potential opposition or repercussions.

- **Take a risk.** Jump boldly into a new challenge, even if it scares you a little. Don't jump blindly; make sure the risk is calculated and well thought out, and then move forward.

Don't just think like a WOW, be bold and act like a WOW. Anything less is just the same old, same old.

Bold Career Move

Anthony E. Zuiker, creator of the TV phenomenon known as *CSI*, wasn't always in the entertainment business. He was on a completely different career track as a tram driver when he conjured up the idea for the forensics-based crime drama. Knowing "absolutely nothing" about script writing proved to be a boon, not a bust, for Zuiker. He's admitted that "breaking all the rules" for TV writing is what gives the show its unique and instantly recognizable storytelling style.

Acting with bold initiative and not succumbing to self-imposed doubts, boundaries, or limitations on what could or couldn't be done gave Zuiker an edge in a highly competitive field. Had he given in to an "old" attitude—a mindset of being too late to the game to succeed—he would have missed the opportunity of a lifetime. And millions of viewers would have missed out on the *CSI* experience: a franchise that's been going strong and building upon its success since the year 2000.

Go Back to Move Forward

WOW leaders are decision makers and problem solvers, but that doesn't mean they're immune to life's ups and downs. Sometimes creativity, motivation, and drive stalls or wanes, and you need to refresh your attitude, change your perspective, or enhance your spirit to keep moving forward in a WOW way. But amid all the pressures and expectations, how do you do it? Perhaps to move forward, you need to go back.

Remember what it was like when you were just starting out? Maybe you had no idea what you were doing, but you were excited to be doing it! You were eager to be on the road to fulfilling a dream, starting a new venture, or becoming a leader. Each step forward was a small but substantial victory. You were on your way and loving every minute of it!

Like the title character in the coming-of-age TV series *Felicity*, you probably once felt the fresh-faced excitement and anticipation of youth on the cusp of a great unknown. In *Felicity*, the pilot episode introduces a newly graduated young woman who is preparing to enter college and begin the next chapter of her life. Her story is just beginning to be written, and with that blank canvas of potential comes the blissful freedom of naive but confident inexperience. Starting from scratch, she has nothing to lose and everything in front of her to gain. Certainly she wants to succeed in her studies, make her parents proud, and work toward a viable career. Yes, she's anxious and worried about what's to come (and often distracted by the usual dating and dorm-room adventures)—but it's a thrilling sort of fear: an idealistic precipice on which to stand and look toward the rest of her life. As adults, we've outgrown so much of that blind innocence. We know better. We're wise to the ways of the world and the realities of life. We've been there, done that. We can't go back—can we?

Once you're established in your profession, grounded as a breadwinning adult, and heading down a particular path, the last thing you want to do is go backward, right? Maybe not. Although it may sound counterproductive, going back to the start can be just what you need to catapult yourself past a career or personal roadblock—not by having a reckless, excitable, laissez-faire, or careless attitude, but by recalling what motivated and drove you in the first place: remembering the excitement and eagerness that once gave you purpose.

Here are a few ways to go back and, ultimately, move forward:

- Try something new
- Take a (calculated) risk
- Dream bigger, think better
- Do something fun or out of character . . . step out of your box
- Laugh at yourself
- Do what you think is right, not what's expected
- Cut yourself some slack—allow mistakes
- Challenge yourself
- Establish a goal and start working to achieve it
- Think differently. Think "what if . . ." and then insert the best-case scenarios, rather than the worst potential outcomes
- Be happier!!

Being a respectable, responsible professional doesn't mean you have to stop dreaming, wondering, or changing. WOW leaders are constantly striving to be better and to keep moving forward. Like Felicity, the young woman immersing herself in a new reality, look at each new day as a new chance to start fresh. Go back to that idealistic, energetic, unapologetic way of thinking that you once knew, and instead of trudging along without enthusiasm, you'll be moving full speed ahead toward your next WOW achievement.

Stay Tuned

Remember, when all is said and done, people don't leave companies, they leave leaders. Are you a leader who motivates, inspires, and encourages your followers to thrive under your guidance, or is your lack of WOW driving them out the door?

Although many leaders want to WOW, few actually do—not because they don't have the skill set to rise to leadership greatness, but because they settle for good enough and fail to break the ceiling of their perceived limitations. They push themselves, but not far enough; they challenge themselves, but stop just short; they want it, but not badly enough. Or they get too comfortable with the security of their status, relying on title, tenure, and authority instead of genuine leadership.

When you think about the history of television programming—how it started, how it has grown, and how the characters, shows, genres, and story lines have developed over the years—it's a timeline of progression, dedication, drive, and creativity. TV done right moves us, inspires us, and teaches us. We loyally tune in to see what's next. We set our DVRs so we don't miss a show.

However, when TV shows miss the mark, they leave us unimpressed, bored, and disengaged. We give up. We turn the channel. We look elsewhere.

It's the same with leadership. Uninspired, lackluster, and ineffective leaders only breed more of the same from their staff. The bar is set so firmly in the position of mediocrity that no one bothers to rise above it. Good becomes good enough. But for those who want more—from themselves and those they lead—nothing short of WOW will do. Those who keep their employees engaged, motivated, and empowered will help them rise to the level of greatness they possess within.

The question is, do you want to simply be a boss with a title, a healthy paycheck, and the prestige that goes with that power? Or do you want to tune in to the greatness within, make a difference in the lives of those you lead, and truly be a WOW leader?

The remote control that navigates your WOW path is in your hands—how you use it is up to you.

Appendix

Quick Lists for WOW Leaders

I n *Tune In to WOW Leadership*, you've read lots of lists that described WOW qualities, provided suggestions, or highlighted steps toward WOW leadership. In this appendix, I've collected some of my favorites into one place for quick reference. Each list is also cross-referenced to the chapter in which it appears, so you can go back for a quick read in context if you need a bit more detail.

Building Trust (Chapter 1)

- Be yourself 24/7
- Focus on strengths
- Let them speak
- Macro-manage
- Encourage calculated risks
- Share the spotlight
- Accept responsibility
- Protect your people
- Follow through

Repairing Trust (Chapter 1)

- Be fair
- Be self-aware
- Keep in touch
- Face the facts
- Communicate and investigate
- Be the bridge
- Trust your instincts
- Make a decision

Cultivating Respect (Chapter 2)

- Reward
- Empathize
- Share
- Protect
- Empower
- Communicate
- Trust

Evaluating EIQ (Chapter 2)

- Self-awareness
- Self-management
- Social awareness
- Relationship management

Learning to WOW Daily (Chapter 3)

- Listen
- Ask
- Do
- Fail
- Change

Seeing Your Blind Spots (Chapter 3)

- Be self-aware
- Be proactive
- Be present
- Be communicative
- Be responsive
- Be diligent

Recharging and Refreshing (Chapter 3)

- Say no
- Clear your head
- Change your perspective
- Step out of your comfort zone
- Laugh
- Compliment someone
- Seek out inspiration
- Pay it forward

Being Authentic (Chapter 4)

- Rein in the rhetoric
- Do what's right, not what's popular
- Turn off the power
- Eat some humble pie
- Expect initiative, not perfection

Fostering Creativity (Chapter 5)

- Take the time
- Communicate
- Reserve judgment
- Allow mistakes
- Reward creativity

Mastering Goal-setting (Chapter 5)

- Define the goal
- List the steps
- Think ahead
- Set a timeline
- Celebrate victories

Choosing When to Text (Chapter 6)

- When an immediate yes or no is required
- To clarify or facilitate logistics
- For simple reminders
- To reach out or touch base

Choosing When to Email (Chapter 6)

- When attaching documents
- For multiple recipients
- As a follow-up to a follow-up
- For CYA situations

Choosing When to Call (Chapter 6)

- When forming a new relationship
- When the message is complex
- When understanding is critical
- When it's not public knowledge

Choosing When to Meet (Chapter 6)

- For pivotal conversations
- To brainstorm
- When giving reviews
- When the topic is touchy

Combating Negativity (Chapter 6)

- Identify the source
- Check yourself
- Confront with caution
- Be the change
- Find out why
- Channel the negative energy
- Align with a mentor
- Don't be a pushover
- Pick your battles

Mentoring Successfully (Chapter 7)

- Take the "me" out of mentor
- Be passionate
- Devote the time
- Preach practicality
- Be objective
- Teach transparently

Empowering the Life/Work Balance (Chapter 7)

- Harness human resources
- Create job share opportunities
- Adjust PTO
- Provide life services

Investing in the Psychological Paycheck (Chapter 7)

- Listen
- Show empathy
- Be honest/authentic
- Praise publicly
- Reinforce regularly
- Encourage growth

Empowering Employees (Chapter 8)

- Clear communication
- Accountability
- Reinforcing the good
- Trusting their decisions
- Consistency

Dealing with Fear (Chapter 9)

- Face your fears
- Be fearless, not reckless
- Be focused, not fearful
- End the vortex of fear

Saying No Tactfully and Resolutely (Chapter 10)

- Answer the request immediately
- Keep it simple
- Stick to your word
- Stay positive, even when the answer is negative
- Offer an alternative

Mastering Delegation (Chapter 10)

- Be selective
- Be strategic
- Be supportive
- Be proactive
- Be realistic

About the Author

Sheri Staak has a BS in Marketing from the University of Central Florida and has participated in programs at Thunderbird School of Global Management at the University of Michigan, the Ross School of Business, and the Kellogg Graduate School of Management. Her affiliations include the Healthcare Business Women's Association where she sat on the board for the Chicago Chapter and led the Executive Engagement Strategy. Sheri has held various vice president positions, at The Upjohn Company, Pharmacia, and Pfizer. She has mentored and groomed numerous young professionals. Her business and leadership acumen has been used to consult small business start-ups.

A strategic and innovative business leader, Sheri has held key leadership roles at both large privately held companies and publicly traded global companies. She has worked with and managed more than one thousand sales representatives in highly aggressive and competitive marketplaces in the U.S. By harnessing her passion for leadership and teamwork, she has become a trusted adviser and coach. Sheri further shares her wealth of knowledge through her blog, The STAAK Report. She is married and has two children.